EGGPLANT AND SQUASH

a Versatile Feast

EGGPLANT

With Illustrations by the Author

AND SQUASH

A Versatile Feast

Sheryl London

Atheneum   New York   1976

Library of Congress Cataloging in Publication Data
London, Sheryl.
Eggplant and squash, a versatile feast.
Includes index.
1.   Cookery (Eggplant)   2.   Cookery (Squash)
I.   Title.
TX803.E4L66   1976   641.6′5′62   75-41858
ISBN 0-689-10709-1

Published simultaneously in Canada by
McClelland and Stewart Ltd.
Composition by American Book–Stratford Press, Inc., Brattleboro, Vermont
Printed and bound by Halliday Lithograph Corporation,
West Hanover and Plympton, Massachusetts
Designed by Kathleen Carey
First Edition

I lovingly dedicate this book to Mel London, voluntary guinea pig for the testing of the recipes. His encouragement and his stoic ability to tolerate two-and-a-half years of eggplant or some kind of squash for lunch and dinner every day have been truly beyond the duties of a good husband.

Contents

CONTENTS

ONE

Squash

HISTORY AND INTRODUCTION

THE SQUASH IS PROBABLY the most ancient vegetable grown by man. Seeds and rind have been found in archeological excavations dating back to 2,000 B.C. The squash is also a truly native American vegetable, eaten by the Indians long before the first settlers came to the United States. Pumpkin and her sister squashes were first grown in the Western Hemisphere 4,000 years ago in the Mexican highlands. In the northern part of the continent all the Indian tribes planted pumpkins in their cornfields—from the Zuñi Indians of the Southwest to the Wampago Indians of the Northeast who helped the Pilgrims. Pumpkins, therefore, have had time to establish a long relationship with man, nourishing him physically and spiritually. They have also developed an interesting place in fable and legend. Pumpkins, as the Europeans call all squash, have been an inspiration for poets, like John Greenleaf Whittier in "The Pumpkin."

> What moistens the lip and what brightens the eye?
> What calls back the past like the rich pumpkin pie?

A pumpkin even took on political overtones during the 1950s McCarthy era, when it played a historic role in the "Pumpkin Papers," microfilm supposedly hidden in a pumpkin for safe-keeping.

Perhaps the pumpkin has the richest lore of all the squashes in the United States, and why not? Who can resist the appeal of a round, yellow-orange pumpkin with its heart-shaped leaves heralding the fall harvest? What other vegetable so truly spreads its golden cheer over the rural American autumn countryside? Just the sight of it evokes an older era of our Indian past. Nestled between dried cornstalks are the artistic potentials of the grinning, candle-lighted jack-o'-lanterns of Halloween. They conjure up witches, ghosts, and skeletons, and will someday become the featured dishes that grace our tables throughout the happy holiday season.

Perhaps our pumpkin nostalgia goes back to the early English settlers. They were the ones who were saved from starving in Jamestown and Plymouth by the native-grown pumpkins. In fact, if it weren't for the life-giving food of the pumpkins at that time, where would we all be now? When the crops that the Pilgrims planted failed, and all there was to eat throughout the winter were the hearty pumpkins, this poem written in 1630 shows that there truly were pumpkin eaters a-plenty.

> For pottage, and pudding and custards and pies
> Our pumpkins and parsnips are common supplies.
> We have pumpkins at morning and pumpkins at noon.
> If it were not for the pumpkins we should be undone.

In fact, the grumbling colonists sounded as if they could use this cookbook to find different ways to serve their bounty. The Indians were there first, however, and did teach them how to prepare it in many different ways. Some of these ways are still retained today. In New England some people still dry thin slices of pumpkin, string them together, and hang them in garlands from their kitchen ceilings. Or, Indian fashion, dehydrate them in the sun and grind the dry slices of pumpkin into a "flour."

The word "squash" is adapted from the American Indian word "asq," the plural of which is "asquash," meaning gourds. The Indians used every part of these gourds—nothing went to waste. The shell, scooped out and dried, became a container for carrying water. Sometimes it held grain or stored corn. When use dictated individual needs and different shapes, some pumpkins and gourds were shaped by pressure or bandaging while growing in the fields. They were used as mixing bowls and masks for religious ceremonies. The stringy fibrous parts of the pumpkin were dried and made into fabric, and after some seeds were set aside for next year's crop, the rest of the seeds were toasted and eaten as a nourishing snack.

The settlers, seeing how versatile and adaptable the pumpkin was, started to invent their own uses for it. At one time pumpkin shells were made into guides for barbers giving haircuts to the settlers.

The early pumpkin pies that were made in America before there was milled wheat for flour were somewhat different from pies we know today. They were baked in the pumpkin shells in hot ashes for several hours, and then eaten with a spoon.

Today, the "field pumpkin," grown in all sizes up to the mammoth exhibition pumpkins weighing 200 pounds or more, is no longer grown in cornfields as it once was. The introduction of corn-harvesting machinery has stopped this custom of planting pumpkins in cornfields and then, after the corn is harvested, having them occupy the ground until they mature.

It is in the form of pumpkin pie that pumpkins have achieved their greatest fame. They are still a seasonal treat after a holiday dinner. The rewards of the pumpkin as a basic ingredient in soups, stews, and other dishes, however, are taste treats not to be missed. All over the world, the pumpkin, or squash, has made its way from the garden patch through an entire dinner, ending up on the dessert tray. Pumpkins are even fed to hogs and cattle, so if you eat a sirloin steak or a pork chop, you're probably eating part pumpkin.

There seem to be lots of "pumpkin poets" that express the universal appeal and simple, homely quality of the pumpkin. Thoreau, in *Walden Pond,* was one who wrote "I would rather sit on a pumpkin and have it all to myself, than be crowded on a velvet cushion." And another nineteenth-century poet wrote:

> The old yellow pumpkin
> The mud-covered pumpkin
> The big-bellied pumpkin
> That makes such good pies.

I hope the collection of recipes in Part I of this cookbook will be a guide and inspiration for an inexhaustible repertoire of savory dishes. It should show that there is more to pumpkin than "such good pies." In fact, the book started because of my own need to use up our harvest in as many different ways as I could. I also found out that the versatility of squash prevented it from being a bore and we ate it a new way each day for three months.

VARIETIES

The varieties of pumpkins and squash are so numerous throughout the world, and come in so many shapes, sizes, colors, and textures that it boggles the mind. Many varieties are grown together in the fields and cross-pollinate, making even more varieties to keep track of. It has, therefore, been difficult to keep them pure. However, we now know enough about the culture of true squashes to be able to keep them pure, so they do not hybridize as easily.

Basically, they can be classified as two general kinds. The "bush" varieties, or summer squash, known botanically as *Cucurbita Pepo,* and the "long-running" varieties, or winter squash, known as *Cucurbita Moschata* or *Maxima.*

Summer squash, obtainable easily in the United States, include cucuzzi or cocozelle, chayotes or mirleton, straight neck and crook neck, yellow squash, zucchini, white scallop varieties called pattypan or cymling in the South, and a tiny variety of the same pattypan called button squash. There are also tropical varieties that have appeared in markets throughout the country and are worth trying. If you live in a section of the country where these squash are available, try the soft-skinned, dark-green, striped calabaza found in Spanish markets. It looks like a large buttercup squash but tastes more like acorn squash (see illustration).

Calabaza   Cocozelle

The upo squash is another one, to be found in Philippine markets. It is a pale-green, bottle-shaped gourd with a light, delicate taste (see illustration).

Upo

Chayote

The most easily obtainable, unusual variety of squash is the chayote (see illustration). The chayote is known by various names throughout the world, as are all international vegetables. It was known to the Mayans and Aztecs and has been a favorite on Mexican tables since pre-Columbian times, when it was called ayotli. Creole cooks in Louisiana call it the mirliton or mirleton. It is a tropical squash also native to Central and South America, and the West Indies as well. It is known in Florida and California, where it is called vegetable pear, mango squash, or christophene. It was also introduced into France from Algeria, and is still imported seasonally for French tables. These pale-green, gnarled-surfaced, pear-shaped squash (see illustration) have only one central seed. They can be used in primarily the same recipes as the summer squash in this book, but choose recipes that are mildly spiced, so that their delicate taste is not overpowered.

The other worthwhile novelty that you may want to try, if you have access to a Chinese market, is the fuzzy squash or hairy melon. This pale-green, furry-surfaced Chinese squash is about 6 inches long and looks like this (see illustration). It is used mostly in soups by the Chinese.

Summer squash are warm-season, frost-sensitive plants. They contain large amounts of water, and usually have small, edible seeds and very tender skins that can be easily pierced with a fingernail. The skins of small and medium-size squash are also totally edible. When well washed they do not need peeling. In fact, peeling takes away some of the already delicate taste of these young vegetables. With very large summer squash, one can peel them if the skins seem particularly tough. Some of the larger seeds and pulpy center may also be removed from the more mature vegetable. Summer squash are more perishable than the winter varieties. They will keep well when refrigerated for a week to ten days before using.

Winter squash have heavy skins. The skins are usually retained when baked or used as containers for soups and stews. This saves the moisture and vitamin content as well. Winter squash have large, removable seeds, some of which, like pumpkin seeds, can be saved, toasted, and eaten as a snack. They also have a stringy, fibrous center portion which must be removed by scraping with a spoon. When winter squash is to be steamed, the skin can be removed before or after it is cooked until tender. Removing the skin after cooking is somewhat easier, but the cooked pieces are more fragile and easily broken. If the vegetable is to be puréed, peel it after it is cooked. If it has to retain its shape, peel it before cooking.

The varieties of winter squash one finds locally in the United States are pumpkin, acorn, butternut, Hubbard, buttercup, gold nugget, Turks turban, and ornamental gourds, just to mention a few.

gold Nugget　　　　　*Buttercup*

Turks Turban

The squash or gourd family has the greatest diversity in its variety, shape, and size. To add to the confusion, there sometimes are many different musical names throughout the world for each variety as well. For example, zucchini is known as zucchette, Italian marrows, courgettes. In French, potiron. In German, kurbis. Pattypan is called pattison in French and custard squash or cymling in certain parts of the United States. Pumpkin is zucca in Italian, calabaza in Spanish, and calabash in Israel. Then again, there is the courgerone, cocozelle, or cucuzzi. All different names for the same vegetable. There is the Chinese fuzzy squash or hairy melon. The Philippine squash called upo, opu, or bottle squash, and there is the spaghetti squash, a new strain that has become a popular novelty with gardeners throughout the country. There are no doubt lots of others too numerous to mention.

In this selection of recipes, most of the summer squash and winter squash are interchangeable. In other words, don't panic if your garden or market only has yellow squash or pattypan instead of zucchini. They can all be prepared in the same way. Some of the pumpkin recipes can also be made with butternut, buttercup, Hubbard, or acorn squash. There will be a slight flavor difference. The variation in using a substitute squash will be a nice taste surprise. As in all cookbooks, this one should be an inspirational guide for your own creativity and inventiveness, so don't be afraid to experiment.

TIPS ON SELECTION AND PREPARATION

PUMPKIN: Buy bright-colored, unblemished, firm vegetables. Remove seeds and stringy, fibrous parts. The skins are tough, and therefore not edible, but help to hold its shape when cooking, if this is necessary. Use 3 pounds of raw pumpkin to yield about 3 cups of purée.

ACORN SQUASH: Buy ridged, acorn-shaped squash that are firm, dark green, and splashed with dark yellow. Split in half and remove the seeds and stringy parts. Here, too, the skin helps retain the shape when cooking, so do not peel. The ridged surface makes peeling difficult, so the skin is generally used as a container to hold the purée, or the pulp is eaten directly from the shell. Allow 1 acorn squash for 2 people.

BUTTERNUT AND BUTTERCUP: The butternut and buttercup squash can be treated the same as the pumpkin when buying and preparing. Allow about 1½ pounds for 2 people.

HUBBARD: This squash should have a rough, warty, hard, firm skin. Prepare the same as pumpkin. Allow about 1½ pounds for 2 people.

SUMMER CROOKNECK OR STRAIGHTNECK YELLOW SQUASH: Buy with curved or straight neck and tender, pale-yellow, bumpy, wartlike surface. Wash well, and cut off ends. Do not peel or seed if young and tender. Allow about 1 pound for 2 people.

PATTYPAN: Choose flat, scalloped, disc-shaped, pale-green squash. Do not peel or seed. Prepare the same as other summer squash. Allow about 1 pound for 2 people.

ZUCCHINI: They come in all sizes and look like a cucumber with a mottled, dark-green, striped surface and smooth, tender skin. Wash well and cut off ends. Remove seeds and skin only if vegetable is very large and mature. Allow about 1 pound for 2 people.

COCOZELLE: Buy these long, medium-green squash with their smooth surfaces when they can be found locally. Sometimes their shapes are straight and sometimes they have a crookneck. Prepare the same as other summer squash.

GROWING SUMMER SQUASH

Zucchini is the kind of prolific, bush-type summer squash that grows so quickly, and bears so heavily, that after the seeds are planted and watered, you must step back quickly and watch them grow.

Make sure there is no danger of frost when planting the seeds. Sow 3 or 4 seeds in a row about 2 to 3 feet apart, and in full sun. They have huge leaves, and take up lots of room in the garden, but 2 or 3 plants will provide you with enough zucchini to try almost all the recipes in this book.

Thin to 2 or 3 plants if all 4 seeds come up. Water the roots, not the leaves. Fertilize with well-rotted manure or Miracle-Gro twice during the growing season, which is 40 to 55 days. The first small squash are ready to eat when they are about 4 inches long. Leave them on the vines for a few days if you want larger ones for stuffing.

The fruits develop from the bright, marigold-yellow female blossoms which are found on short stems. The male blossoms are found on long, thin, upright stems and pollinate the female blossoms, and then drop off. (See Squash Blossoms, page 14.)

Keep the vegetable picked to encourage more bearing. If a recipe calls for a monster-sized zucchini, at the end of the season you are bound to have those also. Just let a few mature on the vine. These larger ones will keep for several weeks in a cool place. Cut with at least a 1-inch stem. Several good varieties to grow are aristocrat hybrid; golden zucchini; chefini hybrid, dark green; and courese, a white French variety.

All these rules for growing zucchini apply to the other summer-squash varieties as well. Seed varieties for these other bush-type, tender-skinned summer squash are as follows: Early golden summer yellow crookneck, St. Pat scallop hybrid, pale green hybrid cocozelle, Seneca butterbar, straightneck yellow buttercup, and dark green.

GROWING WINTER SQUASH

Winter squash are generally vine types, although some are semi-bush types. These vine-type squash sometimes trail 10 feet or more. Most of them have orange flesh and require about 100 to 125 days to mature. They also have a longer keeping power when stored in a cool, dry place. Botanically they are known as *Cucurbita Maxima* and *Cucurbita Moschata.* They are generally larger and weigh a great deal more. The strains of *Cucurbita Maxima,* like the Canada or winter crookneck, the Hubbard, Turks turban, and some varieties of pumpkins, can be grown to enormous sizes. Some weigh up to 200 pounds or more and one sees them on exhibition at country fairs.

Winter squash should be grown the same way as summer squash. Allow more room between rows when size is a consideration. Acorn squash, which are smaller, take up less room in small gardens. Remember to let them mature fully on the vines until their skins are extremely hard. Harvest before the first frost to keep for long storage.

To harvest, cut from the vine, leaving a 2- to 3-inch stem. Let them cure in the sun for at least a week, and then store in a cool, dry place over the winter.

Good varieties to grow are buttercup, blue Hubbard, Waltham butternut, and the semi-bush types, which are smaller and therefore suited to tiny gardens, such as gold nugget, table queen, and acorn squash.

SQUASH BLOSSOMS

Squash blossoms are a bit of exotica that are now more readily available since people are growing their own vegetables in small gardens across the country.

They are familiar to our Southwest and also to Mexico, South and Central America, and Italy. The brilliant saffron-colored blossoms were also the artistic inspiration of much American Indian silverwork. In the United States, the Indian squash blossom pattern is a lovely and familiar classic design that is still used in jewelry.

Squash blossoms have two sexes: the females, which form the vegetable, and the male flowers, which do not develop past the blossom stage.

The male blossoms are found on long, thin stems. These are the ones to pick, since otherwise they drop off to the ground and wither. The male blossoms must be picked before 10 A.M. or the sun will close them, making them harder to wash. Leave a few male blossoms on the plant for good pollination.

To keep and prepare the squash blossoms, harvest the long-stemmed male blossoms before 10 A.M., leaving 3 to 4 inches of stem. Rinse carefully under gently running cold water. Handle the blossoms most carefully, as they are very fragile. Let them drain on paper towels. When they are dry, put only the stem part in a wide jar of ice water. Cover the tops of the blossoms loosely with plastic wrap and keep them fresh in the refrigerator until ready to use. Before cooking, pinch out the center stamen part with the thumb and forefinger.

A WORD ON ORNAMENTAL GOURDS

Although not eaten in this country, ornamental gourds are most interesting and attractive to grow. Their colorful fruits come in a wide variety of shapes and textures. Some are striped and bicolored, and their patterns are lovely.

The dried fruits make a marvelous winter display. Grow them the same way as winter squash. They can be grown over an arbor or trellis, since they are smaller in size than most winter squash, and are most decorative when grown this way. The mature gourds have brown stems and hard, tough skins. Harvest before frost touches them. They can then be scrubbed and dried. If you wish to bring out their colors and give them longer life, spray them with a clear acrylic spray. They will become a lasting, carefree centerpiece to decorate your dining table throughout the fall and winter months.

TIPS ON COOKING SQUASH

Summer squash and people have one thing in common. They are both more than half water. Summer squash exudes large amounts of water during cooking and sometimes produces watered-down sauces in a casserole. The excess water can also cause spattering when the squash is fried in hot oil.

To eliminate this excess water without any loss of flavor to the vegetable, use one of the following methods.

METHOD ONE

When summer squash is to be sautéed, used whole, or cut in half for stuffing:

Place the entire squash in boiling, salted water and blanch it by boiling for about 8 to 10 minutes. Remove and plunge into cold water. Drain dry on paper towels. Cut in half for stuffing or, if the vegetable is to be left whole, scoop out the center with a long-handled spoon and proceed with the recipe directions.

METHOD TWO

For a recipe that calls for grated or sliced summer squash:

Either grate or slice the vegetable, according to the recipe directions. Sprinkle with salt and let sit in a bowl for 15 to 20 minutes, until it gives up some of its excess water. Rinse off the excess salt in a strainer or colander and dry on paper towels. Proceed with the recipe. In the case of grated squash, gently squeeze out the excess moisture between the palms of the hands. For soups or stews, it is not necessary to blanch or pre-salt the vegetable first. The liquids will be incorporated into the dish.

Winter squash does not need this pre-preparation unless grated raw in a recipe.

TABLES OF SIZES AND WEIGHTS

Generally the size and weight of a squash in a recipe is confusing, since squash come in different shapes, sizes, and dimensions, as well as weights and lengths. It's somewhat like buying toothpaste that comes in the small size, traveling size, family size, hospital size, giant size, economy size, large size, and super size. This doesn't tell you too much about the actual contents of a tube of toothpaste.

When you grow your own vegetables, if you do not have a scale to weigh them, there is a problem as to what size and weight to use. This table will help select the proper size and approximate weight to use in each recipe and avoid confusion.

SUMMER SQUASH

1 pound of summer squash yields 2 to 3 portions.

1 summer squash 4 inches long and 1½ inches at its widest point, weighs about ¼ pound. Therefore, 4 small squash of this size equal about 1 pound.

1 pound of raw, cubed, or sliced summer squash equals about 3½ cups.

1 pound of grated summer squash equals about 2 cups.

A. Small	3 to 4 inches	= ¼ pound
B. Medium	6 to 7 inches	= ½ pound
C. Large	9 to 10 inches	= ¾ to 1 pound
D. Very large	12 inches and over	= 1 to 2 pounds

WINTER SQUASH

A. Small	size of a baseball	= 1 pound
B. Medium	size of a child's rubber ball	= 2 pounds
C. Large	size of a football	= 4 to 5 pounds
D. Very large	size of a basketball	= 8 to 10 pounds
E. Giant	size of a beach ball	= 10 to 12 pounds

HORS D'OEUVRES

TOASTED PUMPKIN SEEDS   [Armenian]
ZUCCHINI AND HORSERADISH DIP   [United States]
ZUCCHINI AND BACON HORS D'OEUVRES   [United States]
ZUCCHINI AND CORNICHON   [French]
CRESCENT PUMPKIN CHIPS   [West Indian]
STUFFED COLD ZUCCHINI IN TOMATO SAUCE   [Italian]
SWEET AND SOUR PUMPKIN   [United States]
YOGURT PASTRY TURNOVERS FILLED WITH ZUCCHINI AND
   CHEESE   [Turkish]

TOASTED PUMPKIN SEEDS
[Armenian]

YIELD: TWO 1-PINT JARS

4 cups pumpkin seeds
1 ½ qts. cold water
1 cup salt

[18]

Remove seeds from pumpkin and spread them out on paper towels. Let them dry slightly for 30 minutes. Then to a large pot add water, salt, and pumpkin seeds. Simmer for 30 minutes and drain in a colander. Spread again to dry on paper towels for 10 minutes. Preheat oven to 250°. In a large, flat baking pan, spread out the seeds and toast in the oven about 1 hour, until seeds are light tan.

Test by cracking 1 or 2 seeds between the teeth to make sure the inside kernel is dry and toasted. Let cool, and store in a covered glass jar to prevent moisture from entering.

ZUCCHINI AND HORSERADISH DIP
[*United States*]

SERVES 4

3 small zucchini, unpeeled and chopped fine (about 2 cups)
1 Tbs. horseradish
¼ cup mayonnaise
¼ cup chili sauce

Mix thoroughly and chill.

ZUCCHINI AND BACON HORS D'OEUVRES
[*United States*]

SERVES 4

3 small zucchini, unpeeled and left whole
4 oz. cream cheese, softened
3 slices bacon, fried and crumbled
1 clove garlic, peeled and minced
1 tsp. parsley, chopped
¼ tsp. black pepper

Cut off ends of zucchini and scoop out center with apple corer or long-handled iced-tea spoon. Mix cream cheese, bacon, garlic, parsley, and pepper together and stuff into center of zucchini. Chill. Cut ½-inch-thick slices across the width of the vegetable and serve arranged on plate with crackers.

ZUCCHINI AND CORNICHONS
[French]

SERVES 4

3 small zucchini, unpeeled and
   diced into ½-inch cubes
1 Tbs. olive oil
1 Tbs. onion, minced
⅔ cup tomato sauce
Salt to taste
4 oz. cream cheese, cut into
   chunks

4 to 5 drops Tabasco sauce
3 to 4 small cornichons (French
   pickles), chopped, or 1
   medium-sized Kosher dill
   pickle, chopped

Heat oil and sauté onion until wilted. Add zucchini, tomato sauce, and salt to taste. Simmer 15 to 20 minutes. Let cool. When cool, put into blender, add cream cheese and Tabasco sauce. Remove from blender, stir in chopped cornichons and chill. Serve as spread for crackers.

CRESCENT PUMPKIN CHIPS
[West Indian]

SERVES 4

1 small pumpkin (the size of a baseball, about 1 lb.)
½ cup flour
Salt and pepper
1 cup peanut oil

Wash and peel the pumpkin and cut into wedges. Cut each wedge into slices ¼ inch thick. They should look like crescents. Mix flour with salt and pepper, and dip the slices into it. Heat oil and fry until slices are crisp and light brown. Sprinkle with additional salt before serving.

STUFFED COLD ZUCCHINI IN TOMATO SAUCE
[Italian]

SERVES 6 TO 8

7 medium zucchini (about ½ lb. each)

With long-handled iced-tea spoons, scoop out centers of the zucchini, leaving firm, hollow shells, and set aside.

STUFFING

1 slice white bread, crust removed *3 Tbs. Parmesan cheese, grated*
 ½ lb. ground beef *1 Tbs. parsley, minced*
 1 egg, beaten *Salt and pepper*
 1 clove garlic, minced *¼ tsp. nutmeg*

Put bread in water to soak, and then squeeze out and crumble. Add to ground beef. Add egg, garlic, Parmesan cheese, parsley, salt, pepper, and nutmeg. Mix well and stuff the zucchini shells.

SAUCE

2 Tbs. olive oil *Salt and pepper to taste*
 1 medium onion, chopped *Lemon wedges*
 3 Tbs. dry white wine *1 Tbs. parsley, minced*
 2 cups tomato sauce, canned

Heat an oval casserole, preferably a heavy iron one. Add 2 Tbs. olive oil and the chopped onion. Stir until onion is golden, add white wine, tomato sauce, and salt and pepper. Cook until flavors are blended, about 2 minutes. Then add the stuffed zucchini to the sauce, laying the shells side by side. Bake in a 300° oven for about 20 minutes. Then turn the zucchini over and continue to bake for another 20 minutes. Let cool, then chill and serve cold with lemon wedges dipped into minced parsley.

SWEET AND SOUR PUMPKIN
[United States]

SERVES 8 TO 10

1 large pumpkin (the size of a football, about 5 lbs.), peeled, strings and seeds removed, and cut into 1-inch squares
1 cup white cider vinegar

2 cups sugar
2 sticks cinnamon, broken
6 whole cloves
½ tsp. dried thyme
1 bay leaf, broken
¼ tsp. nutmeg

Boil vinegar, sugar, and broken cinnamon sticks together. Remove from heat and add all other spices. Put pumpkin into a large, sterilized jar. Pour liquid over. Close the jar and shake it. Let marinate for 10 days, shaking the jar occasionally. Serve cold.

YOGURT PASTRY TURNOVERS FILLED WITH ZUCCHINI AND CHEESE
[Turkish]

YIELD: 3 DOZEN

FILLING

2 medium zucchini (about 1½ lbs.), peeled, grated, and with liquid squeezed out
2 eggs, beaten
*¼ lb. mozzarella cheese, cubed**
4 fresh mint leaves, chopped
Salt and pepper to taste

 * A soft, white Turkish cheese is used in Turkey. Mozzarella is substituted here because the Turkish cheese is rarely imported.

Salt the grated zucchini and let stand. Then squeeze out as much liquid as possible. Mix with eggs, cheese, mint, salt, and pepper. Set filling aside and make pastry. If filling accumulates too much liquid, drain in strainer. If still too liquid, sprinkle filling with 1 Tbs. flour.

PASTRY

½ lb. margarine	Flour to make a stiff dough
2 Tbs. olive oil	¼ tsp. baking soda
2 eggs, beaten separately	¼ tsp. salt
8 oz. plain yogurt	

Preheat oven to 400°. Melt margarine and add olive oil. Let cool slightly and add 1 beaten egg and yogurt. Gradually add flour, baking soda, and salt to this mixture, until dough is somewhat stiff. Then knead it for 5 minutes until it becomes more pliable. On floured pastry board, roll out pastry about ¼ inch thick and cut into 3-inch rounds with cookie cutter. Place 1 tsp. of filling near edge of circle, moisten edge with water, fold over in half, and press down edge with a fork to seal. Brush the second beaten egg over the tops of the turnovers. Butter a baking pan and place the turnovers on it about 1 inch apart. Bake for 20 minutes and serve hot.

SOUPS

PUMPKIN SOUP WITH GRAND MARNIER   *[French]*

ZUCCHINI WITH CREAM AND CURRY SOUP   *[United States]*

PUMPKIN CONTAINER FOR CHINESE SOUP   *[Chinese]*

BUTTERNUT SQUASH SOUP   *[Italian]*

SPICED ACORN SQUASH SOUP WITH PINE NUTS   *[United States]*

ZUCCHINI AND CARROT SOUP WITH TARRAGON AND SHRIMP
   [French]

ZUCCHINI SOUP WITH VERMICELLI   *[Italian]*

LEEK AND PUMPKIN SOUP   *[Italian]*

PUMPKIN SOUP WITH SALT PORK   *[West Indian]*

YELLOW SQUASH SOUP   *[United States]*

CREAM OF PUMPKIN WITH HAM AND CURRIED CROUTONS
   [English]

ZUCCHINI AND YOGURT SOUP   *[Armenian]*

COLD, GREEN SUMMER SOUP   *[United States]*

HOT ZUCCHINI SOUP WITH GREEN PEAS AND CHERVIL
[*United States*]

FUZZY SQUASH SOUP   [*Chinese*]

PUMPKIN SOUP WITH GRAND MARNIER
[*French*]

SERVES 8

1 pumpkin (the size of a football, about 5 lbs.), peeled, strings and seeds removed, and cut into 2-inch pieces
3 beef marrow bones
½ lb. chuck beef, cut into 1-inch cubes
1 carrot, grated
1 small turnip, grated
2 medium potatoes, peeled and cut into cubes
2 stalks celery, chopped
1 large leek, white part only, chopped

1 tsp. fresh ginger root, peeled and grated
¼ tsp. allspice
¼ tsp. thyme
Salt to taste
2½ qts. water
2 cups light cream
2 cups corn kernels, frozen or canned
½ cup Grand Marnier
4 drops Tabasco sauce
2 pieces candied ginger, chopped fine

In a large pot with a lid, combine pumpkin, bones, cubed beef, carrot, turnip, potatoes, celery, leek, and all seasonings except Tabasco and candied ginger. Add the water and cook slowly, covered, for 2 hours, skimming the foam that forms, when necessary. Remove meat and bones and purée the soup in a blender a few batches at a time. When cool, add cream, corn, Grand Marnier, and Tabasco. Serve cold, sprinkled with candied ginger.

This is a most elegant, sophisticated first course for a summer's day.

ZUCCHINI WITH CREAM AND CURRY SOUP
[United States]

SERVES 10

6 medium zucchini (about 2½
lbs.), unpeeled and sliced ½
inch thick
6 Tbs. butter
1 large onion, chopped
3 cloves garlic, minced

1 Tbs. curry powder
Two 15-oz. cans chicken broth
Salt to taste
3 cups light cream
4 drops Tabasco sauce

Melt butter in a very large, flat-bottom skillet. Add onion, garlic and zucchini slices, and sprinkle with curry powder. Sauté over medium heat until tender, 20 to 25 minutes, stirring occasionally so it doesn't burn. Add chicken broth and salt and heat to boiling point. Lower heat and simmer for 10 minutes to blend flavors. Whirl in a blender, a few batches at a time. Add the cream and Tabasco and taste for additional salt. Serve ice cold.

This recipe came to me by way of a fellow Fire Islander. Last year, after growing a huge zucchini crop and running out of ways to prepare this bounty, a kindly neighbor parted with her own secret recipe.

PUMPKIN CONTAINER FOR CHINESE SOUP
[*Chinese*]

SERVES 12

1 very large pumpkin (the size of a basketball, about 8 to 10 lbs.)

8 cups chicken broth, fresh or canned

1 cup peanut oil

1 lb. chicken breasts, boned, skinned, and cut into narrow strips

1 lb. shrimp, peeled and cut lengthwise into halves

2 cups bok choy, both white and green parts, slivered*

½ lb. mushrooms, sliced thin, lengthwise

¼ lb. fresh snow peas, left whole

½ lb. fresh bean sprouts

4 scallions, cut into 1-inch pieces

1 tsp. M.S.G.**

1 tsp. ginger root, peeled and grated

1 Tbs. sugar

5 Tbs. soy sauce

8 drops Tabasco sauce

4 Tbs. cornstarch

Make a horizontal cut 2 inches from the top of the pumpkin. This will make a lid. Scrape out seeds and stringy part from bottom half of the pumpkin. Choose a very large pot that can accommodate the pumpkin. Put a large cloth napkin, torn sheeting, or a towel in the bottom of the pot and allow the ends of the fabric to hang out. (These ends will be tied diagonally over the whole pumpkin so that it can be lifted out when finished.) Place bottom half of pumpkin on the fabric in the pot. In a second pot, heat the chicken broth to boiling and pour 4 cups inside the pumpkin. Reserve the rest of the chicken broth for the sauce.

In a wok or large frying pan, heat ½ cup peanut oil, add the chicken, and quickly, over high heat, stir-fry 2 minutes. Remove chicken from wok with slotted spoon, set aside, and add the shrimp.

---

* Bok choy is a crisp, delicate cabbage-like vegetable found fresh in Chinese and Asian markets.

** M.S.G. is short for monosodium glutamate. It is composed of white crystals that have no taste of their own, but enhance the natural flavor of foods.

Stir-fry shrimp for 2 minutes and put in same dish as the cooked chicken. In same wok, add another ½ cup oil and let it get very hot. Add the bok choy, stir-fry 2 minutes, and remove to another bowl. Then add the mushrooms, also stir-fry for 2 minutes, and remove to bowl with bok choy. Add the snow peas, stir-fry for 2 minutes, remove, and lastly, add the bean sprouts, scallions. Cook these 1 minute. There will be two bowls—one with the chicken and shrimp and one with the vegetables. Sprinkle both the vegetables and the shrimp and chicken with M.S.G. in equal amounts.

Bring the pot with reserved chicken broth to a boil. In a bowl blend ginger root, sugar, soy sauce, Tabasco, and cornstarch. Slowly stir this mixture into the boiling chicken broth; stir constantly so there are no lumps. Pour this mixture into the pumpkin shell. Place the lid of the pumpkin on the bottom half and tightly tie the four corners of the fabric over the whole pumpkin to make a knotted handle to lift it out. Pour boiling water around the pumpkin so that the water level is about 2 inches below the cut where the lid was made. Cover the pot and boil gently for approximately 5½ hours, replacing the boiling water around the fabric-wrapped pumpkin if necessary. After 4½ hours, open the knot of the fabric (use potholders, it's hot), remove the lid of the pumpkin and add the shrimp and chicken. Tie ends loosely again and cook for ½ hour. Then open pumpkin again, add the vegetables, and cover with pumpkin lid. Tie knot tightly. Cover pot and cook 15 to 20 minutes more. This method assures a tender pumpkin, which needs long cooking, a flavorful broth infused with pumpkin and meat, and shellfish and vegetables that are not overcooked and limp. Lift the towel out by the topknot and place on a serving dish. Cut away excess cloth. Remove lid and serve from pumpkin tureen.

This festive "meal in a pumpkin" recipe sounds complex but is really very simple when you read it through first. It's worth doing for the oohs and aahs when presented at the table. It is very impressive.

BUTTERNUT SQUASH SOUP
[*Italian*]

SERVES 8

2 *large butternut squash**
(*about 10 to 12 inches,*
about 5 lbs.), *peeled, seeded,*
and sliced
1 *large onion, chopped*
4 *Tbs. butter*
3 *Tbs. olive oil*
6 *medium potatoes, peeled and*
sliced

8 *cups chicken broth, fresh or*
canned
1 *Tbs. cornstarch*
Salt and pepper
1 *cup light cream*
½ *cup Parmesan cheese, grated*

In a large pot with a cover, sauté onion in butter and oil until onion is wilted. Add the slices of squash and potato. Stir over low heat to blend flavors, then add the chicken broth and the cornstarch dissolved in a little cold water. Season to taste with salt and pepper and simmer for 1 hour, stirring occasionally. Whirl the soup in a blender in small batches at a time. Add the cream and 1 Tbs. of extra butter for a smooth texture. Heat slowly to serving temperature and serve with grated Parmesan.

* The variety of Italian pumpkin called zucca is used in Italy for this soup. It is more like our butternut squash than our native pumpkin, therefore it can be more closely duplicated by using the butternut squash.

SPICED ACORN SQUASH SOUP
WITH PINE NUTS
[United States]

SERVES 6

3 acorn squash (each the size
of a baseball, about 1 lb.),
unpeeled, seeded, and cut
into 2-inch cubes
1 medium onion, chopped
1 stalk celery, chopped
2 Tbs. butter
3 cups chicken broth, fresh or
canned

¼ tsp. sugar
1 tsp. cinnamon
¼ tsp. mace
1 cup heavy cream
Salt and pepper to taste
1 Tbs. pine nuts

Add squash to a saucepan of boiling water and simmer for 15 to
20 minutes. Drain and peel. Sauté onion and celery in butter until
wilted. Add chicken broth and squash and simmer for 20 minutes.
Purée in blender, a few batches at a time. Return to saucepan, add
sugar, cinnamon, mace, and cream. Reheat slowly, but do not boil.
Add salt and pepper to taste and garnish with pine nuts.

ZUCCHINI AND CARROT SOUP
WITH TARRAGON AND SHRIMP
[French]

SERVES 6

1 very large zucchini (about 2
lbs.), unpeeled and diced
2 Tbs. butter
1 cup carrots, diced
1 medium onion, chopped
1 clove garlic, minced
2 cups chicken broth, fresh or
canned

2 cups milk
Salt and pepper to taste
1 Tbs. fresh tarragon, minced
¼ lb. shrimp, cooked, shelled,
and halved lengthwise

In a 4-quart covered pot, heat butter and sauté carrots, zucchini, onion, and garlic for 10 minutes, stirring occasionally. Add chicken broth, milk, salt, and pepper. Simmer for 20 minutes and purée in small batches. Add tarragon, stir, and garnish with halved shrimp.

Tarragon

ZUCCHINI SOUP WITH VERMICELLI
[*Italian*]

SERVES 4 to 6

*1 very large zucchini (about
   2 to 3 lbs.), unpeeled and
   diced
2 Tbs. butter
2 Tbs. olive oil
1 tsp. salt
½ tsp. black pepper
6 cups chicken broth, fresh or
   canned*

*2 eggs, beaten
¼ cup Pecorino cheese
3 leaves basil, minced
¼ lb. fine noodles (capellini
   or vermicelli)
1 Tbs. parsley, minced*

In a 5-quart pot, sauté zucchini in butter and oil for 10 minutes. Add salt and pepper. Add chicken broth and stir. Cook, covered, for 25 minutes over low heat. In a bowl, beat the eggs with a whisk, add cheese, basil, and parsley. Add the vermicelli to the zucchini soup and cook for a few minutes until tender. Then gradually add the egg mixture to the hot soup. Stir and cook 1 minute over low heat. Sprinkle with parsley.

LEEK AND PUMPKIN SOUP
[Italian]

SERVES 6

1 medium pumpkin (the size of a child's rubber ball, about 2 lbs.), peeled, strings and seeds removed, and cut into 1-inch cubes
6 Tbs. butter
1 large onion, chopped
2 large potatoes, peeled and diced
½ cup fava beans, or string beans, cut into 1½-inch pieces
2½ cups milk
Salt to taste
3 drops Tabasco sauce
1 large or 2 small leeks, white parts only, cut into strips
3 cups chicken broth, fresh or canned
1 cup heavy cream
1 cup cooked rice
4 Tbs. parsley, chopped

Melt 3 Tbs. butter in a saucepan and cook the onion until wilted. Add pumpkin, potatoes, beans, and milk. Bring to a boil, then reduce heat and simmer for 40 minutes, stirring occasionally.

Purée in a blender, pour into a clean saucepan, and add salt and Tabasco to taste.

Melt the remaining 3 Tbs. of butter in another saucepan and cook the finely cut leeks until soft. Add to pumpkin-potato mixture. Heat chicken broth, add to pumpkin mixture, and bring slowly to a boil. Just before serving, stir in the heavy cream and simmer 1 minute to heat through. Add cooked rice and chopped parsley. Serve hot.

PUMPKIN SOUP WITH SALT PORK
[*West Indian*]

SERVES 6 to 8

1 pumpkin (the size of a   *½ bay leaf*
football, about 4 to 5 lbs.),   *½ tsp. thyme*
peeled, strings and seeds   *4 to 6 drops Tabasco sauce*
removed, and cut into 2-inch   *Salt to taste*
pieces   *½ tsp. nutmeg, grated*
¼ lb. salt pork, minced
4 cups chicken broth, fresh or
canned

In a 6-quart pot, simmer the salt pork in chicken broth with the bay leaf and thyme for 30 minutes. Add pumpkin and cook for 20 minutes more. Whirl in blender to purée in small batches. Add Tabasco, salt to taste, and reheat to serving temperature. Sprinkle with nutmeg.

YELLOW SQUASH SOUP
[*United States*]

SERVES 6

1 very large, yellow summer   *1 large onion, chopped*
squash (about 1½ lbs.),   *Salt and pepper to taste*
unpeeled and cut into   *2 egg yolks*
chunks   *1 cup heavy cream*
6 cups chicken broth, fresh or
canned

Heat chicken broth in a 4-quart saucepan, add onion and squash, and cook gently until tender, about 10 to 15 minutes. Remove vegetables from broth with a slotted spoon and whirl in blender. Return to chicken broth, add salt and pepper to taste. Beat the egg yolks and heavy cream with a wire whisk. Gradually add 1 cup of the hot soup to the egg-cream mixture, using wire whisk. Then return to chicken broth mixture and let it heat through. Do not allow soup to boil, or it will curdle.

Note: This soup is excellent served ice cold and topped with snipped chives.

CREAM OF PUMPKIN SOUP
WITH HAM AND CURRIED CROUTONS
[English]

SERVES 6

1 medium pumpkin (the size of a child's rubber ball, about 2 lbs.), peeled, strings and seeds removed, and cut into 1-inch cubes
1 small onion, chopped
1 small carrot, diced
Two ¼-inch-thick slices ham, minced
4 Tbs. butter
1 Tbs. flour
Salt and pepper to taste

3 cups hot chicken broth, fresh or canned
1 fresh tomato, peeled and diced
½ bay leaf
2 whole cloves
¼ tsp. thyme
1 cup heavy cream
Bread cubes (3 slices white bread, crusts trimmed, cut into ½-inch cubes.)
½ tsp. curry powder

In a 5-quart pot, sauté onion, carrot, and ham (reserving some ham for garnish) in 2 Tbs. butter over low heat for 5 minutes. Sprinkle with flour, salt and pepper, and mix together. Add hot chicken broth, tomato, bay leaf, cloves, thyme, and pumpkin. Cover and cook slowly for 1 hour. Remove from heat and purée in a blender in small batches. Return to pot, add cream and heat through. Sprinkle with minced ham and croutons of cubed bread sautéed in remaining butter and curry powder until golden.

ZUCCHINI AND YOGURT SOUP
[*Armenian*]

SERVES 8

*4 large zucchini (about 3 lbs.),
unpeeled and cut into 1-inch
cubes
1/4 lb. sweet butter, or margarine
4 cups onion, coarsely chopped
4 cups chicken broth, fresh or
canned*

*1 clove garlic, minced
Salt and pepper to taste
1 pt. plain yogurt
1/2 cup scallions, green parts
only, cut fine*

Melt butter in a 7-quart pot and add onions. Cook, stirring, until onion is golden. Add zucchini and cook for 5 minutes. Add chicken broth, garlic, salt, and pepper. Cover and simmer for 10 minutes. Zucchini must be tender-crisp, not mushy. Purée in blender and chill. When chilled, stir in yogurt and sprinkle with scallions. Serve ice cold.

COLD, GREEN SUMMER SOUP
[*United States*]

SERVES 6

*1 large zucchini, unpeeled
and chopped (reserve 6
slices)
2 cups string beans, chopped
2 cups Romaine lettuce,
chopped
2 cups peas*

*1 cup celery, chopped
1/2 cup shallots, chopped fine
5 cups chicken broth, fresh or
canned
Salt and pepper to taste
1/4 cup parsley, coarsely
chopped*

In a 7-quart pot, simmer all vegetables in chicken broth for 15 to 20 minutes with the lid of the pot half off. Purée in a blender in small amounts. Add salt and pepper to taste. Chill and serve topped with thin slices of raw zucchini and chopped parsley.

Note: This is a very light, cold soup for the "dog days" of summer. With the addition of a sliced hard-boiled egg topping the soup, it can be a whole luncheon.

HOT ZUCCHINI SOUP WITH GREEN PEAS AND CHERVIL
[United States]

SERVES 6

1 large zucchini (about 1 lb.), unpeeled and cut into chunks
2 quarts chicken broth, fresh or canned
1 large onion, sliced

2 Tbs. fresh chervil
½ tsp. dried oregano
Salt and pepper to taste
1 cup peas (frozen), thawed and cooked

In a 7-quart pot, combine chicken broth, onion, 1 Tbs. chervil, oregano, salt and pepper and bring to a boil. Add the zucchini, lower heat to medium, and cook about 25 minutes or until zucchini is very soft. Remove from heat and add peas.. Purée in a blender, a few batches at a time. Return to pot to just heat through. Serve hot. Sprinkle with remaining 1 Tbs. chervil.

Chervil

FUZZY SQUASH SOUP
[Chinese]

SERVES 4

*1 medium Chinese fuzzy squash
(about ¾ lb.), peeled and
cut into slices ½ inch thick*
8 cups canned chicken broth
*3 pieces orange peel, cut into
thin strips*
¼ cup water
*1 whole chicken breast, skinned,
boned, and cut in strips*

*3 scallions, cut into 1-inch
pieces*
*2 celery stalks, cut into 1-inch
pieces*
4 Tbs. light soy sauce*
Salt and pepper to taste
2 cakes dried shrimp noodles**

Soak orange peel in ¼ cup water for 20 minutes. Heat chicken broth to boiling in a 6-quart pot. Add chicken, orange peel, squash, 2 scallions, celery, soy sauce, salt and pepper. Cook for 15 minutes. Add dried shrimp noodles and cook for 5 minutes more. Serve hot, garnished with remaining scallion.

Variation: Substitute ½ pound lean pork, cut in strips, for chicken and use regular soy sauce.

* Light soy sauce is more delicate than regular soy sauce and is generally used with chicken, fish, and seafood. (See Sources for Ingredients, page 289.)
** Dried shrimp noodles come in packages and are shaped like cakes. They also can be bought in Chinese markets.

SALADS

ZUCCHINI AND SHREDDED BEEF SALAD   [*Thai*]

ZUCCHINI SALAD WITH OLIVES AND CAPERS   {*Italian*}

ZUCCHINI AND BROCCOLI SALAD   [*Italian*]

YELLOW SQUASH SALAD WITH YOGURT AND MINT   [*Israeli*]

ZUCCHINI FINGERS WITH HERBS AND CAPERS   [*French*]

ZUCCHINI AND AVOCADO SALAD   [*United States*]

YELLOW SQUASH AND AVOCADO WITH RED AND GREEN
    PEPPERS   [*Spanish*]

ZUCCHINI AND MUSHROOM SALAD WITH COCKTAIL ONIONS
    [*United States*]

ZUCCHINI CHAIN SALAD   [*United States*]

TOMATO SALAD STUFFED WITH ZUCCHINI AND RAW
    MUSHROOMS   [*United States*]

ZUCCHINI AND SHREDDED BEEF SALAD
[Thai]

SERVES 4

3 small zucchini (about 1 lb.), unpeeled and sliced ½ inch thick
½ pound cold, leftover roast beef, shredded ¼ inch thick
2 cups iceberg lettuce, shredded

DRESSING

1 clove garlic, minced	*¼ tsp. M.S.G.*
2 tsp. soy sauce	*Salt to taste*
½ cup lemon juice	*2 drops Tabasco sauce*
3 tsp. sugar	*1 Tbs. parsley, minced*

Cook zucchini in ½ inch boiling water for 4 to 5 minutes, until tender-crisp. Drain and cool. Mix beef shreds and lettuce together and arrange zucchini slices around platter. Combine dressing and pour over salad. Garnish with parsley.

ZUCCHINI SALAD WITH OLIVES AND CAPERS
[Italian]

SERVES 6

6 small zucchini (about ¼ lb. each), unpeeled and cut into ½-inch slices	*6 Tbs. olive or safflower oil*
	3 Tbs. lemon juice
	6 stuffed olives, sliced across
6 Tbs. butter	*2 Tbs. capers, rinsed and drained*
6 Tbs. water	
1 tsp. vinegar	*2 Tbs. parsley, chopped*
1 tsp. fresh dill, snipped	*1 scallion, minced*
Salt to taste	*1 egg, hard-cooked and chopped fine*
Lettuce leaves	

Melt 6 Tbs. butter and add 6 Tbs. water, 1 tsp. vinegar, dill, and salt to taste. Cook zucchini in this mixture for 8 minutes over low

heat, stirring carefully until tender-crisp. Drain well and arrange on lettuce leaves. Make a vinaigrette sauce of oil and lemon juice and pour over slices of zucchini. Sprinkle with sliced olives, capers, parsley, scallion, and chopped egg. Serve cold.

ZUCCHINI AND BROCCOLI SALAD
[Italian]

SERVES 8

4 small zucchini (about ¼ lb. each), unpeeled and sliced 1 inch thick
1 small bunch broccoli
Lettuce
1 tsp. fresh tarragon, minced
6 Tbs. safflower oil
3 Tbs. tarragon vinegar

2 canned pimientos, washed, drained, and cut into small strips
2 Tbs. capers, washed and drained
1 tsp. shallots, chopped fine
Salt and pepper to taste

Cut flowers of broccoli from stems and cook broccoli in steamer for 8 minutes. Drain and chill. Do the same to steam zucchini for 5 minutes. Vegetables should be slightly crisp. Place the broccoli and zucchini in a lettuce-lined salad bowl. Mix the tarragon, oil, vinegar, pimiento, capers, shallots, and salt and pepper. Pour over and chill.

YELLOW SQUASH SALAD WITH YOGURT AND MINT
[Israeli]

SERVES 8

8 small summer squash (about ¼ lb. each), unpeeled and sliced ¼-inch thick
8 oz. plain yogurt

Salt and pepper to taste
1 clove garlic, minced
2 Tbs. fresh mint leaves, chopped

Steam sliced squash in a collapsible steamer for 3 minutes. Remove and chill. Mix yogurt with salt, pepper, garlic, and mint and pour over chilled squash.

Variations:

1. 4 Tbs. mayonnaise and 4 Tbs. sour cream can be added to the yogurt.
2. Freshly snipped dill can be used instead of mint.
3. A combination of small, young green zucchini and yellow squash can also be used.

ZUCCHINI FINGERS WITH HERBS AND CAPERS
[French]

SERVES 8

8 small zucchini (about ¼ lb. each), unpeeled and left whole
6 Tbs. safflower oil
2 Tbs. wine vinegar*
1 clove garlic, minced
1 small onion, grated
Lettuce leaves
4 small tomatoes, peeled and cut into cubes

½ small green pepper, cut into ¼-inch strips
1 scallion, minced
1 Tbs. capers, rinsed and drained
1 tsp. parsley, minced
1 tsp. fresh basil, minced
Salt and pepper to taste

Steam whole zucchini for 5 to 8 minutes until tender-crisp. Cut in half lengthwise and then into quarters, so they are finger-shaped sticks. Mix oil, vinegar, garlic, and onion together and pour one-half mixture over zucchini fingers. Cover and marinate for 4 hours in the refrigerator. When ready to serve, lift zucchini out of mari-

* Dessaux Fils is a good French wine vinegar. It is available white with tarragon and also red. It can be bought in specialty food shops. (See Sources for Ingredients, page 289.)

nade with slotted spoon and arrange on lettuce leaves. To the other half of the vinaigrette sauce, add chopped tomatoes, green pepper strips, scallion, capers, parsley, basil, salt and pepper and pour over the zucchini and lettuce.

ZUCCHINI AND
AVOCADO SALAD
[*United States*]

SERVES 6

6 *small zucchini* (*about* ¼ *lb.*   3 *Tbs. olive oil*
   each), *unpeeled and sliced*   1 *Tbs. lemon juice*
   ¼ *inch thick*   *Salt to taste*
3 *scallions, minced*   4 *drops Tabasco sauce*
1 *large avocado, peeled and*   *Lettuce leaves*
   cubed

Steam zucchini slices over boiling water in vegetable steamer for about 6 minutes until tender-crisp. Drain thoroughly on paper towels and chill. Add scallions and avocado and mix carefully. Mix olive oil, lemon juice, salt, Tabasco and pour over zucchini. Chill and serve on lettuce leaves.

YELLOW SQUASH AND AVOCADO
WITH RED AND GREEN PEPPERS
[Spanish]

SERVES 6

6 *small summer squash and zucchini (about ¼ lb. each), unpeeled and sliced thin*
2 *cups scallions, minced fine*
2 *green peppers, cut into small slivers*
1 *sweet red pepper, cut into small slivers*

1 *medium avocado, peeled and sliced into ½-inch wedges*
3 *Tbs. olive oil*
1 *Tbs. white wine vinegar*
1 *Tbs. fresh basil, minced, or 1 tsp. dried basil*
Salt and black pepper to taste
Lettuce leaves

Cook scallions and squash in small amount of water until tender-crisp, about 3 to 4 minutes. Drain and mix with peppers and avocado. Combine oil, vinegar, basil, salt, and pepper. Pour over vegetables and chill. Serve on lettuce leaves.

ZUCCHINI AND MUSHROOM SALAD
WITH COCKTAIL ONIONS
[United States]

SERVES 6 TO 8

4 *medium-small zucchini (about 2 lbs.), cut 1 inch thick*
2 *Tbs. olive oil*
1 *lb. tiny mushrooms, stems removed*
2 *sprigs of parsley*
2 *cloves garlic*

2 *Tbs. pickled cocktail onions, rinsed well and drained*
1 *Tbs. mixed pickling spice*
1 *cup dry white wine*
Salt to taste
Tabasco sauce to taste
Lettuce leaves

Sauté zucchini in olive oil until browned on all sides. Add the mushroom caps, parsley sprigs, and whole garlic cloves. Cover and simmer 10 minutes over low heat. Remove garlic and parsley. With a slotted spoon, remove vegetables, leaving juices in pan, and add the cocktail onions to the vegetables. To the skillet with the vegetable juices, add the pickling spice, wine, salt, and Tabasco to taste. Bring to a boil and boil for 5 minutes. In a strainer lined with cheesecloth, pour the boiling liquid over the vegetables. Let cool, then chill for several hours or overnight to blend flavors. Serve on lettuce leaves.

ZUCCHINI CHAIN SALAD
[United States]

SERVES 6

3 small zucchini (about 1/2 lb.), unpeeled

DRESSING

2 Tbs. lemon juice	*2 Tbs. olive oil*
Salt and pepper to taste	*Lettuce leaves*
1/2 tsp. Dijon-style mustard	*Pimiento strips*
3 Tbs. safflower oil	

With a wire whisk, beat the lemon juice, salt, pepper, and mustard and gradually add the safflower and olive oils, beating all the while. Makes about 1/2 cup.

Run the tines of a fork lengthwise over the skins of the zucchini to score the surfaces and then slice across 1/8 inch thick. Lay slices flat and with the point of a sharp knife, remove a small circle in the center of each slice. Make one cut through the side of each slice, except one, and fit one ring into the other by opening and then closing each ring. In an oval dish spread lettuce leaves, then the zucchini chain, and pour the vinaigrette dressing on top. Chill for 1 hour or more and serve with strips of red pimiento as a garnish.

TOMATO SALAD STUFFED WITH ZUCCHINI AND RAW MUSHROOMS
[*United States*]

SERVES 4

*1 large zucchini (about 1 lb.),
unpeeled, center pulp and
seeds removed, shredded,
salted, and drained
4 large tomatoes
½ tsp. salt
¼ tsp. black pepper
Pinch sugar*

*½ cup mushrooms, sliced very
thin
1 clove garlic
1 clove garlic, minced
1 Tbs. olive oil
4 tsp. mayonnaise
1 tsp. lemon juice
Black olives*

Slice off tops of tomatoes and scoop out pulp. Chop and put in a colander to drain. Mix the tomato pulp and shredded zucchini and let drain again for 20 minutes. Sprinkle inside of tomato with salt, pepper, and sugar. Invert on paper towels and drain in the refrigerator for 20 minutes. Then mix sliced, raw mushrooms, garlic, and parsley together and add to the zucchini-tomato mixture. Mix oil, mayonnaise, lemon juice, additional salt and pepper to taste. Toss with zucchini mixture and stuff tomato shells. Garnish with black olives and serve chilled.

SIDE DISHES

PUMPKIN RING WITH GREEN PEAS   [*United States*]

ZUCCHINI WITH BÉCHAMEL SAUCE   [*Italian*]

SKEWERED ZUCCHINI AND ONIONS   [*French*]

ZUCCHINI WITH SOUR CREAM, DILL, AND PAPRIKA   [*Hungarian*]

STUFFED ZUCCHINI WITH ALMONDS, EGGS, AND CHEESE
   [*United States*]

YELLOW SQUASH WITH BUTTON MUSHROOMS   [*United States*]

POTATOES AND YELLOW SQUASH WITH GARLIC   [*Greek*]

CROOKNECK SQUASH WITH RICE AND DILL   [*Israeli*]

YELLOW SQUASH LOAF   [*Israeli*]

LEMON ZUCCHINI FANS FOR ZUCCHINI FANS   [*French*]

SEVEN VARIETIES OF BAKED STUFFED ACORN SQUASH
   [*United States*]

ZUCCHINI WITH ONION AND TOASTED SESAME SEEDS
   [*Chinese*]

ZUCCHINI WITH LEMON PEEL   [*French*]

CROOKNECK SQUASH IN SOUR CREAM WITH DILL
  [*United States*]
ZUCCHINI WITH CHINESE VEGETABLES [*Chinese*]
SOUTHERN FRIED ZUCCHINI [*United States*]
ZUCCHINI WITH ANCHOVIES, TOMATO SAUCE, AND BLACK
  OLIVES [*Italian*]
ZUCCHINI WITH CURRY SAUCE [*Indian*]
ZUCCHINI WITH TARRAGON AND SOUR CREAM [*French*]
PUMPKIN CURRY [*Indian*]
ZUCCHINI BAKED WITH EGGPLANT [*Greek*]
MAPLE-GLAZED BUTTERNUT SQUASH [*United States*]
SUMMER SQUASH HALVES WITH LEEKS, BACON, AND
  CHEDDAR CHEESE [*United States*]
HUBBARD SQUASH WITH CRANBERRIES [*United States*]
SIMPLE HUBBARD SQUASH [*United States*]
SUMMER SQUASH TRIO WITH GARLIC CROUTONS
  [*United States*]
GREEN AND YELLOW SUMMER SQUASH [*United States*]
STUFFED ZUCCHINI WITH SAUSAGE AND ROSEMARY [*Italian*]
STUFFED ZUCCHINI WITH MUSHROOMS, BACON, BASIL, AND
  SAGE [*Italian*]
ZUCCHINI STUFFED WITH PROSCIUTTO AND MOZZARELLA
  [*Italian*]
ZUCCHINI WITH MOZZARELLA AND ANCHOVIES [*Italian*]
ZUCCHINI, CHEESE, AND CHILI PEPPERS [*Mexican*]
CROOKNECK YELLOW SQUASH WITH SPINACH [*United States*]
PUMPKIN AMANDINE [*United States*]
ZUCCHINI WITH NUTS, RAISINS, AND ANCHOVIES [*Italian*]
YOUNG ZUCCHINI WITH YOGURT AND SHALLOTS [*Turkish*]
YELLOW SQUASH WITH CREAM CHEESE AND CHIVES
  [*Central American*]
BAKED YELLOW SQUASH [*United States*]
PUMPKIN BOORTHA [*Indian*]

PUMPKIN RING WITH GREEN PEAS
[*United States*]

SERVES 8

*1 pumpkin (the size of a child's
    rubber ball, about 2 lbs.),
    peeled, and with strings and
    seeds removed*
1 Tbs. onion, grated
¼ cup heavy cream

3 eggs, well-beaten
4 Tbs. butter, softened
¼ cup bread crumbs
Salt and pepper to taste
*1 lb. fresh peas, shelled, or 1
    package frozen peas, cooked*

Preheat oven to 350°. Cut pumpkin into small pieces and cover
with boiling water. Cook 20 minutes. Drain and mash thoroughly,
or whirl in a blender. Add the cream, onion, beaten eggs, butter,
bread crumbs, salt, and pepper. Mix well. Pour mixture into a
1-quart buttered ring mold and set it into a pan of boiling water.

Bake 45 minutes to 1 hour until firm. When slightly cooled, turn out mold onto serving dish and fill center hole with green peas.

ZUCCHINI WITH BÉCHAMEL SAUCE
[*Italian*]

SERVES 6 TO 8

3 medium zucchini (about 1½ to 2 lbs.), unpeeled and sliced ½ inch thick
4 Tbs. butter
4 Tbs. olive oil

BÉCHAMEL SAUCE

6 Tbs. butter	*4 Tbs. Parmesan cheese, grated*
8 Tbs. flour	*1 egg yolk*
1 tsp. salt	*Black pepper*
4 cups hot milk	*¼ tsp. nutmeg*

Sauté zucchini gently in mixture of butter and olive oil until soft and golden, about 15 minutes.

Preheat oven to 450°. In a double boiler, melt butter, add the flour and salt, and cook, stirring constantly. Then gradually add the hot milk. Using a wire whisk, cook and stir until sauce is thick, about 10 to 15 minutes. Remove from heat and beat in the Parmesan cheese, egg yolk, pepper, and nutmeg. Arrange zucchini in an ovenproof dish, pour the sauce over, and brown in oven for a few minutes.

SKEWERED ZUCCHINI AND ONIONS
[*French*]

SERVES 6

6 *small zucchini* (¼ *lb. each*),
unpeeled, cut ½ *inch thick,*
and reassembled
12 *small white onions, cut into*
4 *slices each and reassembled*
¼ *lb. butter, melted*

2 *tsp. fresh dill, snipped*
Salt and pepper to taste
2 *eggs, hard-boiled and chopped*
fine
3 *Tbs. chives, minced*

Thread zucchini on 6 short skewers so that they look whole. Do the same on separate skewers with the onions. Melt butter and put the onion skewers in a pan, turning to coat with butter. Add dill, and salt and pepper. Cover pan and cook onions on low heat for 10 minutes, turning skewers occasionally in butter. Then add the zucchini skewers. Keep turning the skewers occasionally while they cook for 15 minutes. Arrange alternate skewers of onions and zucchini on a platter and carefully draw out the skewers so the vegetables appear whole. Pour the pan juices over the vegetables and sprinkle with finely chopped egg and chives.

ZUCCHINI WITH SOUR CREAM, DILL, AND PAPRIKA
[*Hungarian*]

SERVES 8

2 *large zucchini* (*about* 2 *lbs.*),
unpeeled and chopped
Salt to taste
6 *Tbs. butter, melted*
6 *Tbs. flour*

2 *cups light cream*
2 *tsp. fresh dill, snipped*
2 *Tbs. tarragon vinegar*
1 *cup sour cream*
1 *tsp. paprika*

Sprinkle chopped zucchini with salt and spread on paper towels to remove excess moisture. Let stand 20 minutes. Meanwhile, melt butter and flour and cook over low heat for a few minutes. Gradually add light cream and dill and stir constantly for about 15 minutes until sauce is thickened. Add the drained, chopped zucchini, tarragon vinegar, and simmer, stirring frequently, for about 6 minutes until tender. Mix sour cream with dill. Place vegetable in warm serving bowl. Make a well in the center and spoon the sour cream–dill mixture into the well. Sprinkle with paprika and additional salt to taste.

STUFFED ZUCCHINI WITH ALMONDS, EGGS, AND CHEESE
[United States]

SERVES 6 TO 8

3 large zucchini (about 3 lbs.), unpeeled and split lengthwise
1½ cups bread crumbs
½ cup milk
½ cup slivered almonds
2 eggs, hard-cooked and chopped

½ cup Swiss or Gruyère cheese, grated
2 Tbs. parsley, minced
Salt and pepper to taste
3 Tbs. butter

Scoop out centers of zucchini and chop the pulp. Drop the zucchini shells into boiling, salted water for 10 minutes. Drain and set aside. Add bread crumbs to milk to soak, and then squeeze dry. Add to chopped zucchini pulp. Add almonds, eggs, cheese, parsley, salt and pepper, and mound mixture in shells. Preheat oven to 350°. Butter a baking dish and place stuffed zucchini in dish side by side. Dot with butter and bake for 15 minutes until browned.

YELLOW SQUASH WITH BUTTON MUSHROOMS
[United States]

SERVES 6

6 small yellow squash (about
2 lbs.), unpeeled and cut
into 1-inch cubes
1 large onion, chopped
1 Tbs. butter
One 8-oz. can tomato sauce

½ cup dry white wine
½ lb. small, fresh mushrooms,
wiped with damp paper
towels and left whole
½ tsp. dried oregano
Salt and pepper to taste

In large saucepan, combine squash, onion, and butter. Sauté for 2 minutes over low heat, stirring until coated with butter. Add tomato sauce, wine, mushrooms, oregano, salt, and pepper, and simmer about 7 minutes. Serve hot.

POTATOES AND YELLOW SQUASH WITH GARLIC
[Greek]

SERVES 6

2 medium yellow squash
(about 2 lbs.)
1½ lbs. potatoes
1 cup olive oil
¼ tsp. black pepper
1 large onion, chopped

1½ Tbs. tomato paste, diluted
with 1 cup water
8 cloves garlic, minced
½ cup parsley, chopped
1 cup feta cheese, crumbled*
½ cup bread crumbs

Preheat oven to 375°. Peel squash and potatoes and slice thinly in round slices. Heat oil and fry; sprinkle with black pepper. Remove from pan. In same pan sauté onions and add diluted tomato paste, garlic and parsley. Cook for 20 minutes until thickened. Remove from heat and add ¾ cup feta cheese and 3 Tbs. bread crumbs.

* Feta cheese can be bought at Middle Eastern Specialty Shops. (See Sources for Ingredients, page 289.)

Oil a baking dish. Spread the sliced potatoes and squash in a layer and cover them with a layer of sauce. Continue until all are used up. Top with remaining cheese and bread crumbs. Drizzle a little oil over top and bake for 30 minutes.

CROOKNECK SQUASH WITH RICE AND DILL
[Israeli]

SERVES 6

4 medium yellow crookneck
   squash (about 2 lbs.),
   unpeeled and cut into 2-inch
   slices
1 large onion, minced
3 Tbs. butter

1 fresh tomato, peeled and cut
   in quarters
1/4 cup uncooked rice
2 tsp. lemon juice
Salt and pepper to taste
1 tsp. fresh dill, snipped

Sauté onion in butter until wilted in 10-inch skillet. Add squash, tomato, and rice. Cover and cook over very low heat until squash is tender and rice has absorbed excess liquid, about 20 minutes. After 15 minutes uncover the pot and check to see if additional water is needed; continue cooking. Season with lemon juice, salt, and pepper, and sprinkle with dill.

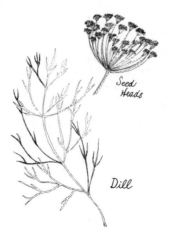

Seed Heads

Dill

YELLOW SQUASH LOAF
[*Israeli*]

SERVES 4

2 *medium yellow squash* (*about*
1 ½ *lbs.*), *peeled and*
coarsely grated
3 *Tbs. peanut oil*
1 *small onion, grated*

2 *eggs, beaten*
½ *cup matzoh meal**
1 *tsp. caraway seeds*
Salt and pepper to taste

Preheat oven to 350°. Oil a 9 × 5 × 2¾-inch loaf pan. Mix grated squash, onion, eggs, matzoh meal, caraway seeds, salt, and pepper, and pour into loaf pan. When loaf is firm after ½ hour, brush 1 Tbs. oil on surface to brown and return to oven. The total baking time is 45 minutes. Slice and serve as an accompaniment for roasted veal or beef.

LEMON ZUCCHINI FANS FOR ZUCCHINI FANS
[*French*]

SERVES 4

4 *small zucchini* (*about* 1 *lb.*), *unpeeled* (*cut as illustrated*)
½ *cup flour*
Salt and pepper
Olive oil for frying
2 *Tbs. lemon juice*
1 *Tbs. parsley or chervil, chopped*

Steam whole, unpeeled zucchini in vegetable steamer for 6 minutes. Drain and dry thoroughly on paper towels. When cool enough to handle, cut lengthwise into ⅓-inch slices, leaving a 1-inch base (see illustration). Shape them gently into a spreading

---

* Matzoh meal can be bought locally in supermarkets. Substitute cracker crumbs if difficult to find.

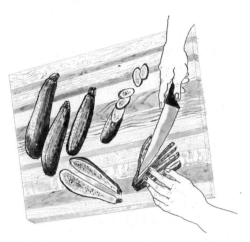

fan. Sprinkle flour, salt, and pepper over the fans, and sauté in hot oil until browned on both sides. Remove carefully to platter and add lemon juice to pan drippings. Pour over fans and sprinkle with chopped parsley or chervil.

SEVEN VARIETIES OF BAKED STUFFED ACORN SQUASH
[United States]

SERVES 4

2 acorn squash (the size of a baseball), cut in half, and strings and
   seeds removed
¼ tsp. mace
2 Tbs. butter, softened
2 tsp. dark brown sugar
Pinch salt

Preheat oven to 375°. Season the cut squash with mace, butter, sugar, and salt. Put in a baking pan and add 1 inch water to bottom of pan. Bake for 45 minutes, or longer if squash is larger.

Variations: Omit mace and proceed with one of the following:

1. Stuff with creamed spinach, hard-boiled egg cut into quarters, ¼ tsp. nutmeg, and strips of red pimiento.
2. Sauté crumbled Italian sweet or hot sausage. Drain and stuff squash.
3. Before baking squash, fill with chopped, peeled apple and, for each squash, 1 tsp. of chutney. (Major Grey's is a good brand.)
4. Omit sugar; use only butter and salt. Fill center of squash with ½ cup hot green peas or Brussels sprouts.
5. Without the sugar or mace, 3 or 4 cubes of sharp Cheddar cheese can be added 5 minutes before removing squash from oven.
6. Omit sugar and butter and add 1 Tbs. grated onion and 2 Tbs. light cream. When cooked, scoop out squash from center of shell, mash, and return mixture to shells. Stud with sliced almonds standing on end and reheat for 5 minutes before serving.

Note: Acorn squash seems to go beautifully with any pork or poultry dish.

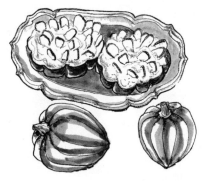

ZUCCHINI WITH ONION AND TOASTED SESAME SEEDS
[*Chinese*]

SERVES 4

4 very small zucchini (about ¼
   lb. each), unpeeled and cut
   crosswise into ¼-inch slices
2 Tbs. peanut oil
1 small onion, sliced thin

1 clove garlic, minced
1 pinch sugar
2 Tbs. soy sauce
1 Tbs. sesame seeds, toasted

In a skillet or Chinese wok, heat peanut oil. Add onion and garlic and stir-fry for 1 minute. Add zucchini and toss for 1 more minute. Sprinkle with sugar, cover, and cook 2 minutes. Uncover, add soy sauce, and toss 2 minutes more. Sprinkle with toasted sesame seeds before serving.

Variation: Yellow summer squash or a combination of yellow and green squash can be used.

ZUCCHINI WITH LEMON PEEL
[*French*]

SERVES 4 TO 6

6 small zucchini (about ¼
   lb. each), unpeeled and cut
   crosswise into ¾-inch slices
½ tsp. salt
3 Tbs. butter

½ cup onion, chopped fine
1 tsp. lemon peel, grated
3 Tbs. lemon juice
½ cup parsley, minced
Salt and pepper to taste

In a 10-inch skillet with cover, put about 1 inch of water and ½ tsp. salt, and bring to a boil. Add zucchini and cook covered about 8 minutes, until tender but crisp. Drain thoroughly in a flat bowl lined with paper towels. Heat butter in same pan and add onion.

Cook, stirring, until onion is wilted. Add lemon peel and lemon juice. Transfer drained zucchini into a heated serving dish and pour lemon sauce over it. Add parsley, salt and pepper to taste, toss gently to mix.

Variation: Instead of grated lemon peel, mince 1 small, green pepper and use 1 Tbs. fresh tarragon instead of parsley.

CROOKNECK SQUASH IN SOUR CREAM WITH DILL
[*United States*]

SERVES 4

2 *medium crookneck squash*	*1 cup sour cream*
(about 1½ lbs.), unpeeled	*1 tsp. salt*
and cut into 1-inch pieces	*½ tsp. black pepper*
2 *Tbs. butter*	*1 Tbs. fresh dill, snipped*
1 small onion, chopped	

Steam squash in vegetable steamer for 10 minutes. Drain. Melt butter in skillet and sauté onion until wilted. Add the drained squash and stir gently so they won't be crushed. Lower heat and add sour cream, salt and pepper. Do not allow to boil or sour cream will separate. When heated through, transfer to serving dish and top with freshly snipped dill.

ZUCCHINI WITH CHINESE VEGETABLES
[*Chinese*]

SERVES 6

*1 very large zucchini (about
1½ lbs.), unpeeled and
sliced paper thin
1 Tbs. peanut oil
1 clove garlic, minced
¼ lb. snow peas**
*2 large dried Chinese black
mushrooms,** or ½ cup
fresh mushrooms, sliced
paper thin*

*1 stalk celery, sliced diagonally
and paper thin
1 Tbs. soy sauce
1 tsp. cornstarch, dissolved in
a bit of cold water
½ lb. fresh bean sprouts****

In a large, heavy pan or Chinese wok, heat oil and add garlic, snow peas, mushrooms, celery, and zucchini. Stir-fry for 3 minutes. Add soy sauce and cornstarch and then bean sprouts. Cook 30 seconds more, stirring constantly.

* Snow peas can be found in Chinese markets or easily grown in your garden.

** Black Chinese mushrooms come dried. They must be soaked in warm water for 1 hour until soft, and the center stem removed. They are then sliced. They are very strong in flavor and most succulent.

*** Bean sprouts can also be found in Chinese markets, and they are also fun to sprout at home. Use 2 Tbs. mung beans, a large jar covered with cheesecloth, and a rubber band. Let beans soak in water in jar overnight. Rinse and drain in the morning. Then, 3 times a day for the next 2 or 3 days, rinse with cold water and drain until the sprouts are ½ to ¾ of an inch long.

SOUTHERN FRIED ZUCCHINI
[United States]

SERVES 4

2 medium zucchini (about 1
lb.), unpeeled and sliced
¼ inch thick
1 cup buttermilk

¾ cup white cornmeal
½ cup flour
Salt and black pepper
4 Tbs. peanut oil

Soak zucchini slices in buttermilk for 1 hour. Mix cornmeal, flour, salt, and pepper together. Lift slices out of buttermilk with tongs and dip into cornmeal mixture. Heat oil until very hot and quickly fry slices, turning once when browned. Do not overcook. Slices should be tender inside and crisp outside.

ZUCCHINI WITH ANCHOVIES, TOMATO SAUCE, AND BLACK OLIVES
[Italian]

SERVES 6 TO 8

2 large zucchini (about 2
lbs.), unpeeled and sliced ¼
inch thick
1 Tbs. olive oil
2 cloves garlic, minced
6 flat anchovies, each cut into
3 pieces

2½ cups Italian tomatoes,
drained (reserve liquid)
½ tsp. dried oregano
2 Tbs. parsley, chopped
Black pepper to taste
6 black olives, pitted and cut
in half

In a saucepan, heat olive oil, add garlic and anchovies, and, with the back of a wooden spoon, crush the anchovies until they are melted. Add tomatoes, oregano, and 1 Tbs. parsley. Simmer for 15 minutes, stirring occasionally. Add the zucchini slices and stir. Cook over low heat until barely tender. Add black pepper to taste and transfer to serving bowl. Garnish with black olives and the other tablespoon of minced parsley.

ZUCCHINI WITH CURRY SAUCE
[Indian]

SERVES 4

1 large zucchini (about 1 lb.),	*1 Tbs. clarified butter**
unpeeled and cut into ¾-inch	*1 clove garlic, minced*
cubes	*2 Tbs. white raisins*

CURRY SAUCE:

2 Tbs. clarified butter*	*1 Tbs. curry powder*
2 Tbs. flour	*4 drops Tabasco sauce*
1 cup hot chicken broth, fresh	*Salt to taste*
or canned	*½ cup shredded coconut*

In a large pan, heat 1 Tbs. clarified butter and add garlic and raisins. Toss to coat and add the cubed zucchini. Let cook 5 minutes, stirring until tender-crisp. Remove to warm serving dish and set aside.

In the same pan, melt the 2 Tbs. clarified butter and add flour. Stir until slightly tan and add hot chicken broth, curry powder, Tabasco, and salt to taste. Sauce should be thickened in 5 minutes of low-heat cooking. Then add the zucchini and simmer for a few minutes to heat through and blend flavors. Sprinkle with shredded coconut.

* See Method for Clarifying Butter, page 287.

ZUCCHINI WITH TARRAGON AND SOUR CREAM
[*French*]

SERVES 6

*1 very large zucchini (about 2 lbs.), unpeeled, and with center
pulp and seeds removed*
¾ cup sour cream*
2 Tbs. butter, melted
1 sprig fresh tarragon leaves, or ½ tsp. dried tarragon
Salt and pepper to taste

After centers of zucchini have been removed, shred the firm part.
There should be about 3 cups. Sprinkle with salt and let stand until
liquid forms, about 10 minutes. Then strain in a strainer. Heat
melted butter, add zucchini, and stir for about 5 minutes. Drain
again. Add sour cream, salt and pepper, and tarragon. Heat only
until heated through. Do not boil or it will curdle. This a good
way to use up those extra-large zucchini found in the garden in late
August.

Variations: This dish can also be made by using 8 ounces of yogurt,
and substituting freshly snipped dill for the tarragon, or mint with
the addition of ½ clove of minced garlic.

---

* In France, *crème fraiche,* which is somewhat more subtle than sour
cream, is generally used. A reasonable facsimile can be made as follows:

1 pt. heavy, sweet cream
3 Tbs. buttermilk

Mix and let stand at room temperature for 24 hours.

PUMPKIN CURRY
[*Indian*]

SERVES 4

*1 pumpkin (the size of a child's
rubber ball, about 2 lbs.),
peeled, and with seeds and
strings removed*
*2 Tbs. clarified butter**
2 small onions, sliced thin

*1 Tbs. curry powder****
Salt to taste
*1 large tomato, peeled and
chopped*
3 drops Tabasco sauce

Cut the pumpkin into thick slices. Melt the butter and fry the
onions until slightly brown. Add the curry powder and salt and
mix together. Add the tomato, and if there is not enough liquid,
add 1 to 2 Tbs. water. Add pumpkin slices and let curry simmer
over very low heat until pumpkin is tender and sauce is thickened.
Add Tabasco, stir, and serve hot.

ZUCCHINI BAKED WITH EGGPLANT
[*Greek*]

SERVES 8

*6 small zucchini (about 3
lbs.), unpeeled*
*2 small eggplants (about ½ lb.
each)*
8 shallots, chopped
1 clove garlic, minced
½ tsp. dried oregano
Salt and pepper to taste

Pinch of sugar
3 Tbs. tomato paste
*¾ cup chicken broth, fresh or
canned*
2 Tbs. bread crumbs
2 Tbs. olive oil
*6 black olives, pitted and cut in
half*

* See Method for Clarifying Butter, page 287.
** Sun Brand Curry is a good blend. (See Sources for Ingredients,
page 289.)

Slice zucchini into ½-inch slices. Prepare eggplants, using Method 1 (see page 174). Oil a baking dish. Preheat oven to 350°. Layer baking dish with eggplant slices. Sprinkle with shallots, garlic, oregano, salt, and pepper. Then cover with a layer of zucchini sprinkled with the same herbs and spices. Alternate these layers until dish is filled. Mix sugar, tomato paste, and chicken broth. Pour over vegetables. Sprinkle with bread crumbs and pour oil over. Bake for 1 hour. Garnish with pitted, black olives cut in half, and serve hot or cold.

MAPLE-GLAZED BUTTERNUT SQUASH
[*United States*]

SERVES 6

1 medium butternut squash	*3 Tbs. butter, melted*
(about 2 lbs.), peeled, strings	*2 Tbs. lemon juice*
and seeds removed, and cut	*1 tsp. lemon rind, grated*
into quarters	*1 tsp. salt*
3 Tbs. maple syrup	

Preheat oven to 400°. Parboil squash for 15 minutes, then cut into 4-inch pieces and place in a buttered baking dish. Combine maple syrup, butter, lemon juice and rind, and salt. Pour mixture over pieces of squash. Bake 30 minutes, covered. Remove cover and baste for about 10 minutes more until a glaze forms.

Note: This is good with turkey or other poultry as a change from sweet potatoes.

SUMMER SQUASH HALVES WITH LEEKS, BACON AND CHEDDAR CHEESE
[*United States*]

SERVES 6

3 medium summer squash
  (about 1½ to 2 lbs.), un-
  peeled and cut in half length-
  wise
1 cup bread crumbs
Salt and pepper to taste

¼ cup butter, melted
2 leeks, white part only, minced
6 slices bacon
½ cup sharp Cheddar cheese,
  grated
¼ cup chicken broth

Parboil squash halves for 15 minutes. Drain well. Preheat oven to 375°. Combine bread crumbs, salt, and pepper. Dip each squash half into melted butter and then roll in bread-crumb mixture. Place in a baking dish. Add minced leeks. Top with a slice of bacon and grated Cheddar cheese. Pour chicken broth into bottom of dish and bake 10 to 15 minutes, until bacon is crisp and cheese melted.

HUBBARD SQUASH WITH CRANBERRIES
[*United States*]

SERVES 4 TO 6

2 medium Hubbard squash
  (about 3 lbs.)
1 egg, beaten slightly
¼ cup butter, melted
Salt and pepper to taste

1 cup fresh cranberries, coarsely
  chopped
2 Tbs. sugar
Pinch of nutmeg

Preheat oven to 400°. Cut squash into 4-inch pieces, remove stringy parts and seeds, and boil in 2 inches of salted water for 30 minutes. Drain. Separate pulp from rind and mash pulp. With an egg beater, beat together egg, squash pulp, half the melted butter, and salt. Then stir in cranberries and sugar. Butter a 1-quart casserole and spoon in mixture. Drizzle rest of butter over top and sprinkle with nutmeg. Bake uncovered 30 minutes.

SIMPLE HUBBARD SQUASH
[*United States*]

SERVES 2 TO 3

1 medium Hubbard squash (about 1½ lbs.), unpeeled
Salt and pepper to taste
1 Tbs. butter, melted
1 Tbs. cream
1 tsp. parsley, chopped

Remove seeds and strings from squash. Cut in quarters. Boil in 2 inches of salted water for 30 minutes. Drain and scoop from shells. Discard shells. Mash pulp, add salt, pepper, butter, and cream, and sprinkle with chopped parsley.

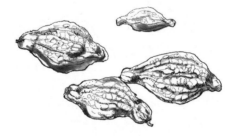

Variation:
1. Prepare recipe the same way, but instead of parsley, add either grated cheese, minced onion sautéed in butter, or powdered ginger.
2. Omit parsley and add ½ cup pitted and chopped prunes, dates or figs.

SUMMER SQUASH TRIO WITH GARLIC CROUTONS
[*United States*]

SERVES 6 TO 8

2 to 3 small, very young, yellow summer squash (*about 1½ lbs.*)
2 to 3 small green zucchini (*about 1½ lbs.*)
2 to 3 small white pattypan squash (*about 1½ lbs.*)
4 Tbs. butter
3 slices white bread, crusts trimmed, and cut into 1-inch cubes
1 clove garlic, minced
Salt and pepper
1 small, canned pimiento, cut into strips

Cut the three kinds of squash into 1-inch slices; do not peel. Drop into 2 inches of boiling, salted water and cook covered until just tender-crisp, about 8 minutes. In the meantime melt 2 Tbs. butter and toss with bread cubes and minced garlic. When squash is finished, drain thoroughly. Add salt and pepper to taste and the other 2 Tbs. butter. Sprinkle with red pimiento strips and garlic croutons.

GREEN AND YELLOW SUMMER SQUASH
[*United States*]

SERVES 4

1 medium zucchini (*about ½ lb.*), *sliced across ¼ inch thick*
1 medium yellow summer squash (*about ½ lb.*), *sliced across ¼ inch thick*

6 Tbs. butter
½ cup fresh bread crumbs
1 Tbs. garlic, peeled and minced
1 Tbs. salt
½ tsp. black pepper
½ tsp. dried thyme, crushed

Preheat oven to 325°. Melt 2 Tbs. butter in a small pan and stir in bread crumbs, stir until they are lightly browned. Butter an

8-cup casserole and alternately add the yellow squash and zucchini. Dot with butter and sprinkle with ¼ tsp. garlic, salt, pepper, and some of the thyme and bread crumbs. Repeat until all ingredients are used. Cover casserole with aluminum foil, if it has no cover, and bake for 45 minutes.

STUFFED ZUCCHINI WITH SAUSAGE AND ROSEMARY
[*Italian*]

SERVES 4

2 medium zucchini (about 1 lb.)
½ lb. Italian sausage, removed from casing and crumbled
1 tsp. garlic, minced
1 tsp. rosemary, fresh or dried, minced fine
3 Tbs. parsley, minced
½ cup toasted bread crumbs

2 Tbs. heavy cream
¼ cup Parmesan cheese, grated
1 tsp. salt
¼ tsp. black pepper
1 egg, lightly beaten
¼ cup butter
½ cup dry white wine
½ cup tomato purée

Preheat oven to 350°. Trim off ends of zucchini. Cut in half lengthwise and, using a small spoon or melon-ball cutter, scoop out pulp in center of zucchini, leaving ½ inch to form a "boat." Reserve the pulp. Cook sausage in skillet until browned slightly. Pour off fat. Then add pulp of zucchini, garlic, rosemary, parsley, bread crumbs, heavy cream, half the cheese, salt and pepper. Blend mixture well with beaten egg and fill zucchini boats. Sprinkle with the remaining cheese and dot with butter.

Arrange in a shallow, buttered baking dish. Mix wine and tomato purée and pour around bottom of pan. Bake 30 minutes until zucchini is tender and filling is golden brown.

ZUCCHINI STUFFED WITH MUSHROOMS, BACON, BASIL, AND SAGE
[*Italian*]

SERVES 8 TO 10

5 *medium zucchini (about 3 lbs.)*
5 *slices bacon*
2 *cloves garlic, minced*
1 *cup onion, chopped fine*
½ *lb. fresh mushrooms, chopped fine*
1 *Tbs. fresh basil, chopped, or 2 tsp. dried basil*

1 *tsp. sage, crushed*
1 *Tbs. tomato paste*
Salt and pepper to taste
1 *Tbs. Parmesan cheese or Gruyère cheese, grated*
½ *cup toasted bread crumbs*

Preheat oven to 400°. Drop whole zucchini into boiling, salted water to cover and cook 8 minutes until tender. Drain, let cool, and cut in half lengthwise. Scoop out inner pulp, leaving a firm shell for stuffing. Chop the reserved pulp and set aside.

Cook bacon in a skillet until crisp. Drain and reserve. Pour off all the bacon fat, except for 2 Tbs., and add the garlic and onion. Cook over low heat until wilted. Then add the chopped mushrooms and cook 5 minutes, stirring frequently. Add the chopped zucchini pulp, basil, sage, tomato paste, salt, pepper, and cheese. Add the bread crumbs and stir until mixture is slightly dry. More crumbs may be needed. Fill the zucchini with this stuffing and sprinkle crumbled bacon over them. Place in an oiled baking dish and bake 20 minutes.

ZUCCHINI STUFFED WITH PROSCIUTTO AND MOZZARELLA

[*Italian*]

SERVES 8

*4 large zucchini (about 4 lbs.),
  unpeeled
4 Tbs. olive oil
1 large onion, chopped
2 cloves garlic, minced
1 egg, beaten
½ cup prosciutto or ham, diced
¼ cup mozzarella, diced into
  ½-inch cubes*

*1 Tbs. fresh basil, minced
½ tsp. dried marjoram
Salt and pepper
¼ cup bread crumbs, toasted,
  or packaged poultry stuffing
¼ cup Parmesan cheese, grated*

Preheat oven to 350°. Parboil the zucchini in boiling, salted water to cover for 5 minutes. Drain and cool. Then scoop out the pulp, leaving a firm shell; chop pulp and reserve. Heat olive oil in a frying pan, and sauté onion and garlic for 5 minutes, stirring occasionally. Add to chopped pulp. Then add beaten egg, prosciutto, mozzarella, basil, and marjoram. Add a very little salt, as prosciutto may be salty, then add black pepper to taste. Stuff zucchini with the mixture and top with bread crumbs and grated Parmesan cheese. Place in an oiled, flat casserole and bake 20 to 25 minutes.

ZUCCHINI WITH
MOZZARELLA AND ANCHOVIES
[Italian]

SERVES 6

6 small zucchini (about ¼
lb. each), unpeeled and
sliced ⅛ inch thick
3 Tbs. olive oil
1 medium onion, chopped fine
One 1-lb. can Italian plum
tomatoes

4 tsp. tomato paste
3 sprigs fresh basil, minced
Salt
½ tsp. black pepper
½ lb. mozzarella cheese, sliced
4 anchovy filets, cut in half
lengthwise

Preheat oven to 375°. Fry zucchini slices in 2 Tbsps. hot olive oil until golden, turning once. Drain on paper towels. In skillet, add remaining 1 Tbsp. olive oil. Wilt the onion over medium heat, then add tomatoes, tomato paste, and basil. Cook for 10 minutes over high heat. Taste for salt and pepper and add if necessary.

Brush a round baking dish with oil. Place slices of zucchini on bottom so they overlap. Spoon on tomato sauce and then place slices of cheese and anchovy in a circular design on top. Sprinkle with black pepper and bake for 25 minutes until cheese is melted and bubbly.

ZUCCHINI, CHEESE, AND CHILI PEPPERS
[Mexican]

SERVES 6

2 medium zucchini (about 1
lb.), unpeeled and sliced
1 inch thick
Peanut oil for frying
One 1-lb. can of tomatoes
3 oz. tomato paste
4 cloves garlic, minced
3 sprigs fresh coriander,
chopped*

2 mild chilies, fresh or
canned**
½ tsp. dried rosemary, crushed,
or 1 sprig fresh rosemary
1 tsp. salt
½ lb. sharp Cheddar cheese, or
Monterey Jack, sliced

Preheat oven to 400°. Heat a small amount of peanut oil until
very hot and fry the sliced zucchini until the slices are tender and
transparent. Turn once and then drain on paper towels.

Put tomatoes and tomato paste in saucepan and add garlic,
coriander, chilies, rosemary, and salt. Stir and cook for 5 minutes
to blend flavors.

Butter a 12 x 15-inch flat casserole and spread the slices of
zucchini on the bottom. Pour the sauce over and top with the
cheese. Cover with aluminum foil and bake 40 minutes.

* Fresh coriander, also called Chinese parsley, can be found in local
Chinese markets, or in Spanish markets, as cilantro. If unobtainable, substitute
fresh parsley.
** Chilies can be bought canned in Spanish groceries. Use a few drops
of Tabasco sauce as a substitute.

CROOKNECK YELLOW SQUASH WITH SPINACH
[United States]

SERVES 6 TO 8

6 medium crookneck squash
(about ½ lb. each),
unpeeled
1 package frozen chopped
spinach
½ cup sour cream

1 Tbs. butter
Salt and pepper to taste
3 scallions, minced
¼ cup bread crumbs
¼ cup Gruyère cheese, grated

Preheat oven to 350°. Cut squash in half, lengthwise. Spoon out center part, leaving a ¾-inch shell. Cook shells in boiling, salted water until tender. Remove and drain upside down on paper towels. Meanwhile, cook spinach as directed and then drain in a strainer by pressing out excess liquid with back of spoon against the strainer. Mix drained spinach with sour cream, butter, salt, pepper, and chopped scallions. Fill squash shells with mixture, sprinkle with bread crumbs and cheese. Place in oiled baking dish and bake for 20 minutes.

PUMPKIN AMANDINE
[United States]

SERVES 6

1 pumpkin (the size of a child's
rubber ball, about 2 lbs.),
peeled, seeded, strings removed, and cut into ½-inch
cubes
¼ cup flour
6 Tbs. butter, melted

2 cups light cream, scalded
2 egg yolks, beaten
Salt and pepper to taste
¼ tsp. nutmeg
¾ cup almonds, sliced and
blanched

Cook cubed pumpkin in salted water to cover for 20 minutes. Drain. In saucepan add flour to 4 Tbs. of the butter. Cook over low heat, stirring until foamy. Remove from heat and add scalded cream. Return to heat and cook, stirring until thick and smooth. Add egg yolks, salt, pepper, and nutmeg and beat again. Then add pumpkin and mix well. Butter a 6-cup baking dish and spoon mixture into it. Drizzle the other 2 Tbs. melted butter over the pumpkin mixture and sprinkle with almonds. Put under the broiler until almonds are lightly toasted. Watch carefully so they don't burn.

This dish goes very well with roast pork.

ZUCCHINI WITH NUTS, RAISINS, AND ANCHOVIES
[Italian]

SERVES 6

6 medium zucchini (about
   ½ lb. each), unpeeled and
   cut into quarters
2½ Tbs. olive oil
1 clove garlic, crushed
2½ Tbs. wine vinegar
2½ Tbs. water

3 Tbs. pine nuts
3 Tbs. seedless white raisins
2 flat anchovies, rinsed, drained,
   and chopped
Pepper to taste
4 pitted black olives, quartered

Heat olive oil in skillet and sauté garlic. Removed and discard. (Do not brown or it will be bitter.) Add zucchini, toss, cover pan and cook for 2 minutes. Add vinegar and water and cook over medium heat for 10 minutes. Add nuts, raisins, and chopped anchovies. Cook 2 minutes longer, add pepper, stir in olives, and cook for 1 minute more. Serve hot.

YOUNG ZUCCHINI WITH YOGURT AND SHALLOTS
[Turkish]

SERVES 4

6 to 8 very small zucchini
(about 2 lbs.), unpeeled
and cut lengthwise into ⅜-
inch slices
4 Tbs. olive oil

Salt and pepper to taste
8 oz. plain yogurt
1 Tbs. parsley, chopped fine
1 tsp. shallots, chopped fine

Heat olive oil and sauté zucchini quickly until lightly browned. Drain on paper towels and sprinkle with salt and pepper. Keep warm. Arrange on a serving plate. Combine yogurt, parsley, and shallots. Spoon the sauce over the zucchini and serve warm.

YELLOW SQUASH WITH CREAM CHEESE AND CHIVES
[Central American]

SERVES 6

3 medium yellow squash (about
2 lbs.), unpeeled and cut in
half
1 tsp. salt

¼ lb. cream cheese, softened
4 Tbs. chives, minced
½ tsp. black pepper
½ cup butter, melted

Cook squash in boiling water to which salt has been added. Boil 10 minutes or until tender and then drain and sprinkle with salt and pepper to taste. Preheat oven to 375°. Mash cream cheese with chives and black pepper and spread the mixture on squash halves. Cover with the other halves like sandwiches. Butter a baking dish and place the squash, which now look whole, next to each other and pour melted butter over them. Bake for 30 minutes, basting occasionally with the melted butter in the pan. Serve hot.

BAKED YELLOW SQUASH
[United States]

SERVES 6 TO 8

6 medium yellow squash (about 3 lbs.), cut into 1-inch pieces
Salt for boiling
½ cup onion, minced
½ cup bread crumbs

2 eggs, lightly beaten
¼ lb. butter, melted
1 tsp. salt
½ tsp. pepper
1 Tbs. sugar

Preheat oven to 375°. Cook squash in boiling, salted water to cover for 10 minutes. Drain well and, when cooled, purée in a blender for a few seconds. Transfer to a bowl and add onion, half the bread crumbs, beaten eggs, half the melted butter, salt, pepper and sugar. Butter an ovenproof baking pan and add the squash purée. Pour the rest of the melted butter over the squash and sprinkle the remaining bread crumbs on top. Bake for 1 hour or until the squash is puffed and the crumbs are browned.

This recipe was wormed out of the cook at Aunt Fanny's Cabin in Smyrna, Georgia. Simple and good.

PUMPKIN BOORTHA
[Indian]

SERVES 4

1 pumpkin (the size of a child's rubber ball, about 2 to 3 lbs.), peeled and cut into 4-inch pieces
2 oz. clarified butter*
1 medium onion, minced
1 clove garlic, minced
1 tsp. fresh ginger root, peeled and grated

½ tsp. ground cumin
6 drops Tabasco sauce, or 2 green chilies, coarsely cut
1 Tbs. coconut, grated
1 tsp. lemon juice
Salt to taste

* See Method for Clarifying Butter, page 287.

Boil pumpkin in salted water until tender. Drain. Melt the clarified butter and sauté onion, garlic, and ginger. Add pumpkin. Remove from heat and mash thoroughly. Add cumin, Tabasco, coconut, lemon juice, and salt. Serve warm.

This boortha, which is a Moslem savory dish, can also be made with zucchini or yellow squash.

MAIN DISHES

ZUCCHINI WITH BREAST OF VEAL   [*Egyptian*]

STUFFED ZUCCHINI RINGS WITH SHRIMP   [*Chinese*]

PUMPKIN AND LAMB SHANKS WITH MINT   [*Armenian*]

ZUCCHINI STUFFED WITH LAMB AND BULGUR WHEAT
    [*Armenian*]

ZUCCHINI AND SHREDDED CHICKEN   [*Turkish*]

YELLOW SQUASH, SWISS CHARD, AND CRABMEAT CUSTARD
    [*United States*]

YELLOW SQUASH STUFFED WITH COTTAGE CHEESE   [*Israeli*]

BUTTERNUT SQUASH WITH BEEF, PRUNES, AND CHICK PEAS
    [*Israeli*]

SUMMER SQUASH, CORN, AND TOMATO WITH CHEESE
    [*Mexican*]

BEEF, VEGETABLES, AND FRUIT BAKED IN A PUMPKIN
    [*Argentinian*]

PUMPKIN STEW WITH MEAT AND CABBAGE   [*North African*]

ZUCCHINI AND PORK WITH GARLIC   [*Mexican*]

SUMMER SQUASH WITH PORK SAUSAGES PATTIES
   [*United States*]

BAKED, STUFFED PUMPKIN, OR "MEAT-IN-THE-MOON"
   [*Jamaican*]

SUMMER SQUASH WITH CHILIES AND CHEESE   [*Mexican*]

STUFFED ZUCCHINI WITH NUTS AND YOGURT   [*Indian*]

ZUCCHINI, VEGETABLE, AND EGG MEDLEY   [*Italian*]

ZUCCHINI PIE   [*Greek*]

ROAST LAMB WITH GREEN AND YELLOW SQUASH   [*Greek*]

MIRLETON, STUFFED WITH BEEF AND CURRY   [*United States*]

BAKED CHICKEN BREASTS WITH ZUCCHINI AND MUSHROOMS
   [*United States*]

STUFFED PATTYPAN SQUASH WITH EGGS AND CHEESE
   [*United States*]

ZUCCHINI AND CORN BAKED IN CUSTARD   [*United States*]

PUMPKIN, CORN, AND TOMATO STEW   [*South American*]

STUFFED PUMPKIN WITH RAISINS, BEEF, CAPERS,
   AND GREEN OLIVES   [*South American*]

ZUCCHINI FOR DIETERS   [*United States*]

ZUCCHINI WITH HAM, MUSHROOMS, AND SWISS CHEESE
   [*United States*]

ZUCCHINI WITH HOT SAUSAGE AND BASIL   [*Italian*]

STUFFED ZUCCHINI RINGS WITH RICE, HAM, AND CHEESE
   [*United States*]

ZUCCHINI TACOS WITH BEEF, CHILIES, AND CHEESE   [*Mexican*]

ZUCCHINI RING WITH CHICKEN AND PROSCIUTTO   [*Italian*]

MIRLETON SQUASH STUFFED WITH CRABMEAT   [*United States*]

UPO AND SHRIMP WITH GARLIC   [*Philippine*]

ZUCCHINI WITH BREAST OF VEAL
[Egyptian]

SERVES 4

2 medium zucchini (about 1
lb.), unpeeled, cut lengthwise, and then cut into 1-inch
pieces
1 lb. breast of veal, cut into
riblike pieces
2 cloves garlic, minced
1 Tbs. dill, snipped
2 tsp. tarragon, chopped fine

Salt and pepper
4 Tbs. butter
1 large onion, chopped fine
2 large tomatoes, peeled and
cut in quarters
2 cups chicken broth, fresh or
canned
1 tsp. paprika

In a flat dish or glass pie plate, place meat, garlic, half the dill and tarragon, and salt and pepper, and let marinate for 1 hour. Turn once after 30 minutes.

Melt half the butter in a large skillet; add onion and mari-nated veal and cook over low heat for 30 minutes, shaking the pan occasionally so that meat doesn't burn. Add tomatoes and cook for 10 minutes more. Remove from heat and set aside.

Melt the remaining butter and put the zucchini in a clean pan. Add chicken broth and cook covered, for 10 minutes.

Preheat oven to 350°. In a buttered baking dish, alternate meat and zucchini. Add the chicken broth in which the zucchini was cooked and any other accumulated liquid. Cover with alumi-num foil and bake for 1 hour. Remove foil and sprinkle with re-maining dill, tarragon, and paprika. Serve hot.

STUFFED ZUCCHINI RINGS WITH SHRIMP
[*Chinese*]

SERVES 4 TO 6

2 *medium zucchini* (*about 1
lb.*), *unpeeled, ends removed, and cut crosswise
into 2-inch circular pieces*
1 *lb. raw shrimp, peeled, de-
veined, and chopped*

2 *tsp. light soy sauce**
1 *Tbs. cornstarch*
2 *scallions, minced*
1 *Tbs. peanut oil*
1 *medium onion, minced*
2 *cloves garlic, minced*

With the point of a sharp knife cut a circle in the center core of each 2-inch slice of zucchini, leaving about ¾ of an inch around. Steam in steamer for 5 minutes. Drain and set aside.

Mix the shrimp, soy sauce, cornstarch and scallions together. Heat the peaut oil in a wok or skillet. Add the onion and garlic and stir-fry 1 minute. Add the shrimp mixture and stir until it loses color, about 2 minutes. Allow shrimp mixture to cool slightly and, with fingers, stuff the center core of the zucchini circles with mixture. Put stuffed circles on a heavy plate on a rack over a pan of boiling water. Cover the plate and steam 8 minutes more.

* Light soy, or "thin" soy, can be purchased in Chinese food markets. It is generally used with the more delicate dishes, such as fish or chicken, instead of the regular soy sauce.

PUMPKIN AND LAMB SHANKS WITH MINT
[Armenian]

SERVES 6

1 pumpkin (the size of a child's rubber ball, about 2½ to 3 lbs.), peeled, seeded and strings removed, and cut into 2-inch pieces

3 lbs. lamb shanks, cut into 2-inch pieces

2 tsp. salt

Pepper to taste

2 cloves garlic, minced

1½ qts. water

3 cups canned tomatoes, mashed with fork

3 Tbs. tomato paste

¼ cup lemon juice

1 green pepper, seeded and cut into 1-inch squares

4 Tbs. fresh mint leaves, chopped, or 2 Tbs. dried mint leaves, crushed

In a large pot, sprinkle salt, pepper, and garlic over lamb and brown on all sides over medium heat until lightly browned. Add water and bring to a boil. Skim froth from top with a spoon as it accumulates. Add tomatoes, tomato paste, and lemon juice and simmer for 1½ hours until meat is partly tender and may be separated from the bones. Lift out meat with a slotted spoon and cool. Strain liquid in pan, pressing tomatoes against strainer. Let liquid cool until fat rises to the surface and skim with a spoon. Remove meat from bones and put back into the pot with the liquid. Add pumpkin and green pepper and bring to a boil. Lower heat and simmer for 1 hour more until pumpkin and meat are tender. Add more salt, pepper, and lemon juice, if necessary. Add the mint and cook for 1 minute more. Serve over hot rice or steamed bulgur wheat.

ZUCCHINI STUFFED WITH LAMB AND BULGUR WHEAT
[Armenian]

SERVES 6

3 medium zucchini (about 1½
   lbs.), unpeeled, whole
1 cup raw lamb, ground
1 cup canned tomatoes, drained
   and juice reserved
2 Tbs. tomato paste
1 clove garlic, minced
½ cup bulgur wheat, coarse

grind, washed and drained
½ green pepper, seeded and
   diced
3 to 4 drops Tabasco sauce
Salt to taste
1 cup water
Lemon wedges

Boil zucchini in water to cover, 10 to 15 minutes. Drain and scoop out center pulp with a long-handled spoon, leaving ¼-inch-thick shell. Chop pulp fine and mix with lamb, tomatoes, tomato paste, garlic, green pepper, bulgur, Tabasco, and salt in a large mixing bowl. Stuff the zucchini with this mixture and put in a large, flat saucepan. Add reserved tomato juice to water and pour into bottom of pan. Cover pan and cook 30 minutes. After 10 minutes, baste the stuffed zucchini with pan juices, and then again after another 10 minutes, to make sure there is enough liquid to steam the bulgur. Serve with lemon wedges.

ZUCCHINI AND SHREDDED CHICKEN
[Turkish]

SERVES 4

4 small zucchini (about 1 lb.),
   unpeeled and cut lengthwise
One 2-lb. chicken, cut in quarters
1 cup water
1 cup dry white wine
Salt and pepper

4 Tbs. butter
3 Tbs. flour
1 cup chicken stock
1 cup light cream
1 Tbs. fresh tarragon, chopped
½ cup Gruyère cheese, grated

In a saucepan, put chicken, water, wine, and salt and simmer gently for 2 hours. Remove chicken and let cool. Remove skin and bones and shred the chicken fine. Boil the liquid in the pot rapidly, uncovered, to reduce to 1 cup. Cook zucchini in 2 inches boiling salted water for 10 minutes. Drain and arrange in a buttered baking pan.

Preheat oven to 350°. Melt butter in saucepan and add flour. Over low heat, cook until slightly tan, stirring constantly. Slowly add reduced hot chicken stock, stirring constantly. When sauce has thickened, add cream, stir constantly, and let it come to a boil. Reduce heat to simmer, add salt and pepper to taste, tarragon, and half the grated Gruyère cheese. Simmer for 5 minutes more and then add the shredded chicken. Pour over the zucchini, sprinkle with the other half of the cheese, and bake for 15 minutes until top is brown. Serve hot.

YELLOW SQUASH, SWISS CHARD, AND CRABMEAT CUSTARD
[United States]

SERVES 6

3 small yellow squash (about ¾ lb.), unpeeled and cut into 1-inch cubes	2 cups Gruyère cheese, grated
	Salt and white pepper to taste
	½ tsp. dried oregano
1 small onion, sliced thin	1 tsp. fresh basil, chopped
½ lb. Swiss chard, chopped	½ lb. crabmeat, fresh or frozen
4 eggs	and defrosted
1 cup light cream	

Steam squash and onion in steamer for 5 minutes. Remove and drain on paper towels. In same steamer, steam chopped chard for 3 minutes, remove, and drain. Beat eggs until frothy, and add cream, grated cheese, salt, pepper, oregano, and basil. Butter a round, 3-inch-deep baking dish. Add the squash, chard, and crabmeat to

the egg mixture and spoon into dish. Bake in a preheated 325°
oven for 40 to 45 minutes, until custard is set.

Variation: Instead of crabmeat, use shrimp or cooked chicken.

YELLOW SQUASH STUFFED WITH COTTAGE CHEESE
[Israeli]

SERVES 6

6 small, yellow summer squash (about 1½ lbs.), unpeeled
1 cup cottage cheese
2 eggs, beaten
3 Tbs. scallions, minced
Salt and pepper to taste
¼ cup sour cream

Preheat oven to 400°. Cook unpeeled squash whole in small
amount of water until tender but firm. Slit lengthwise and remove
seed section with spoon. Mix cheese, eggs, most of the scallions,
salt and pepper and fill the squash boats. Bake in a buttered baking
dish until filling has set, about 30 minutes. Top with sour cream.
Sprinkle with additional scallions.

Note: This dish can be served hot or cold.

BUTTERNUT SQUASH WITH BEEF, PRUNES, AND CHICK PEAS
[Israeli]

SERVES 8

*One 2-lb. butternut squash,
peeled, strings and seeds removed, and cut into 3-inch
chunks*
¼ cup peanut oil
2 lbs. brisket of beef

*One 2-lb. can chick peas, rinsed
and drained*
2 cups water
8 prunes, pitted and halved
1 tsp. cinnamon
Salt and pepper to taste

Heat oil and sear the meat on both sides until browned. Add chick peas and water. Simmer together about 2½ hours over low heat. Oil a casserole and put butternut squash on bottom. Add prunes, cinnamon, salt, and pepper. Cover this layer with the meat, chick peas, and liquid in pot. Preheat oven to 350°, and bake until liquid is almost absorbed and squash is tender—1 hour, if necessary. Remove meat and slice before serving; put back into casserole and baste with sauce. Serve hot.

Note: In Israel, a type of pumpkin called calabash is used for this dish. Our butternut squash is closer in flavor than the American pumpkin.

SUMMER SQUASH, CORN, AND TOMATO WITH CHEESE
[*Mexican*]

SERVES 4

*1 large summer squash
(about ¾ lb.), unpeeled
and sliced thin*
3 Tbs. butter
1 small onion, chopped
1 clove garlic, minced
*1 fresh tomato, peeled and
chopped*
*1 package frozen corn kernels,
or 2 ears fresh corn kernels,
cut off the cob*

*1 sprig fresh mint leaves,
chopped, or ½ tsp. dried
mint*
¼ tsp. ground coriander
1 tsp. salt
1 cup light cream
3 to 4 drops Tabasco sauce
3 oz. cream cheese, diced

In a heavy oval flat casserole, melt butter and wilt onion and garlic. Add squash, tomato, corn, and toss in the butter. Add mint, coriander, and salt, cover pan, and cook very slowly for 20 minutes. Stir occasionally to prevent scorching. Add cream and simmer, covered, for 20 minutes more. Add Tabasco and toss. Top with small pieces of diced cream cheese, which should be partially melted when brought to the table.

Variations:
1. Cream cheese with chives can also be used, or Gruyère cheese in place of the cream cheese.
2. A mixture of yellow and green squash can be used.

BEEF, VEGETABLES, AND FRUIT BAKED IN A PUMPKIN

[Argentinian]

SERVES 8 TO 10

1 very large pumpkin (the size of a basketball, about 8 to 10 lbs.)
¾ cup light brown sugar
¼ lb. butter, melted
2 Tbs. olive oil
2 lbs. beef chuck, cut into 1-inch cubes
Salt and pepper to taste
1 large onion, chopped
½ green pepper, seeds removed, diced
2 cloves garlic, minced
2 cups beef broth, canned
1 cup canned Italian tomatoes, drained and chopped

½ tsp. dried oregano
1 bay leaf
3 medium white potatoes, peeled and cut into ½-inch cubes
2 yams or sweet potatoes, peeled and cut into ½-inch cubes
1 medium zucchini (about ½ lb.), unpeeled and cut into ½-inch slices
2 ears corn, shucked and cut into 1-inch round pieces
5 or 6 peach halves, drained and rinsed in water

Preheat oven to 375°. Scrub pumpkin with a stiff brush and cut off top part with stem, to make a lid. With a large metal spoon scrape out stringy parts and seeds, leaving a 3-inch-thick shell to hold the stew. Melt the brown sugar and butter together and pour into the pumpkin, tilting it to coat the insides. Put the lid on and bake in a shallow pan for 1 hour with 1 inch of water in the bottom of pan. While pumpkin is baking, prepare stew. On top of stove, in a large, heavy pot, heat the oil and brown the meat, adding salt and pepper, and turn to brown evenly. When meat is brown, remove with slotted spoon to plate. In the same pan, add onion, green pepper, and garlic. Stir, and cook 5 minutes. Add the beef broth and the reserved meat, tomatoes, oregano, bay leaf, and salt and pepper to taste. Cover and simmer over low heat for 15 minutes. Add the two kinds of potatoes, stir, and cook covered again for 15 minutes more. Add the sliced zucchini and cook an additional 10 minutes, then add pieces of corn and peaches and cook for 5 more minutes.

Ladle this stew into the pumpkin and pour pan juices over stew. Cover the pumpkin with its lid and return to oven to bake for 15 more minutes. To serve, remove entire pumpkin filled with stew to large serving platter, and after stew is served, scrape pieces of the insides of the pumpkin near the top onto each plate.

Note: The calabaza, or Spanish pumpkin, is used in South America for this dish. It tastes like a cross between our American pumpkin and acorn squash.

PUMPKIN STEW WITH MEAT AND CABBAGE
[North African]

SERVES 6

1 large pumpkin (the size of a football, about 4 lbs.), peeled, strings and seeds removed, and cut into 2-inch squares
1 Tbs. olive oil
1 ½ lbs. veal, lamb, pork, or beef, minced and cooked

1 clove garlic, minced
4 shallots, minced
Salt and pepper to taste
½ lb. cabbage, shredded
½ cup beef broth, canned or fresh

Heat olive oil and fry meat lightly in a 12-inch skillet. Add garlic, shallots, and salt and pepper to taste. Then add shredded cabbage and the pumpkin. Stir, cover, and simmer over very low heat for 1 hour. The pumpkin and the cabbage will give up some of their liquid, but more may be necessary—if so, add the beef broth. Serve hot over cooked rice.

ZUCCHINI AND PORK WITH GARLIC

[*Mexican*]

SERVES 8

2 *medium zucchini* (*about 1 lb.*), *unpeeled and cut into 1-inch slices*

1½ *lb. pork tenderloin, with some fat, cut into thin slices*

1 *cup* (*yes, 1 cup!*) *garlic, peeled and minced**

Salt to taste

1 *large onion, chopped*

1 *cup tomato purée*

1 *Tbs. chili powder*

1 *cup frozen corn kernels, defrosted and separated*

1 *cup Monterey Jack cheese, shredded*

In a heavy oval casserole, cook sliced pork in its own fat until brown. When almost brown, sprinkle with garlic and salt to taste. Toss, and add onion and tomato purée. Cover and cook 1 hour, very slowly, so that garlic will not overpower the dish. Add chili powder, zucchini, and corn, cover, and cook 20 minutes more. Cover with shredded cheese, which will melt on top. Serve hot.

* Remove center bud from garlic. Cut clove lengthwise and in center will be a light, green core. Remove this before mincing to give a more subtle flavor. Also, when cooked slowly in any kind of liquid, garlic will not insinuate itself as much.

SUMMER SQUASH WITH PORK SAUSAGE PATTIES
[United States]

SERVES 4

1 medium summer squash,
parboiled and drained (about
2 cups)
2 Tbs. butter
1 egg, beaten
½ cup heavy cream

2 Tbs. brown sugar
½ tsp. mace
Salt and pepper to taste
½ lb. pork sausage removed
from casing

Preheat oven to 400°. Mash the cooked squash well and add butter, egg, cream, sugar, mace, and salt and pepper. With wet hands, form the sausage into flat, 3-inch patties and flatten with back of spatula. Put squash mixture into a buttered baking dish and lay the pork patties on top. Bake for 25 minutes until sausage is brown.

BAKED, STUFFED PUMPKIN, OR "MEAT-IN-THE-MOON"
[Jamaican]

SERVES 6

1 medium pumpkin (the size
of a child's rubber ball, about
2 to 3 lbs.), unpeeled
1 lb. ground beef
1 medium onion, chopped
¼ cup bread crumbs

½ tsp. oregano
1 Tbs. pine nuts
Salt and pepper to taste
Melted butter
1 cup water
Parsley

Cut off the pumpkin top one-quarter of the way down and reserve. Scoop out stringy parts and seeds with a spoon. Put both pieces of pumpkin into a large pot of boiling, salted water and parboil for 15 minutes. Meanwhile, mix beef, onion, bread crumbs, oregano, pine nuts, and salt and pepper to taste. Drain bottom of pumpkin well, upside down on paper towels, then reverse and fill with meat mixture. Add the top as a cover. Place in a buttered baking dish, brush the outside of the pumpkin with melted butter, and add 1 cup water to bottom of dish. Bake at 350° for 45 minutes. To test for doneness, remove top of pumpkin, and pierce the inside flesh with a knife to see if it is tender. Remove carefully with two wide spatulas to a serving dish and ring with sprigs of curly parsley.

SUMMER SQUASH WITH CHILIES AND CHEESE
[*Mexican*]

SERVES 6

2 medium summer squash (about 1 lb.), unpeeled, and cut into ½-inch-thick slices	2 canned Jalapeño chilies, rinsed, dried, seeded, and cut into strips
1 onion, chopped	½ tsp. ground coriander
2 cloves garlic, minced	Salt to taste
2 medium tomatoes, peeled and chopped	¼ lb. Monterey Jack cheese, cut into strips

Combine squash, onion, garlic, tomatoes, chilies, coriander, and salt in a saucepan. Cook over low heat for 10 minutes until tender. Put vegetables into a colander and drain excess liquid. Oil a flame-proof serving dish and put vegetables into it. Add strips of cheese and run under broiler for 2 minutes. Serve hot when cheese bubbles.

STUFFED ZUCCHINI WITH NUTS AND YOGURT
[Indian]

SERVES 6 to 8

2 large zucchini (about 2 lbs.)
4 Tbs. clarified butter*
½ cup onion, chopped
1 Tbs. scallion, minced
½ tsp. turmeric
1 black cardamom seed, peeled
  and crushed with mortar and
  pestle

2 Tbs. plain yogurt
½ cup heavy cream
½ cup ground almonds and
  cashew nuts, mixed
1 tsp. lemon juice
1 tsp. salt
½ tsp. black pepper
1 tsp. ground coriander seed

Preheat oven to 350°. Split zucchini lengthwise and scoop out center, leaving a firm shell. Chop and reserve pulp. Heat 2 Tbs. butter in a large skillet and add pulp, onion, scallion, turmeric, and cardamom. Cook, stirring, until soft, about 5 minutes. Lower heat, add yogurt, and cook until mixture is fairly dry, stirring constantly. Add heavy cream, ground nuts, and cook until quite thick. Add lemon juice, salt, and pepper.

Fill zucchini shells with mixture and place in a shallow, buttered casserole. Sprinkle with additional black pepper and coriander and pour remaining 2 Tbs. melted clarified butter over stuffed zucchini. Bake about 15 to 20 minutes, until tender.

* See Method for Clarifying Butter, page 287.

ZUCCHINI, VEGETABLE, AND EGG MEDLEY
[Italian]

SERVES 8

3 medium zucchini (about 1½
  lbs.), unpeeled and diced
5 Tbs. olive oil
1 lb. raw spinach, coarsely
  chopped
1 cup onion, coarsely chopped
1 cup string beans, cut into
  1-inch pieces

½ tsp. garlic, minced
2 tsp. fresh basil, chopped, or
  1 tsp. dried basil
1 tsp. salt
½ tsp. nutmeg
¼ tsp. black pepper
4 eggs, lightly beaten
½ cup Parmesan cheese, grated

Preheat oven to 350°. Heat 3 Tbs. olive oil in a 12-inch skillet and add spinach. Cook until wilted, stirring with a wooden spoon. Add the rest of the oil to skillet, and then the diced zucchini, onion, and string beans. Lower heat and stir occasionally. Cook 5 minutes. Add garlic, basil, salt, nutmeg, and pepper and then transfer to a buttered, 2½-quart casserole.

Pour eggs over the vegetables. Sprinkle with cheese and bake 45 minutes until eggs are set and top is browned. Cut into wedges to serve.

Basil

ZUCCHINI PIE
[Greek]

SERVES 8 to 10

3 large zucchini (about 3 lbs.),   *Black pepper to taste*
    or yellow squash, unpeeled   *4 eggs, lightly beaten*
Salt   *1 cup bread crumbs, toasted*
1 lb. feta cheese, rinsed and   *3 Tbs. parsley, minced*
    dried*   *4 Tbs. fresh dill, minced*
1 lb. clarified butter**   *1 lb. phyllo****

Grate zucchini coarsely, sprinkle lightly with salt, and place in a plastic colander to drain for 1 hour. After 1 hour, rinse under cold, running water and let drain for 10 more minutes. Squeeze excess moisture out of grated zucchini between the palms of the hands, until it is very dry. Crumble feta cheese into small pieces about the size of green peas. Preheat oven to 250°. In a large skillet, heat one-quarter of the butter. Add the grated zucchini and black pepper to taste. Toss a few times to coat, then remove from heat and set aside. In a large separate bowl, beat the eggs and then add the bread crumbs, cheese, parsley, and dill. Add this mixture to the zucchini and stir again.

Melt the remaining butter. Butter a baking pan slightly smaller than the sheets of phyllo, and about 1½ inches deep, allowing a 2-inch overlap of the phyllo on both sides. Work quickly and gently so the thin sheets of phyllo do not dry out and become brittle. Using two sheets of phyllo at a time, place the phyllo in a buttered pan. With a pastry brush, brush melted butter on the phyllo. Repeat this process until half the phyllo is used up. Then spread the zucchini mixture evenly over the phyllo. Fold the over-

---

* Feta is a dry, salty Greek cheese that can be found in Middle Eastern groceries. (See Sources for Ingredients, page 289.)

** See Method for Clarifying Butter, page 287.

*** Phyllo, or filo, is a paper-thin pastry or strudel dough. It comes frozen in supermarkets and freshly made in Middle Eastern groceries.

hanging phyllo up and over the zucchini mixture to contain it. Then repeat the phyllo layers and butter on top until all is used up. Trim the top layers at the edges very carefully with a very sharp knife and butter the top well. With a sharp knife, score the dough (see illustration) and bake for 1 hour. Cool slightly before cutting through where you have scored the dough to the bottom of the pan.

ROAST LAMB WITH GREEN AND YELLOW SQUASH
[Greek]

SERVES 6

6 medium summer squash and zucchini (about 3 lbs.), unpeeled
One 3-lb. leg of lamb, boned and rolled
Salt and pepper to taste

2 cloves garlic, slivered
1 tsp. rosemary
1 Tbs. lemon juice
1½ lbs. fresh, ripe tomatoes, peeled
¼ lb. butter

Preheat oven to 350°. Sprinkle lamb with salt and pepper and pierce it in several places. Insert slivers of garlic and a few leaves of rosemary into each slit. Pour lemon juice over. Cut the tomatoes into thin slices and spread them out in bottom of a 14-inch heavy oval casserole. Place meat on the tomatoes. Melt the butter and pour over meat. Roast for 30 minutes. Cut the unpeeled squash into pieces 2 to 3 inches across. Sprinkle with salt and pepper and add to the meat and tomatoes in the pan. The squash will exude water, so do not add any other liquid. Cook until all the liquid is absorbed and the butter that remains is a sauce. Roast until the meat and squash are tender, about 1 hour longer.

Serve hot, carving slices at the table.

MIRLETON STUFFED WITH BEEF AND CURRY
[United States]

SERVES 6

3 large mirleton squash	*3 medium, fresh tomatoes,*
2 Tbs. safflower oil	*peeled and chopped*
1 large onion, chopped fine	*Salt and black pepper to taste*
1 clove garlic, minced	*2 Tbs. butter, softened*
1 lb. ground beef	*½ cup Parmesan cheese, grated*
1 Tbs. curry powder	

Boil whole squash in salted water, about 30 minutes. Cut in half lengthwise, remove seed, scoop out pulp, and mash. Reserve shells. Heat oil in skillet and add onion and garlic. Stir until wilted and then add ground beef. Cook for 15 minutes, stirring occasionally. Add the curry powder, stir, and cook 2 minutes more. Then add the tomatoes and pulp of the mirleton squash. Cook, stirring, until the mixture is fairly dry. Preheat oven to 350°. Season mixture well with salt and pepper and return to shells. Dot with butter and sprinkle with grated cheese. Bake in a flameproof casserole for 15 minutes.

BAKED CHICKEN BREASTS WITH ZUCCHINI AND MUSHROOMS
[United States]

SERVES 6

2 lbs. zucchini, cut into ½-inch
slices
1 lb. fresh mushrooms, sliced
1 medium onion, chopped
1 fresh tomato, peeled and
chopped
1 clove garlic, minced

Salt to taste
3 drops Tabasco sauce
4 chicken breasts, skinned and
boned
2 Tbs. olive oil
2 Tbs. parsley, minced

Preheat oven to 350°. Put vegetables plus garlic in bottom of a flat oval 14-inch casserole. Season with salt and Tabasco and place chicken breasts on top. Pour olive oil over chicken and vegetables and add more salt. Bake for 45 minutes, basting chicken breasts with the accumulating juices. Do not disturb vegetables; use baster to draw up the juices. Sprinkle with parsley before serving.

STUFFED PATTYPAN SQUASH WITH EGGS AND CHEESE
[United States]

SERVES 6

6 medium, pattypan squash
(about ½ lb. each)
3 Tbs. butter, melted
4 scallions, minced
2 eggs, hard-boiled and chopped
¾ cup Gruyère cheese, grated

¾ cup bread crumbs
Salt and black pepper to taste
2 Tbs. fresh tarragon, minced
1 tsp. lemon juice
¼ tsp. paprika

Boil squash in boiling, salted water for 15 to 20 minutes. Scoop out centers with a grapefruit knife, leaving 2-inch sides. Drain upside down while preparing the stuffing. Melt butter and add scallions. Stir for 2 minutes. Chop center pulp of squash and add. Stir for 2 more minutes. Then add chopped eggs, most of the cheese (reserving some for top), bread crumbs, salt, pepper, tarragon, and lemon juice. Stir all together. Preheat oven to 350°. Fill shells with stuffing. Sprinkle with reserved cheese and paprika. Place squash in a baking pan, put ½ inch water in bottom of pan, and bake for 20 minutes. Slip under the broiler for 1 minute to brown cheese.

ZUCCHINI AND CORN BAKED IN CUSTARD
[United States]

SERVES 6 TO 8

6 medium zucchini, unpeeled
   and sliced ½ inch thick
Salt and pepper to taste
¼ cup butter
1 large onion, minced
2 cloves garlic, minced
1 small green pepper, seeded
   and diced

½ tsp. oregano, dried
1½ cups corn kernels, fresh,
   canned, or frozen, cooked and
   drained
½ cup Cheddar cheese, grated
5 eggs, well-beaten
½ cup light cream

Preheat oven to 325°. Steam zucchini slices in vegetable steamer over water. Drain and sprinkle with salt and pepper. Cook only 5 minutes, until tender-crisp. Melt half the butter and sauté onion, garlic, and green pepper until wilted. Add additional salt and pepper to taste, and oregano, and let cool. Then add zucchini, corn, and cheese, then the well-beaten eggs, cream, and rest of the butter. Mix and pour into a buttered baking dish (a 1½-quart soufflé dish is fine). Place this dish in a pan of hot water and bake for 40 minutes, or until custard is firm.

PUMPKIN, CORN, AND TOMATO STEW
[South American]

SERVES 6 TO 8

1 medium pumpkin (the size of a child's rubber ball, about 2 to 3 lbs.), peeled, seeded, strings removed, and cut into 1-inch cubes
2 cups onions, sliced thin
¼ cup lard
3 tsp. achiote seed, ground with mortar and pestle*

1 canned, hot, green chili pepper, minced
2 tsp. garlic, minced
One 35-oz. can tomatoes
2 cups canned corn kernels, drained
4 eggs, hard-boiled and sliced
2 Tbs. fresh coriander, minced**

Sauté sliced onions in lard for 10 minutes in 12-inch skillet, stirring until slightly brown. Add achiote, chili pepper, and garlic, and sauté, stirring for 2 minutes more. Add the pumpkin cubes and tomatoes and cook for 20 minutes. Add the corn and cook for 10 minutes more. Serve when pumpkin is tender, topped with sliced hard-boiled eggs and sprinkled with fresh coriander.

* Achiote seed is available in Spanish specialty shops.
** Fresh coriander (also known as Chinese parsley), or cilantro, can be purchased in either Chinese markets or Spanish groceries. (See Sources for Ingredients, page 289.)

STUFFED PUMPKIN WITH RAISINS, BEEF, CAPERS, AND GREEN OLIVES
[South American]

SERVES 6 TO 8

1 medium pumpkin (the size of child's rubber ball, about 2½ lbs.)
3 Tbs. butter
1 medium onion, chopped
1 small green pepper, diced
1 clove garlic, minced
1 lb. ground beef
1 tsp. black pepper
Salt to taste
½ tsp. dried thyme
½ cup beef broth
8 green olives, pitted and cut in half
1 Tbs. small capers, rinsed and drained
1 bay leaf
4 fresh tomatoes, peeled and chopped
1 Tbs. dry white wine
1 Tbs. raisins
1 cup rice, cooked
¼ cup Parmesan cheese, grated
Parsley sprigs

Put the pumpkin in a large pot and cover with water. Since it is whole, if it does not submerge, weight it down with a heavy object. Cook for about 45 minutes until tender. Drain and cut a circle from the top for a lid, about 3 inches from the stem. Reserve the lid. Scoop out the seeds and strings from the pumpkin, and sprinkle the inside with salt and pepper. Set aside.

In a large skillet, melt the butter and sauté the onion, green pepper, and garlic for 5 minutes. Add the beef, pepper, salt, and thyme and cook over moderate heat, stirring, for 5 minutes. Add the beef broth, olives, capers, and bay leaf and simmer 20 minutes. Then add the tomatoes, wine, and raisins and simmer until the liquid is reduced by half. Remove from heat, add the cooked rice, and stuff the pumpkin with this mixture. Sprinkle the stuffing with the Parmesan cheese and put the whole thing into a shallow baking pan. Bake in a 250°, slow oven for 15 minutes, until cheese is brown. Replace the lid on the pumpkin before serving. Serve with a ring of parsley sprigs.

ZUCCHINI FOR DIETERS
[*United States*]

SERVES 4 to 5

2 medium zucchini (about 1
lb.), unpeeled and sliced ½
inch thick
½ lb. skim-milk mozzarella
cheese, sliced thin

1 Tbs. chives, minced
2 medium tomatoes, sliced
¼ tsp. oregano
Salt and pepper to taste
1 Tbs. safflower oil

Steam slices of zucchini in a vegetable steamer until barely tender. Sprinkle with salt and pepper. Remove and place in a flameproof dish. Top with slices of mozzarella, chopped chives, slices of tomatoes, and then sprinkle with oregano and drizzle some safflower oil over tomatoes. Season again with salt and pepper. Slip under broiler and broil until cheese is melted and tomato grilled. Serve immediately.

ZUCCHINI WITH HAM, MUSHROOMS, AND SWISS CHEESE
[*United States*]

SERVES 6 TO 8

1 very large zucchini (about
1½ to 2 lbs.), unpeeled, split
in half, center core and tough
seeds removed, and diced
5 Tbs. butter
½ lb. fresh mushrooms, sliced
thin
2 cups cooked ham, cut into thin
slivers

1 small onion, minced
3 Tbs. flour
¾ cup milk, scalded
1 cup hot chicken broth, canned
½ cup Swiss cheese, shredded
1 tsp. Dijon-style mustard
Salt and pepper to taste
⅓ cup Parmesan cheese, grated
¼ cup slivered almonds

Steam zucchini in a vegetable steamer until tender-crisp, then lift out and drain. Set aside. In a large skillet, melt butter and sauté mushrooms for about 3 minutes. Add slivered ham and toss. Lift out with a slotted spoon and add to the zucchini. In same skillet, sauté onion, then blend in flour and gradually add hot milk and chicken broth. Cook over low heat, stirring until smooth and thick. Add Swiss cheese, mustard, salt, and pepper, and stir until the cheese melts. Mix with ham, mushrooms, and zucchini and spoon into shallow, buttered casserole. Sprinkle with Parmesan cheese and stud with slivered almonds. Slip under broiler for a few minutes until light brown and bubbly.

ZUCCHINI WITH HOT SAUSAGE AND BASIL
[Italian]

SERVES 6

4 to 6 small zucchini (about ¼ lb. each), unpeeled and sliced crosswise
3 hot Italian sausages
1 large onion, coarsely chopped
1 clove garlic, minced
One 8-oz. can tomato sauce

4 fresh basil leaves, minced, or ½ tsp. dried basil
½ tsp. oregano
¼ tsp. sugar
¼ tsp. black pepper
Salt to taste
2 Tbs. bread crumbs, toasted

Slice sausages very thin and cook in skillet over medium heat until lightly browned. Remove with slotted spoon and set aside. In same skillet, sauté onion and garlic until wilted. Add zucchini slices, stir, and cook, stirring occasionally, until golden. Add tomato sauce, basil, and oregano. Add sugar, pepper, salt. Cook for 5 minutes. Arrange sausage on top. Cover, and cook for 5 minutes more. Sprinkle with toasted bread crumbs.

STUFFED ZUCCHINI RINGS WITH RICE, HAM, AND CHEESE
[United States]

SERVES 6

1 very large zucchini (about 2 lbs.), unpeeled and cut crosswise into ½-inch slices
1 cup rice, cooked
½ cup cooked ham, minced
⅓ cup sharp Cheddar cheese, grated
¼ cup chicken broth, canned
¼ cup white wine
½ tsp. paprika

Remove center pulp and seeds from large zucchini slices. Preheat oven to 350°. Oil a large baking dish and place rings in one layer in dish. Mix together rice, ham, cheese, and half the chicken broth and wine. Spoon into centers of rings. Pour the rest of the chicken broth and wine around the rings. Sprinkle tops with paprika and bake 35 minutes, basting occasionally. Serve hot.

ZUCCHINI TACOS WITH BEEF, CHILIES, AND CHEESE
[Mexican]

SERVES 4

*1 medium zucchini (about ½
  lb.), unpeeled and coarsely
  diced*
1 tsp. olive oil
*1 medium onion, coarsely
  chopped*
¼ lb. ground beef
1 clove garlic, minced
*2 green chilies, canned, drained,
  and chopped*

*2 medium tomatoes, peeled and
  cut into 8 pieces*
1 cup taco sauce, canned*
*4 taco shells, frozen, prepared
  according to directions**
1 cup iceberg lettuce, shredded
*½ cup sharp Cheddar cheese,
  grated*
Salt to taste

Heat oil in skillet and wilt onion. Add ground beef and garlic and stir until beef loses its color. Add diced zucchini, chilies, and tomatoes and cook over low heat for 10 minutes. Add taco sauce. Salt to taste. Spoon into hot taco shells and garnish with shredded lettuce, chopped onion, and grated Cheddar cheese.

ZUCCHINI RING WITH CHICKEN AND PROSCIUTTO
[Italian]

SERVES 6

*1 very large zucchini (about
  1½ to 2 lbs.), unpeeled,
  center pulp and seeds
  removed and grated*
4 Tbs. wheat germ
2 Tbs. butter, melted

1 Tbs. heavy cream
2 eggs, beaten
*1 medium onion, grated and
  drained*
Salt to taste
½ tsp. black pepper

* Tacos, taco sauce, and chilies can be bought at local supermarkets or in Spanish specialty food shops. (See Sources for Ingredients, page 289.)

Salt the grated zucchini and let stand 10 minutes. Squeeze out all liquid between palms of the hands. Rinse and squeeze again. Preheat oven to 300°. In a bowl, mix grated zucchini with wheat germ, melted butter, cream, eggs, grated onion, salt and pepper. Oil a small round tube pan and pour mixture into it. Bake for 45 minutes. Let cool slightly and unmold. Fill center of mold with chicken and prosciutto filling.

FILLING:

2 Tbs. butter	½ tsp. white pepper
3 Tbs. flour	½ cup prosciutto, slivered
1 cup milk, scalded	1 chicken breast, cooked and
3 small shallots, minced	shredded
1 tsp. Marsala wine	½ cup Parmesan cheese

Melt butter and add flour. Stir until thickened over medium heat. Slowly add scalded milk, stirring constantly, until slightly thick. Add shallots, Marsala, pepper, prosciutto, chicken, and Parmesan cheese. Let cook until heated through and pour into center of zucchini ring mold.

MIRLETON SQUASH STUFFED WITH CRABMEAT
[United States]

SERVES 6 TO 8

6 mirletons (about ¾ lb. each)	1 cup wet bread, squeezed
6 Tbs. butter	1 lb. fresh crabmeat
1 large onion, chopped	Salt and pepper to taste
3 scallions, minced	2 eggs, beaten
2 cloves garlic, minced	½ cup bread crumbs
1 small green pepper, seeded and diced	

Boil mirletons in salted water to cover for 20 minutes. Drain. Split in half and remove seeds. Scoop out pulp and chop, leaving ½-inch shell. Melt butter and sauté onion, scallions, garlic, green pepper, and mirleton pulp for 5 minutes. Add wet bread, crabmeat, salt and pepper, and beaten eggs. Preheat oven to 350°. Stuff filling into mirleton shells. Put into ovenproof baking dish. Sprinkle with bread crumbs and bake for 10 minutes.

Note: Mirletons and chayote squash are the same vegetable. They are called mirletons in the southern part of the United States. They are most delicate, go well with crabmeat or chicken, and are a regional specialty of the Louisiana Bayou country.

UPO AND SHRIMP WITH GARLIC
[Philippine]

SERVES 2

1 very small upo, peeled, seeded, and sliced thin (about 2 cups)
¼ lb. fresh shrimp, unshelled
1 cup water
2 Tbs. lard

2 cloves garlic, crushed
1 Tbs. bagoong*
Salt to taste
¼ cup shrimp broth (liquid from cooking shrimp)

Cook shrimp in 1 cup of water for 5 minutes. Reserve ¼ cup of this shrimp broth. Peel and devein the shrimp. Set aside. Heat the lard and fry the garlic. Do not let it brown. Add the bagoong, salt, and shrimp broth. Bring to a boil. Reduce heat and add the upo. Cover and cook for 5 minutes. Add shrimp and continue cooking until upo is just tender-crisp. Serve hot with rice.

* Bagoong is salted and fermented shrimp. It can be found in Philippine groceries. (See Sources for Ingredients, page 289.)

PICKLES AND RELISH

SCAPECE [*Italian*]
PICKLED ZUCCHINI WITH BASIL [*Italian*]
CANDIED ZUCCHINI PICKLES [*United States*]
ZUCCHINI PICKLES [*United States*]
MIRLETON PICKLES [*United States*]
ZUCCHINI PICKLES WITH GARLIC, DILL HEADS, AND
    HORSERADISH ROOT [*United States*]

SCAPECE
[*Italian}*

SERVES 6 to 8

This zucchini dish is a classic Italian one. Eggplant slices can be
used in place of the zucchini, or a combination of the two can be
used.

8 small zucchini (about ¼ to
½ lb. each), unpeeled and
cut into ¼-inch round slices
¾ cup olive oil
Salt and black pepper to taste

10 to 12 sprigs fresh mint, use
leaves only
1 cup white wine vinegar
3 to 4 cloves garlic, minced

Heat heavy skillet and add 2 Tbs. olive oil. Place zucchini slices in one layer to cover bottom of skillet. Turn once when lightly browned and fry the other side. More oil may be necessary. Repeat until all zucchini is used up, removing slices with a slotted spoon into a soufflé or other flat-bottom deep dish. Cover dish with the slices in a single layer, sprinkle with salt, pepper, and a layer of mint leaves. Continue until all is used up, alternating zucchini and mint, and ending with a layer of mint on top. Put vinegar and garlic in small saucepan. Bring to a boil and boil 1 minute. Pour at once over zucchini and mint. If there is any oil left, add this too. Cover with plastic wrap and let stand *outside* of the refrigerator for 24 hours for full flavors to develop.

Note: This dish can also be served as an appetizer, salad, or side dish.

PICKLED ZUCCHINI WITH BASIL
[Italian]

SERVES 6

2 large zucchini (about 2 to 3 lbs.)
½ cup olive oil
Salt and pepper
2 sprigs fresh basil, chopped
2 cloves garlic, minced
½ cup white wine vinegar

Cut zucchini into 1-inch slices and fry in hot oil until light brown, about 3 minutes. Sprinkle with salt and pepper and put into casserole. Sprinkle with basil and garlic.

Boil vinegar for 3 minutes in same pan that slices of zucchini were fried in. Pour over casserole and refrigerate overnight. Serve cold.

Note: This dish will keep for 2 weeks in the refrigerator and may also be served with meat, fish, or poultry as well as a relish.

Variations:
1. Add 1½ Tbs. sugar to vinegar for a sweet-sour taste.
2. Use 2 sprigs of chopped fresh mint instead of basil.
3. Use 1 tsp. dried oregano instead of basil.

CANDIED ZUCCHINI PICKLES
[United States]

YIELD: 3 TO 4 PINTS

*6 medium zucchini (about 3 lbs.), peeled and cut into ¾-inch
   chunks
4 Tbs. alum*
3 qts. water
Ice cubes*

SYRUP:
*9½ cups sugar
4 cups vinegar
25 whole cloves
4 sticks cinnamon
Few drops green food coloring (optional)*

Heat alum in 3 quarts of water. Do not boil. Pour this over the raw zucchini, cover with ice cubes to bring temperature down quickly, and let stand for 2 hours. Drain after 2 hours. Meanwhile, bring 8

* Alum can be purchased from your local druggist.

cups of sugar, the vinegar, cloves, and cinnamon sticks to a boil. When boiled, pour over drained zucchini and let sit overnight. Lift out the zucchini in the morning and add ½ cup of sugar to the syrup and bring just to a boil. Pour over zucchini and let sit overnight again. Repeat this process for 2 more days, adding ½ cup sugar each time, bringing to a boil, and pouring over drained zucchini. On the third day, boil, add a few drops of green food coloring if desired, pack zucchini and syrup into hot sterilized jars, and seal.

ZUCCHINI PICKLES
[*United States*]

YIELD: 6 TO 7 PINTS

5 lbs. zucchini (small or medium), unpeeled and cut crosswise into ¼-inch slices	*¼ cup salt*
	2 tsp. celery seed
	1 tsp. dry mustard
1 qt. white distilled vinegar	*2 tsp. ground turmeric*
2 cups sugar	*5 medium onions, sliced thin*

In a large pot, bring to a boil, vinegar, sugar, salt, celery seed, dry mustard, and turmeric. Put the zucchini and onions in a large bowl and pour the boiling liquid over them. Let stand for 1 hour, stirring occasionally. Then transfer to a large pot again, bring the mixture to a boil, and simmer for 3 minutes. Keep the pot simmering while quickly packing one sterilized jar at a time. Fill to ½ inch of the top, making sure the vinegar mixture covers the vegetables. Cap each jar immediately and process for 5 minutes in a boiling water bath.*

* See Boiling Water-Bath Method for Canning, page 287.

MIRLETON PICKLES
[*United States*]

YIELD: 4 PINTS

5 medium mirleton squash (about 1 lb. each)
½ lb. fresh, hot red chilies*
4 cloves garlic, peeled and left whole
2½ cups cider vinegar
4 tsp. salt

Peel squash and cut in half lengthwise. Remove seeds with tip of a sharp knife, then cut squash lengthwise into ½-inch-thick slices. Wash the chilies under cold water and pull out stems. Discard seeds and cut chilies lengthwise into ¼-inch strips. Into 4 pint-sized, hot, sterilized jars, place 1 clove garlic, then the sliced squash and chilies alternately. Boil the vinegar and salt together and pour into jars a little at a time to allow to flow to bottom. Fill to ⅛ inch of tops. Seal and place in hot water bath with 2 inches of boiling water above jars and boil for 10 minutes.** Remove and let stand for 10 days to develop true flavor.

* Hot chilies must be handled carefully or the oil will burn your hands. Wear rubber gloves.
** See Boiling Water-Bath Method for Canning, p. 287.

ZUCCHINI PICKLES WITH GARLIC, DILL HEADS, AND HORSERADISH ROOT
[*United States*]

YIELD: 6 PINTS

*3 very large zucchini (about 5
lbs.), unpeeled, cut into
chunks, and center core
removed if seeds are too large
6 fresh dill heads**
*6 slices horseradish root, peeled
and cut thin***

*12 garlic cloves, peeled
8 cups water
4 cups white vinegar
⅔ cup kosher salt
1 tsp. alum****

Into each sterilized 1-pint jar, place 1 head of dill, 1 slice of horse-radish root, and 2 cloves of garlic. Pack zucchini chunks into the jars. Boil water and vinegar together, add salt and alum. Pour over zucchini in jars and seal. Put in large pot of boiling water, with 2 inches of water to cover jars, and process for 5 minutes when water starts to boil.**** Let ripen for 6 weeks before eating.

* Use fresh heads of dill, not the leaves.
** Horseradish root can generally be found at specialty produce markets.
*** Alum can be purchased from a druggist. Be sure it is alum for cooking.
**** See Boiling Water-Bath Method for Canning, p. 287.

PASTA, EGGS, PANCAKES, SOUFFLÉS, CRÊPES, STUFFING AND SAUCES

ZUCCHINI AND LAMB CROQUETTES WITH DILL   [*Turkish*]

LINGUINE WITH ZUCCHINI SAUCE   [*Italian*]

CUSTARD BAKED IN CHAYOTE   [*South American*]

ZUCCHINI AND GROUND BEEF SAUCE WITH FETTUCINE
   [*Italian*]

WHITE, GREEN, AND ORANGE VEGETABLE PANCAKES   [*Israeli*]

ZUCCHINI PANCAKES WITH POT CHEESE   [*Israeli*]

CURRIED ZUCCHINI AND ONION FRITTERS WITH
   WHEAT GERM   [*United States*]

ZUCCHINI STICKS AND ONION RINGS WITH TURMERIC
   [*Indonesian*]

YELLOW AND GREEN SQUASH FRITTERS WITH LEMON
   [*United States*]

ZUCCHINI AND PROSCIUTTO FRITTATA   [*Italian*]

[114]

ZUCCHINI AND GRUYÈRE CHEESE SOUFFLÉ [French]
ZUCCHINI AND EGG CRÊPES [French]
PATTYPAN SQUASH STUFFING FOR POULTRY [United States]
ZUCCHINI SAUCE FOR FISH [United States]

ZUCCHINI AND LAMB CROQUETTES WITH DILL
[Turkish]

SERVES 6

1 large zucchini (about 1 lb.),   2 oz. cream cheese
  unpeeled and grated   2 eggs
1 tsp. salt   Pepper to taste
1 lb. raw lamb, chopped   2 Tbs. flour
1 Tbs. fresh dill, snipped   2 Tbs. olive oil
1 large onion, grated

Sprinkle salt on grated zucchini and let drain in bowl until liquid forms. Squeeze out any excess moisture between the palms of hands. Mix well with lamb, dill, onion, cream cheese, eggs, and pepper. Add flour and form into flat hamburgerlike shapes. Heat oil and fry until brown, turning to brown other side. Serve hot, decorated with lemon wedges and a sprig of dill.

LINGUINE WITH ZUCCHINI SAUCE
[Italian]

SERVES 4 TO 6

2 medium zucchini (about 1   1 Tbs. salt
  lb.), unpeeled and sliced   Lots of black pepper
  ¼ inch thick   1 lb. linguine
2 Tbs. olive oil   3 Tbs. Parmesan cheese, grated
4 Tbs. butter

Sauté zucchini slices in the oil and 2 Tbs. of the butter over low heat until they are browned lightly. Drain on paper towels and sprinkle with salt and pepper. Cook the linguine as directed on the package. Drain and toss with the other 2 Tbs. butter. Add more black pepper and serve with slices of zucchini on top. Sprinkle with Parmesan cheese and toss again before serving.

Variation:
1. Sauté 1 small green pepper, diced, and 1 fresh tomato, peeled and chopped, with zucchini for another sauce.

CUSTARD BAKED IN CHAYOTE
[*South American*]

SERVES 4

2 large chayotes (about 1 lb. each)	*¼ tsp. vanilla*
	¼ tsp. ground cardamom
1½ cups milk	*2 Tbs. sugar*
2 egg yolks, beaten	*3 Tbs. brown sugar*

Place whole chayotes in boiling water to cover and cook until tender. Test after 20 minutes with the tip of a knife. Drain, cut in half lengthwise, and scoop out the pulp in center. Remove seed and leave ½ inch of vegetable near the skin. Chop the center pulp and press out excess moisture between palms of hands. Combine milk, egg yolks, vanilla, cardamom, and sugars. Combine with drained pulp and spoon into shells. Place in baking dish with 1 inch hot water in bottom of dish. Bake at 300° for 45 minutes, until custard filling is set and golden brown.

Note: Chayotes can be found in Spanish, Phillipine, and Mexican specialty shops. (See Sources for Ingredients, page 289.)

ZUCCHINI AND GROUND BEEF SAUCE WITH FETTUCINE
[Italian]

SERVES 6

6 small zucchini (about 1½
lbs.), unpeeled and diced
fine
3 Tbs. olive oil
1 medium onion, minced
1 clove garlic, minced
½ lb. ground beef
1 can tomato purée

2 tsp. fresh basil, minced
½ bay leaf
½ tsp. salt
1 lb. fettucine
Lots of black pepper
3 Tbs. parsley, minced
½ cup Parmesan, grated

Heat olive oil and add onion, garlic, and ground beef, and sauté, stirring until meat loses its color, separating it with a wooden spoon. Add diced zucchini and simmer, stirring occasionally, for 5 minutes more. Add tomato purée, basil, and bay leaf and cook over low heat, stirring frequently, for 30 minutes.

Cook the fettucine in boiling, salted water according to package directions. Drain in colander and put into large serving dish. Pour sauce over and add black pepper, parsley and Parmesan cheese. Toss at table before serving.

WHITE, GREEN, AND ORANGE VEGETABLE PANCAKES
[Israeli]

SERVES 4

1 cup butternut squash, peeled,
seeded, chopped fine, and
cooked
1 cup spinach, cooked
1 cup leeks, cooked

¾ cup flour
2 eggs
Salt and pepper to taste
1 tsp. sugar
Oil for frying

Cook the vegetables separately and then chop together. Mix flour, eggs, salt and pepper, sugar, and then add to vegetables. If liquid has accumulated in vegetables, strain first before adding to batter. Form with hands into patties and fry in hot oil, turning once to brown on both sides.

Variation:

1. These pancakes can also be served as they are traditionally by Turkish Jews on Rosh Hashanah to symbolize the variety of the harvest. Use only one vegetable for each batch of pancakes so that there are three different colors.

ZUCCHINI PANCAKES WITH POT CHEESE
[Israeli]

SERVES 4

4 small zucchini (about 1 lb.), unpeeled and sliced
4 Tbs. pot cheese
3 Tbs. matzoh meal*
1 egg
Salt and pepper to taste
Oil for frying

Parboil zucchini slices for 10 minutes, drain, and mash and drain again. Add cheese, matzoh meal, egg, salt, and pepper. Drop by tablespoonsful into hot oil. Fry until edges are brown, then turn and fry on the other side. Drain on paper towels and keep warm while others are frying. Serve hot.

* Matzoh meal can be found in some markets and food shops that carry Israeli or Jewish food. If difficult to obtain, substitute flour.

CURRIED ZUCCHINI AND ONION FRITTERS
WITH WHEAT GERM
[*United States*]

SERVES 4

1 large zucchini (about 1 lb.),	*3 Tbs. flour*
unpeeled and coarsely	*1 tsp. baking powder*
shredded	*Salt and pepper*
2 medium onions, grated	*1 egg, slightly beaten*
2 Tbs. wheat germ	*3 Tbs. peanut oil*
2 Tbs. curry powder	

Shred and drain the zucchini in a colander. Add the grated onion to the colander, stir, and press against sides with a wooden spoon to get rid of excess moisture. Transfer to bowl and add wheat germ, curry powder, flour, baking powder, salt and pepper, and beaten egg. If mixture seems too watery, drain again. Heat oil and drop fritters by tablespoon. Flatten with back of spoon and cook until crisply brown. Turn and brown other side. Drain on paper towels and sprinkle with salt and pepper. Serve hot.

ZUCCHINI STICKS AND ONION RINGS WITH
TURMERIC
[*Indonesian*]

SERVES 4

2 medium zucchini (about 1	*Water to make batter as thick*
lb.), unpeeled	*as sour cream*
1 large onion, sliced thin and	*1 tsp. salt*
separated into rings	*½ tsp. turmeric*
1 cup flour, sifted	*Peanut oil for frying*

Cut unpeeled zucchini into small strips about 2 inches long and ½ inch thick. Separate onion slices into rings. Make batter with flour, water, salt, and turmeric. Dip onion rings and zucchini sticks into batter and fry in hot oil a few pieces at a time. Drain on paper towels and keep warm until all are fried. Add additional salt if needed. Serve hot.

YELLOW AND GREEN SQUASH FRITTERS WITH LEMON
[United States]

SERVES 6

3 small zucchini and 3 small yellow summer squash (about 1 lb. each), unpeeled, cut into 2-inch chunks, parboiled 5 minutes, and drained completely	1 tsp. baking powder ¼ tsp. salt ½ cup milk 2 eggs, separated Oil for deep frying Salt and pepper to taste
⅔ cup flour, sifted	Lemon wedges

Combine flour, baking powder, and ¼ tsp. salt and mix quickly with milk and beaten egg yolks. Beat egg whites separately and, when stiff, combine with egg yolk and flour mixture to make batter. Dip chunks of squash into batter and fry in deep, hot oil until light brown. Sprinkle with salt and pepper and serve hot with lemon wedges.

ZUCCHINI AND PROSCIUTTO FRITTATA
[Italian]

SERVES 6

3 small zucchini (about ¾ lb.), unpeeled and diced fine	2 fresh basil leaves, minced
⅛ lb. prosciutto with fat, cut into strips	Salt and black pepper to taste 6 eggs, beaten
6 scallions, chopped fine	¼ cup Parmesan cheese, grated
1 tsp. parsley, minced	1 Tbs. butter, softened

Fry the prosciutto slowly, stirring, for 3 minutes. Remove with slotted spoon and put in bottom of baking dish. Add the zucchini, scallions, parsley, and basil to the same pan in which prosciutto has been cooked. Toss vegetables, season with salt if needed and black pepper, cover, and cook slowly 6 to 8 minutes. Remove vegetables to baking dish with prosciutto and toss together. Pour beaten eggs over the vegetables and prosciutto and cook slowly for 5 minutes. Sprinkle with grated cheese, dot with soft butter, and slip under a hot broiler to melt cheese and finish cooking eggs. Serve cut into pie-shaped wedges.

Variation:
1. Substitute 8 slices of salami, diced, for the prosciutto.
2. Add half a minced and sautéed sweet red pepper and 10 thin slices of hot pepperoni sausage.

ZUCCHINI AND GRUYÈRE CHEESE SOUFFLÉ
[French]

SERVES 6 TO 8

3 medium zucchini (about 1 ½ lbs.), unpeeled and cut into ½-inch slices
4 Tbs. butter
5 Tbs. flour
1 ¾ cups milk
7 eggs, separated

¾ cup Gruyère, grated
Sprinkle of nutmeg
Salt and pepper to taste
3 Tbs. chives, chopped
Pinch of cream of tartar
¼ cup Parmesan cheese, grated

Preheat oven to 400°. Cook squash in boiling, salted water for 8 minutes until tender-crisp. Drain and set aside. Melt the butter and add the flour, stirring constantly with a wire whisk. Add the milk gradually and beat with wire whisk until sauce is smooth and thickened. Remove from heat and add the egg yolks one at a time, beating after the addition of each one. Fold in the reserved zucchini and Gruyère cheese, nutmeg, salt and papper, and 2 Tbs. of the chives. Beat the egg whites with a pinch of salt and the cream of tartar until very stiff. Fold the squash mixture lightly into the egg whites and pile carefully into a buttered 6-cup soufflé dish. Sprinkle surface with grated Parmesan cheese and bake 25 minutes. Remove and sprinkle with the remaining chives and serve at once.

Note: This is an excellent light summer luncheon dish served with a salad and cold white wine.

ZUCCHINI AND EGG CRÊPES
[French]

SERVES 6

CRÊPE BATTER:

> ¾ cup water
> ⅔ cup milk
> 3 eggs
> 2 Tbs. butter, melted and cooled
> ¾ tsp. salt
> ¾ cup flour, sifted

With a wire whisk, beat the liquid, then add the eggs, butter, and salt to the flour. Beat very well until batter is smooth and let stand covered with plastic wrap for 1 hour. Heat a 6- or 7-inch iron crêpe pan over moderately high heat. Fill ⅛ measuring cup with the batter and pour it into the pan. Quickly tilt and rotate the pan so that the batter covers the bottom of the pan in a thin layer. Return the pan to the heat and loosen the edges of the crêpe with a spatula. When it is lightly brown on one side, turn the crêpe and brown the other side. Transfer to a plate covered with wax paper and continue to make crêpes until batter is used up. If crêpes seem to stick to paper, lift them gently and put fresh paper between them when they cool slightly. Makes about 16 crêpes. They can be made in advance and wrapped in plastic wrap and refrigerated, or frozen.

ZUCCHINI AND EGG FILLING:

1 medium zucchini, unpeeled and cut into thin finger shapes (about 2 cups)
¼ cup butter
1 cup dry bread crumbs
5 Tbs. butter

⅓ cup onion, minced
3 eggs, beaten
Salt and pepper to taste
3 Tbs. parsley, minced
⅓ cup Parmesan cheese, grated
⅓ cup Gruyère cheese, grated

Preheat oven to 375°. Melt ¼ cup butter and add the bread crumbs, tossing them until lightly toasted. Transfer to a bowl and reserve. Add the 5 Tbs. butter to the pan, melt it, and add the onion and zucchini strips. Stir and cook until zucchini is tender and lightly tan. Add the eggs, salt and pepper, and with a fork lightly scramble the mixture over moderate heat; then add to the reserved bread crumbs with the minced parsley. Divide the mixture among 12 crêpes. Roll up and place seam side down in a buttered baking dish. Sprinkle with both cheeses and bake for 10 minutes until crêpes are hot and cheese is golden.

PATTYPAN SQUASH STUFFING FOR POULTRY
[United States]
YIELD: ENOUGH FOR ONE 3-POUND CHICKEN

6 very small pattypan squash (about 1 lb.), unpeeled and cut into 1-inch cubes
6 Tbs. butter, melted
4 medium onions, chopped

2 cloves garlic, minced
6 scallions, chopped
1 cup bread crumbs
Salt and pepper to taste
½ tsp. powdered sage

Steam the squash in a steamer for 5 to 6 minutes until tender-crisp. In 2 Tbs. melted butter sauté onions, garlic, and scallions, until tender. Add the squash and, over medium heat, stir constantly so that liquid evaporates and mixture is somewhat dry; add the rest of the melted butter and the bread crumbs, salt, and pepper, and sage.

This stuffing can be used for Cornish Game Hens as well. For a variation, add the poultry livers, chopped and sautéed.

ZUCCHINI SAUCE FOR FISH
[United States]

YIELD 1½ CUPS

1 medium zucchini (about ½ lb.), unpeeled, grated, salted, and drained
¾ cup sour cream
¼ cup mayonnaise

1 Tbs. chopped dill pickle
1 Tbs. prepared horseradish, drained
1 Tbs. chives, minced
⅛ tsp. white pepper

Mix all together and serve over broiled fish.

BLOSSOMS

SQUASH BLOSSOMS STUFFED WITH BEEF AND RICE   [Italian]
STUFFED ZUCCHINI BLOSSOMS WITH MOZZARELLA
  AND ANCHOVIES   [Italian]
ZUCCHINI MATCHSTICKS AND BLOSSOMS IN BEER BATTER
    [Italian]
SUMMER SQUASH PANCAKES TOPPED WITH BLOSSOMS
    [United States]
SWEET SQUASH BLOSSOM FRITTERS IN BEER BATTER
    [United States]
SQUASH BLOSSOM SOUP   [Mexican]

SQUASH BLOSSOMS STUFFED WITH BEEF AND RICE
[*Italian*]

SERVES 4

Since the times of the Aztecs, pumpkin and squash blossoms have been eaten. In case you grow your own squash or have a pumpkin patch, these recipes are included. Living near a Mexican market helps as well.

16 zucchini or yellow summer squash blossoms	*½ small onion, grated*
½ lb. ground beef	*1 egg*
1 cup rice, cooked	*Salt and pepper to taste*
½ tsp. oregano	*1 cup chicken broth*
	1 Tbs. butter

Wash squash blossoms and remove stamens gently. Put in ice water to crisp. Mix ground beef, rice, oregano, onion, and egg. Add salt and pepper to taste.

Preheat oven to 350°. Butter a flat, ovenproof casserole. Drain flowers well on paper towels and stuff gently with meat mixture. Fold ends of flowers to form a neat packet and lay them close together in casserole. Pour chicken broth in bottom of casserole and dot blossoms with butter. Bake 20 minutes.

Variations:
1. Use ½ cup chopped, cooked chicken mixed with 1 beaten egg white, 1 tsp. chives, ½ tsp. tarragon, 1 Tbs. cream, salt and pepper, and enough bread crumbs to bind the mixture for stuffing.
2. Use ½ cup minced lamb or veal, ½ clove minced garlic, 1 tsp. minced parsley, ¼ tsp. rosemary, 1 Tbs. tomato juice, and enough bread crumbs to bind the mixture.

STUFFED ZUCCHINI BLOSSOMS WITH
MOZZARELLA AND ANCHOVIES
[Italian]

SERVES 3

12 zucchini blossoms
¼ lb. mozzarella cheese, cut
*   into ¼-inch cubes*
Black pepper
1 can flat anchovy filets, drained
*   of oil and washed under*
*   running water, then drained*
*   on paper towels*

Olive oil or peanut oil, for
*   frying*
Lemon wedges

BATTER:
½ cup flour
⅔ cup water

¼ tsp. salt

Remove the stamens of the zucchini blossoms with a sharp knife or pull them out with fingers. Handle carefully, for blossoms are delicate. Wash gently and well under slowly running water. Dry thoroughly on paper towels. Cut the mozzarella into tiny cubes and sprinkle with black pepper. Cut the anchovies into small pieces as well. Stuff the cheese and anchovies into the bottom of the blossom. The petals close naturally and hold the stuffing in.

Blend the flour, water, and salt together. Dip each stuffed flower into the batter and fry in deep fat until golden, only a few minutes. The cheese center should melt and blend with the anchovy. Drain on paper towels, salt lighty, and serve at once with a wedge of lemon to be squeezed over them. This can be served as a side dish or an hors d'oeuvre.

Variations:
1. Stuff blossoms with slivers of prosciutto instead of anchovies.
2. Stuff with 2 Tbs. bread crumbs, 2 anchovy filets crushed in 1 tsp.

olive oil, and 2 sprigs chopped parsley. When served as an hors
d'oeuvre, allow 4 blossoms per portion.

ZUCCHINI MATCHSTICKS AND BLOSSOMS
IN BEER BATTER
[Italian]

SERVES 4

BEER BATTER:

1 cup flour
1 cup light beer, at room
temperature

Sift flour into bowl and make a depression in the center of flour.
Pour in the beer and stir until batter is smooth. If there are lumps,
strain the batter through a sieve. Cover the bowl and let batter
stand at room temperature for 3 hours.

2 medium zucchini (about 1   *Peanut oil for frying*
lb.), unpeeled and cut into   *16 zucchini blossoms*
½-inch-length matchstick   *Salt and black pepper to taste*
shapes   *Lemon wedges*

Make batter first. Dip the zucchini sticks into the batter first, fry in
hot oil until golden, drain on paper towels and keep warm. Then
dip the zucchini blossoms into the batter and fry. Sprinkle liberally
with salt and black pepper, and serve with lemon wedges to be
squeezed over the vegetables at the table. Serve hot.

SUMMER SQUASH PANCAKES TOPPED
WITH BLOSSOMS
[*United States*]

SERVES 4

2 *medium summer squash*
  (*about 1 lb.*), *unpeeled and*
  grated
½ *cup flour*
1 *tsp. baking powder*
½ *tsp. salt*
1 *egg, beaten*
2 *Tbs. parsley, minced*

2 *drops Tabasco sauce*
Oil for frying
1 *Tbs. butter*
Squash blossoms
1 *clove garlic, minced*
2 *Tbs. grated Parmesan cheese*
  (*optional*)

Grate squash and place in a large bowl. Drain and squeeze out moisture. Sift over it flour, baking powder, and salt. Mix together and add beaten egg, parsley, and Tabasco. Mix again, and in a large skillet heat the oil and drop the batter in by the tablespoonful. Fry until brown and turn to brown other side. Drain on paper towels and keep warm.

In another pan, heat 1 Tbs. butter and add minced garlic, stir, and cook for 1 minute. Add squash blossoms and flatten with spatula, sauté quickly, turn blossoms to the other side, with spatula press down for a few seconds, and then remove. Serve pancakes topped with blossoms.

Note: This recipe can also be made with zucchini and its blossoms.

SWEET SQUASH BLOSSOM FRITTERS IN
BEER BATTER
[*United States*]

SERVES 4

16 squash blossoms
½ cup cognac
¼ cup sugar
Peanut oil for frying
½ cup confectioners' sugar, sifted

Prepare Beer Batter (see page 128). Combine cognac and ¼ cup sugar. Put washed blossoms into a bowl and let them marinate in cognac and sugar mixture in the refrigerator for 30 minutes. Drain and dip into fritter batter and fry in hot peanut oil. Lift with a spatula when golden. Drain on paper towels and sprinkle with confectioners' sugar.

SQUASH BLOSSOM SOUP
[*Mexican*]

SERVES 6

1 lb. squash or pumpkin blossoms
4 Tbs. butter
1 small onion, chopped
8 cups chicken broth, fresh or canned
Sprig of epazote*
Salt and pepper to taste

Wash blossoms carefully and remove stems. Cut into 4 pieces. Heat the butter and wilt the onion. Add the squash blossoms and

* Epazote or pazote is a Mexican and Spanish herb also used in Europe as an herbal tea. It is known in the United States as pigweed or wormseed, and sometimes grows wild here. It can be found in Mexican and Puerto Rican markets. (See Sources for Ingredients, page 289.)

cook for 1 minute. Heat the chicken broth with the epazote, and then add the squash blossom and onion mixture. Add salt and pepper to taste, remove the sprig of epazote, and cook gently for 5 minutes.

JAMS AND PRESERVES

YELLOW SQUASH PRESERVES   [Armenian]
YELLOW SQUASH JAM WITH PISTACHIO NUTS   [North African]
PUMPKIN JAM   [United States]
PUMPKIN PRESERVES   [Mexican]
ZUCCHINI GINGER JAM   [African]
PUMPKIN BUTTER   [United States]

YELLOW SQUASH PRESERVES
[Armenian]

YIELD: 5 PINTS

6 medium yellow squash (about
   3 lbs.), peeled and shredded
2 qts. water
2 Tbs. lime powder*
7 cups sugar

8 cups water
3 whole cloves
1 cinnamon stick, 2 inches long
3 Tbs. lemon juice
Peel of 1 lemon, cut in strips

   * Lime powder can be obtained from a druggist. Be sure it is lime for cooking.

Soak shredded squash overnight in the 2 quarts of water with the lime powder added. Remove squash with slotted spoon and drain thoroughly in colander. Rinse with cold water and drain again in colander. Repeat rinsing again and drain thoroughly. About 1 hour before rinsing the squash, mix 6 cups of sugar with the 8 cups of water. Bring the sugar and water to a boil, lower heat, and cook the syrup uncovered for 1 hour. The syrup will then be ready to receive the squash. Pour off some of the syrup into a small saucepan and reserve. Add the grated squash to the first pot. In the saucepan with the small amount of syrup, add cloves, cinnamon, lemon juice and rind, and the last remaining cup of sugar. Bring to a boil, and then add this mixture to the squash and thinner syrup. Simmer all together until thickened, stirring occasionally. When the preserves cling to the spoon, it is finished.

Pour into sterilized jars and seal with wax. (See To Preserve with Paraffin, page 286.)

YELLOW SQUASH JAM WITH PISTACHIO NUTS
[*North African*]

YIELD: 4 PINTS

2 lbs. very small yellow squash, whole and unpeeled
2 lbs. sugar
½ cup shelled pistachio nuts
1 Tbs. orange flower water*

Put squash into heavy saucepan with sugar and cook over low heat for 1½ to 2 hours, until mixture is thick. Add orange flower water and nuts, stir for 1 minute. Pour into hot sterilized jars and seal with wax. (See To Preserve with Paraffin, page 286.)

* Orange flower water can be bought in Middle Eastern Specialty Shops. (See Sources for Ingredients, page 289.)

PUMPKIN JAM
[*United States*]

YIELD: 6 PINTS

1 pumpkin (the size of a foot-   *2½ cups water*
ball, about 5 lbs.), peeled,   *Juice of 2 lemons*
seeds and strings removed,   *One 1-inch piece fresh ginger*
and cut into small cubes   *root, peeled and grated*
One 5-lb. bag sugar   *1 tsp. citric acid**

Boil the sugar and water together for 10 minutes. Add the pumpkin, lemon juice, ginger, and citric acid. Cook at a slow boil for about 2 hours. Pour into hot, sterilized jars and seal with hot wax. (See To Preserve with Paraffin, page 286.)

PUMPKIN PRESERVES
[*Mexican*]

YIELD: 6 PINTS

1 large pumpkin (the size of a   *1 gal. water*
football, about 5 lbs.), peeled,   *4 Tbs. lime powder***
strings and seeds removed,   *Sugar in amount of pumpkin*
and cut into 2-inch cubes   *cubes (see below)*

Place pumpkin cubes in water mixed with lime to cover. Let stand for 12 hours. Drain and wash cubes thoroughly several times with cold water. Weigh the pumpkin and transfer to a large bowl. Add as much sugar as there is pumpkin (i.e., for 3 lbs. pumpkin cubes use 3 lbs. sugar). Let pumpkin stand for 2 hours in the sugar. When liquid starts to form, place in saucepan and cook over very low heat until pumpkin is tender, dark brown, and transparent,

---

* Citric acid can be purchased from a druggist.
** Lime powder can be purchased from a druggist. Be sure it is lime for cooking.

about 2 hours. Pour into hot, sterilized jars and seal with hot wax. (See To Preserve with Paraffin, page 286.)

Variation: The cubes of pumpkin preserves can be dried to make pumpkin candy!

MEXICAN PUMPKIN CANDY: Follow recipe for Pumpkin Preserves. Then remove pumpkin cubes from syrup and place on waxed paper in the sun to dry. Turn frequently. When there is no moisture, the candy is ready to eat. A mesh screen raised above a flat tray can also be used to circulate air freely.

ZUCCHINI GINGER JAM
[*African*]

YIELD: 4 PINTS

1 very large zucchini (about 3 lbs.), peeled
2½ lbs. sugar
1 lemon, juice and peel
One 1-inch piece fresh ginger root
¼ lb. candied ginger, slivered

Cut peeled zucchini into small cubes. If seeds are large, remove center portion. Place in large bowl and cover with sugar. Let stand overnight. Drain off accumulated liquid with the sugar and bring this syrup to a boil, adding the lemon juice and peel. Add ginger root, tied into a cheesecloth bag for later removal, and simmer for 1 hour. Add candied ginger and zucchini to the hot syrup and simmer for another hour or until the zucchini becomes transparent. Remove cheesecloth bag and spoon jam into hot sterilized jars. Seal with melted wax. (See To Preserve with Paraffin, page 286.)

PUMPKIN BUTTER
[United States]

YIELD: 3 CUPS

1 medium pumpkin (the size of a child's rubber ball, about 2½ lbs.), peeled, strings and seeds removed, and chopped fine
4½ cups light brown sugar
½ cup lemon juice
2 Tbs. lemon peel, grated
1 cup water

In a bowl put chopped pumpkin, sugar, lemon juice, and peel. Let stand overnight. Transfer to saucepan and add 1 cup water. Bring to a boil and then lower heat. Let cook 2½ hours, stirring occasionally, until mixture is thick and water has evaporated. Spoon into jars with covers and chill.

Note: This is good on toast for breakfast.

DESSERTS, PIES, CAKES AND COOKIES

PUMPKIN AND RAISIN-FILLED TURNOVERS   [Mexican]

PUMPKIN WITH COCONUT AND WALNUTS   [Turkish]

YELLOW SQUASH AND PEANUTS   [African]

ZUCCHINI WITH WALNUTS   [Iranian]

YELLOW SQUASH AND APPLE COMPOTE   [Israeli]

CANDIED PUMPKIN   [United States]

PUMPKIN PIE   [United States]

THREE WINTER SQUASH WITH CARAMEL SAUCE   [Mexican]

PUMPKIN CHEESECAKE   [English]

PUMPKIN FLAN WITH RUM   [Mexican]

FESTIVE BAKED WHOLE PUMPKIN   [Mexican]

DRUNKEN RUM PUMPKIN   [Mexican]

PUMPKIN HONEY WITH ORANGES   [Mexican]

SWEET PUMPKIN FRITTERS   [West Indian]

PUMPKIN DELIGHT   [Turkish]

ORANGE PECAN SQUASH SQUARES   [United States]

YELLOW SQUASH SPICE CAKE   [United States]

CANDIED ZUCCHINI AND CUSTARD MERINGUE PIE
   [United States]

STEAMED PUMPKIN PUDDING WITH LEMON CREAM SAUCE
   [English]

PUMPKIN ICE CREAM MOLD WITH MINCEMEAT SAUCE
   [United States]

PUMPKIN CUSTARD WITH WHIPPED CREAM AND
   CRYSTALLIZED GINGER   [United States]

PUMPKIN PARFAIT WITH PECANS   [United States]

PUMPKIN DROP COOKIES   [United States]

PUMPKIN MOUSSE WITH VANILLA SAUCE   [United States]

FRIED PUMPKIN RINGS WITH CINNAMON SYRUP
   [South American]

COLD PUMPKIN SOUFFLÉ   [United States]

FROZEN PUMPKIN ALASKA WITH WHEAT GERM   [United States]

BAKED CHAYOTE, STUFFED WITH RAISINS, ALMONDS, AND
   CAKE CRUMBS   [South American]

PUMPKIN AND RAISIN-FILLED TURNOVERS
[Mexican]

YIELD: 3 DOZEN

PASTRY:

1¾ cups flour	¼ lb. butter, softened
¼ tsp. cinnamon	3 oz. cream cheese, softened
Pinch of salt	3 Tbs. heavy cream
2 Tbs. sugar	

In a large bowl, mix flour, cinnamon, salt, and sugar. With a pastry blender, cut softened butter and cream cheese into dry ingredients until it looks like coarse cornmeal. Add the cream and, with floured hands, work into a ball. Do not work too much or pastry will be tough. Chill for 1 hour and then bring to room temperature before rolling out.

FILLING:

1 cup pumpkin purée, canned*
¼ cup light brown sugar
½ cup raisins, soaked overnight in 2 Tbs. cognac
2 tsp. anise seed
Pinch salt

Combine pumpkin, sugar, raisins and cognac, anise seed, and salt. Bring to a boil and simmer 15 minutes. Remove from heat and allow to cool.

Roll out pastry ⅛ inch thick and cut into 3-inch circles with a floured cookie cutter. Place a teaspoon of the filling on the side of each circle. Dampen the edges of the circle, fold over in half, and press the edges together with a fork.

Preheat oven to 400°. Brush a cookie pan with melted butter —you may also brush the tops of the turnovers with melted butter as well. Bake for about 20 minutes. Serve warm, and sprinkled with white sugar and cinnamon if you wish.

---

* Canned pumpkin purée can be used in any recipe in this book that calls for puréed pumpkin. It is good for out-of-season cooking. In season, fresh pumpkin calls for a bit more kitchen labor but is required for certain recipes where the pumpkin must remain in cubes or where a whole pumpkin is used. Also, anything that is fresh and in season is tastier and more economical.

PUMPKIN WITH COCONUT AND WALNUTS
[Turkish]

SERVES 6

*1 medium pumpkin (the size of child's rubber ball, about 2½
  lbs.), peeled, seeded, and cut into 1-inch cubes*
4 Tbs. brown sugar
Juice of 1 lemon
3 Tbs. walnuts, chopped
2 Tbs. shredded coconut

Place pumpkin cubes and sugar in a pot and add enough water to just cover the pumpkin. Simmer until soft but not mushy, about 20 to 25 minutes. Remove pumpkin with slotted spoon to serving bowl, and let the liquid boil down for about 5 minutes more. Add lemon juice and pour over pumpkin. Then sprinkle with coconut and chopped walnuts and serve warm.

YELLOW SQUASH AND PEANUTS
[African]

SERVES 4

*2 medium yellow summer
  squash (about 1 lb.), unpeeled and cut into 1-inch
  cubes*
*1 cup peanuts, shelled and skins
  removed*

¼ tsp. salt
2 Tbs. peanut oil
4 Tbs. dark brown sugar
*½ pt. heavy cream, whipped (or
  vanilla ice cream)*

Steam squash for 10 minutes. Drain. In a blender, whirl peanuts for a few seconds until coarsely chopped. (Or chop coarsely by hand.) Add the nuts to the squash, and add salt to taste. Heat the oil, and cook mixture over low heat for 15 minutes, stirring occasionally. Sprinkle with brown sugar and cook 1 minute more. Serve hot topped with whipped cream or vanilla ice cream.

ZUCCHINI WITH WALNUTS
[Iranian]

SERVES 4

4 to 5 small zucchini (about ½ cup water
1/4 lb. each), peeled 1 Tbs. lemon juice
and cut into 1-inch slices 8 lady fingers, torn apart
1 cup light brown sugar Whipped cream
1 cup apple cider ½ cup walnuts, chopped fine

In a flat-bottom pan, place a layer of zucchini and sprinkle with brown sugar. Mix cider, water, and lemon juice together and pour over zucchini. Cover and cook for 25 minutes over medium heat. Remove from heat and let cool. Chill completely.

In a serving dish, spread a layer of torn lady fingers, and place zucchini and liquid over it. Garnish with whipped cream and chopped walnuts. Serve cold.

YELLOW SQUASH AND APPLE COMPOTE
[Israeli]

SERVES 4

4 small summer squash (about 1/4 lb. each), peeled and diced
   fine
3 cups sugar
1½ cups water
Juice and grated rind of 2 lemons
2 whole cloves
1 tart apple, peeled and diced fine

Boil sugar and water together until syrup forms. Add lemon rind and cloves. Add diced squash and apple and cook until squash becomes clear. Remove from heat and add lemon juice. Let chill and serve cold.

[141]

PUMPKIN PIE
[United States]

MAKES ONE 9-INCH PIE

PASTRY:

1½ cups flour
Pinch of salt
3 Tbs. sugar
4 oz. cream cheese, softened
¼ lb. sweet butter, softened
2 to 3 Tbs. heavy cream

In a large bowl, with a pastry blender, cut flour, salt, and sugar into cream cheese and butter until grainy in texture. Add cream and mix into a ball. Do not overmix or pastry will toughen. Chill in wax paper for 1 hour and then bring to room temperature before rolling out on a floured board. Roll out and crimp edges.

FILLING:

1¾ cups pumpkin, cooked and
mashed, or 16-oz. can
pumpkin purée
¾ cup brown sugar
½ tsp. salt
1 tsp. cinnamon

½ tsp. nutmeg
¼ tsp. ground ginger
¼ tsp. ground cloves
2 eggs, beaten
1 cup light cream

Preheat oven to 375°. In a saucepan, stir pumpkin purée for 10 minutes until slightly dry. Keep warm. Mix together sugar, salt, spices, and add to pumpkin purée. In a separate bowl, beat eggs, add cream, and then add to pumpkin mixture. Pour into pastry-lined 9-inch pan and bake for 40 to 45 minutes, until only 1 inch of the center is still slightly liquid. Cool before cutting.

THREE WINTER SQUASH WITH CARAMEL SAUCE
[*Mexican*]

SERVES 6

1 lb. Hubbard squash, unpeeled and cut into 3 or 4 lengthwise pieces
1 lb. butternut squash, unpeeled, cut in half, strings and seeds removed
1 lb. acorn squash, unpeeled, cut in half, strings and seeds removed

½ cup water
2 cups dark brown sugar
3 Tbs. butter, melted
Pinch of salt
1 cup heavy cream (optional)

Pour the water into a large, heavy pan and bring to a boil. Put pieces of squash into pan, sprinkle with sugar, and drizzle the melted butter over them. Add the salt and lower the heat to the lowest possible setting. Cover the pan and simmer for about 1 hour. Every 10 minutes, remove cover and baste with the caramel sauce that has formed to glaze the squash. Let squash cool to room temperature and serve with caramel sauce.

Whipped cream can be used to top this dish if you like. Whip 1 cup heavy cream until very stiff. Use a spoon for eating to scoop the pulp from the shells.

PUMPKIN CHEESECAKE
[*English*]

SERVES 12

C R U S T :

1½ cups gingersnaps, crushed
½ cup butter, melted

[143]

Preheat oven to 350°. Butter a 9-inch spring-form pan. Mix gingersnap crumbs and melted butter and press onto bottom of pan. Bake 15 minutes, remove from oven, and set aside.

FILLING:

6 eggs, separated

1 lb. cream cheese, at room temperature

2 cups pumpkin purée, fresh or canned

One 15-oz. can sweetened condensed milk

¼ tsp. salt

1½ tsps. cinnamon

½ tsp. ground ginger

½ tsp. nutmeg

¼ cup brown sugar

1 cup sour cream

¼ cup pecans, chopped

Beat egg yolks until thick and lemon colored in electric mixer for 5 minutes. Add softened cream cheese and beat until very smooth. Transfer to a larger bowl and add pumpkin, condensed milk, salt, and spices. Beat again until well blended. In a separate bowl, beat egg whites until stiff and fold into the pumpkin mixture. Pour into baked gingersnap crust and bake for 1 hour until set. Remove from oven and increase temperature to 450°. Combine brown sugar with sour cream and spread on top of baked filling, then sprinkle with pecans. Bake for 5 minutes. Cool and refrigerate until serving time.

PUMPKIN FLAN WITH RUM
[*Mexican*]

SERVES 6 TO 8

2 cups pumpkin purée, fresh or canned

1⅔ cups sugar

1 cup milk

2 cups light cream

1 tsp. salt

½ cup rum

6 eggs

Preheat oven to 350°. Melt 1 cup sugar over a low flame, stirring with a wooden spoon until it turns a light amber color. Immediately remove and pour into a deep baking dish. Turn the dish quickly so sides are coated with sugar. It must be done quickly before sugar starts to harden. Set sugar-coated pan aside.

Scald the milk and cream slowly. When bubbles form at the edge of milk, add the pumpkin, remaining ⅔ cup sugar, salt, and rum. Remove from stove and set aside. Beat eggs until frothy and then spill small amount of the pumpkin mixture into the eggs, beating constantly. Then add this to the remaining pumpkin mixture, beating constantly. Pour the egg and pumpkin mixture into the caramelized baking dish and set it into another pan with 2 inches of boiling water. Bake for 1 hour, until a knife inserted in center comes out clean. Let cool, then chill and invert on serving dish with sides to hold the caramelized liquid.

FESTIVE BAKED WHOLE PUMPKIN
[Mexican]

SERVES 8

1 large pumpkin (the size of a football, about 4 to 5 lbs.)
3 lbs. light brown sugar
3 sticks cinnamon

Cut a wedge into the top of the pumpkin near stem. Pour in brown sugar and cinnamon sticks. Replace the wedge and place the whole pumpkin in an ovenproof baking pan. Bake very slowly at 250° until a toothpick can pierce the shell into the flesh, about 1½ hours.

Serve whole and break apart at the table, where the strings and seeds are removed and the flesh is eaten with a spoon from the shell.

DRUNKEN RUM PUMPKIN
[*Mexican*]

SERVES 8

1 large pumpkin, the size of a
football, about 4 to 5 lbs.
1 bottle rum
3 lbs. brown sugar
*1 tsp. lime powder**

1 qt. cold water
4 oranges, rind included, cut
into chunks
2 sticks cinnamon

The night before, cut a hole about 2 inches in diameter into the top of the pumpkin and pour in the rum. Let stand overnight. In the morning, pour out rum and reserve for other uses. Cut unpeeled pumpkin into chunks, remove seeds and string. Sprinkle lime powder in the cold water to cover pumpkin pieces; let stand for 1 hour. Drain, rinse several times in cold water and dry on paper towels. Mix sugar, oranges, and cinnamon and bring to a boil. Add pumpkin. When pumpkin is tender and syrup thick, in about ¾ hour, remove from stove and cool.

Note: The classic way to serve this is in a deep bowl with cold milk poured over it.

PUMPKIN HONEY WITH ORANGES
[*Mexican*]

SERVES 6 TO 8

1 large pumpkin (the size of a
football, about 4 to 5 lbs.),
peeled, strings and seeds
removed, and cut into 4-inch
pieces
2 lbs. brown sugar

2 oranges, unpeeled and sliced
1 stick cinnamon
10 whole cloves
1 tsp. anise seeds
½ cup water

* Lime powder can be purchased from a druggist. Be sure it is lime for cooking.

Put pumpkin in a heavy pan with lid. Pack the brown sugar around the pieces of pumpkin, tuck in orange slices. Tie cinnamon, cloves and anise into a cheesecloth bag and bury in center of pan. Add ½ cup water and cook covered over very low heat for 1 hour. Pumpkin should be tender and darkly glazed. Remove spice bag, then remove pumpkin to warm serving dish; cook the remaining syrup in the pan until it is reduced and becomes thick. Pour over the pumpkin and top with slices of glazed orange from the pan. Serve at room temperature.

SWEET PUMPKIN FRITTERS
[West Indian]

SERVES 4 TO 6

1 small pumpkin (the size of a
   baseball, about 1 lb.), peeled,
   seeds and strings removed,
   and grated
½ cup milk
2 eggs, beaten
⅔ cup flour
1 tsp. baking powder

¼ tsp. salt
Oil for frying
¾ cup sugar
½ tsp. cinnamon
½ tsp. mace
½ tsp. ginger
¼ tsp. nutmeg

Make batter for fritters by mixing milk and beaten eggs together, combining dry ingredients, and quickly combining the two mixtures. Add finely shredded raw pumpkin to batter. Drop by spoonfuls into hot oil and, when brown on both sides, remove with slotted spoon. Mix cinnamon, mace, ginger, and nutmeg, and sprinkle mixture over fritters.

PUMPKIN DELIGHT
[Turkish]

SERVES 6 TO 8

*1 large pumpkin (the size of a
football, about 4 to 5 lbs.),
and cut into 1-inch slices*
1 lb. sugar

½ cup water
1 tsp. orange flower water*
½ cup walnuts, chopped

Sprinkle sugar over layers of pumpkin slices in a saucepan. Add water, cover, and cook over medium heat until pumpkin is tender but retains its shape. Let cool in pot. Remove pumpkin with slotted spoon. If there seems to be too much liquid, boil syrup to reduce by half. Then, add orange flower water to syrup, pour over pumpkin and remove to serving dish. Garnish with chopped walnuts.

ORANGE PECAN SQUASH SQUARES
[United States]

YIELD: 9 TO 12 PIECES

*1 medium yellow summer
squash, grated and drained of
excess liquid (about 1 cup)*
1½ cups flour
1 cup sugar
1 tsp. baking powder
1 tsp. baking soda
½ tsp. salt

*¾ cup pecans, chopped, with
several whole ones reserved
for topping*
2 egg whites
4 Tbs. corn oil or melted butter
½ cup orange juice
2 tsp. orange peel, grated

Preheat oven to 350°. Mix together flour, sugar, baking powder, baking soda, and salt. Stir in squash and chopped pecans. In a separate bowl, beat egg whites until slightly stiff and then add oil

* Orange flower water can be bought in Middle Eastern specialty shops. (See Sources for Ingredients, page 289.)

or butter and orange juice. Combine with squash mixture and add the grated orange peel. Butter and flour a 9 × 13 × 2-inch baking pan. Spoon batter into it and bake for 45 minutes. After 15 minutes of baking, top with pecan halves so they will not sink into the batter. Cool and cut into squares.

YELLOW SQUASH SPICE CAKE
[United States]

SERVES 6 TO 8

2 medium yellow summer squash (about 3 cups or 1½ lbs.), unpeeled and cubed	1 tsp. salt
	1½ tsp. baking soda
	½ tsp. ground cloves
½ cup applesauce	½ tsp. cinnamon
½ cup butter, softened	1 tsp. mace
1 cup sugar	¼ cup apple juice
1 egg	½ cup walnuts, chopped
2½ cups flour	Confectioners' sugar

Preheat oven to 350°. Mix squash and applesauce together and simmer slowly until tender. When cool, put into blender to purée and set aside to cool. Cream butter and sugar together until light and fluffy. Add egg and continue beating. Add squash and applesauce purée and mix well. In another bowl, mix together flour, salt, and baking soda. Mix cloves, cinnamon, and mace together and add to dry ingredients. Combine with squash mixture and beat well, adding the apple juice so batter is not too stiff. Stir in chopped walnuts. Butter and flour a 9 × 13 × 2-inch pan and bake about 45 minutes. When cake is cooled, invert pan. With a strainer, shake confectioners' sugar over top of inverted cake, covering it.

CANDIED ZUCCHINI AND CUSTARD
MERINGUE PIE
[United States]

YIELD: TWO 9-INCH PIES

PASTRY:

1½ cups flour
Pinch of salt
2 Tbs. sugar
¼ lb. sweet butter, softened
4 oz. cream cheese, softened
2 to 3 Tbs. heavy cream

Put flour, salt, and sugar into a large bowl. Add softened butter and cream cheese. With pastry blender, work into flour until mixture is the size of small peas. Add heavy cream and with hands form dough into a ball. Put in wax paper and chill in the refrigerator for 1 hour. Bring to room temperature before rolling out.

Butter 2 pie tins, roll out pastry, flute the edges. Put a circle of aluminum foil over bottom of pastry and cover with dry lima beans. Bake shell 20 minutes in 450° oven. Remove foil and lima beans.

CANDIED ZUCCHINI FILLING:

7 or 8 zucchini (about 2½   *1 Tbs. vanilla*
lbs.), unpeeled and sliced   *1 lemon, sliced thin*
across into ½-inch slices   *1 cup water*
2 lbs. sugar

Combine sugar, vanilla, lemon, and water and bring to a boil. Add slices of zucchini to the boiling syrup and cook until transparent and slightly candied. Drain in strainer and put on wax paper to dry further. The sugar syrup can be reserved and used for other recipes.

CUSTARD FILLING:

> *3 egg yolks, beaten*
> *4 Tbs. sugar*
> *½ tsp. lemon rind, grated*
> *½ tsp. vanilla*
> *1 tsp. cornstarch*
> *1 cup milk*

Mix egg yolks, sugar, lemon rind, vanilla, and cornstarch. Bring milk to boiling, add egg mixture, and simmer until mixture thickens. Set aside to cool.

MERINGUE:

> *4 egg whites*
> *Pinch of salt*
> *½ tsp. cream of tartar*
> *6 Tbs. sugar*
> *1 tsp. vanilla*

Beat egg whites with salt and cream of tartar until very stiff. Add sugar and vanilla and mix well.

To assemble pie: Spread custard evenly on prebaked pie shells. Top with slices of well-drained candied zucchini slices. Cover with meringue and bake at 300° for 20 minutes until meringue is nicely browned.

Note: This pastry can be made a day before, chilled, and brought to room temperature before rolling out the next day. It also freezes well.

STEAMED PUMPKIN PUDDING WITH LEMON
CREAM SAUCE
[*English*]

SERVES 8

1 cup pumpkin purée, canned	*½ tsp. ground cloves*
¼ lb. butter, softened	*¼ tsp. nutmeg*
1 cup dark brown sugar	*1 tsp. baking powder*
2 eggs, lightly beaten	*½ tsp. baking soda*
1¾ cups flour	*¼ cup heavy cream*
½ tsp. cinnamon	*1 tsp. lemon juice*
½ tsp. powdered ginger	

Cream butter and sugar, add eggs and pumpkin and beat well. Mix together flour, spices, baking powder, and baking soda. Mix the cream with the lemon juice. Gradually stir the flour mixture into the pumpkin mixture alternately with the lemon and cream. Pour into a 1½-quart pudding mold. Cover the top of the mold with a piece of buttered wax paper cut in a shape to fit the mold and tie with a string. Put the mold on a rack in a deep pot and add enough boiling water to reach halfway up the side of the mold. Cover the pot and simmer the pudding for about 2 hours, or until it is firm. Remove the mold from the pot and let cool for 10 minutes before unmolding pudding. Serve warm with Lemon Cream Sauce.

LEMON CREAM SAUCE:

½ pt. heavy cream
2 Tbs. confectioners' sugar, sifted
1 Tbs. lemon juice

Whip the cream, mix with the sugar and lemon juice, and pass in a separate bowl to be served over the pudding.

PUMPKIN ICE CREAM MOLD WITH MINCEMEAT SAUCE
[*United States*]

SERVES 6

ICE CREAM MOLD:

> *1 cup pumpkin purée, canned*
> *½ cup light brown sugar*
> *¼ tsp. salt*
> *¼ tsp. cinnamon*
> *⅛ tsp. ground cloves*
> *1 qt. vanilla ice cream, slightly soft*

Mix the pumpkin purée, sugar, salt, and spices together, and then blend with the ice cream. Put mixture into a 1-quart melon-shaped mold and freeze for 24 hours. To unmold, place mold in warm water for a few minutes, invert on serving plate, and shake out. Serve with warm Mincemeat Sauce.

MINCEMEAT SAUCE:

> *One 14½-oz. jar of prepared mincemeat*
> *½ cup apricot nectar, canned*
> *1 Tbs. orange rind, grated*

Heat mincemeat, apricot nectar, and grated orange rind in saucepan. Stir and cook over low heat for 1 minute. Cool slightly before serving over ice cream mold.

Note: This dessert is a pleasant, unusual departure for the finale of a Thanksgiving Day or Christmas feast.

CANDIED PUMPKIN
[*United States*]

SERVES 8

1 medium pumpkin (the size   *¼ lb. sweet butter*
of child's rubber ball, about   *¼ cup molasses*
2½ lbs.), peeled, seeds and   *¾ cup sugar*
strings removed, and cut into   *Pinch of salt*
1-inch cubes

Parboil pumpkin cubes in skillet with water to cover until tender. Drain and reserve in bowl. In same skillet, add butter, molasses, sugar, and salt and cook, stirring constantly, over low heat until blended. Add pumpkin cubes; cover skillet and cook 10 minutes more. Stir gently to coat but do not break cubes of pumpkin. Preheat oven to 350°. Transfer mixture to baking dish and bake uncovered until brown and candied, basting occasionally with syrup. Serve at room temperature.

PUMPKIN CUSTARD WITH WHIPPED CREAM AND CRYSTALLIZED GINGER
[*United States*]

SERVES 8

2 cups pumpkin purée, canned   *¼ tsp. nutmeg*
3 eggs, lightly beaten   *¾ tsp. salt*
2 Tbs. honey   *¼ cup dry sherry*
1¾ cups light cream   *Whipped cream*
⅓ cup light brown sugar   *Crystallized ginger, slivered*
1 tsp. powdered ginger   *thin*
2 tsp. cinnamon

In a large bowl beat eggs, pumpkin purée, honey, light cream, sugar, spices, salt, and sherry together thoroughly. Preheat oven to 350°. Butter a 1½-quart baking pan and pour custard into it. Set it in a larger shallow pan of boiling water. Bake for 1 hour until 1-inch circle in center is still soft. It will set later and is a good test to make sure the custard is not overdone. Cool. Cover with plastic wrap and refrigerate for several hours. Serve dollops of whipped cream on top, and sprinkle the whipped cream with slivered crystallized ginger.

Note: This dessert is actually a pumpkin pie without the pie crust. It is a bit lighter after a large meal than the usual pumpkin pie.

PUMPKIN PARFAIT WITH PECANS
[*United States*]

SERVES 4

1 cup pumpkin purée, canned
2 Tbs. sugar
¼ tsp. cinnamon
¼ tsp. ground ginger
⅛ tsp. ground cloves
One 3¼-oz. package vanilla
  pudding (*do not use instant*
  pudding)

1½ cups milk
½ pt. heavy cream, whipped
½ cup pecans, coarsely
  chopped, with 4 whole
  pecans reserved

Combine sugar, cinnamon, ginger, and cloves with vanilla pudding. Add milk, stir, and bring to a boil, stirring constantly. Remove from heat and add pumpkin. Chill. Spoon into 4 parfait glasses alternately with the whipped cream mixed with the chopped pecans, so that the parfait is striped. Top each parfait with whipped cream and 1 whole pecan.

PUMPKIN DROP COOKIES
[United States]

YIELD: ABOUT 4 DOZEN

1½ cups pumpkin purée,　　　*1 tsp. cinnamon*
*　canned or fresh*　　　　　*¼ tsp. ground ginger*
¼ lb. butter, softened　　　*½ tsp. nutmeg*
1¼ cups light brown sugar　*½ tsp. salt*
2 eggs, well beaten　　　　*1 cup pecans, chopped*
2½ cups flour　　　　　　*1 cup white seedless raisins*
3 tsps. baking powder

Preheat oven to 400°. Cream butter and sugar together until light and fluffy. Add eggs and pumpkin purée and beat again. Sift flour and baking powder and add the spices and salt. Then add the dry ingredients to the pumpkin mixture and stir until well blended. Add the chopped pecans and raisins. Butter 2 or 3 cookie sheets. Drop the batter with a teaspoon and bake for 15 minutes until light brown. Remove with spatula when slightly cool.

PUMPKIN MOUSSE WITH VANILLA SAUCE
[United States]

SERVES 4 TO 6

1¼ cups pumpkin purée,　　*1 tsp. cinnamon*
*　canned*　　　　　　　　*½ tsp. allspice*
1 Tbs. unflavored gelatin　*½ tsp. nutmeg*
2 Tbs. cold water　　　　　*¼ tsp. mace*
3 egg yolks　　　　　　　*1 cup heavy cream, whipped*
½ cup sugar

Dissolve gelatin: sprinkle over 2 Tbs. cold water to soften, place in bowl over simmering water, and stir until dissolved. Beat the egg yolks well and gradually add the sugar. Then stir in the pumpkin purée, the spices and gelatin. Fold the whipped cream gently into the pumpkin mixture and pour into a mold. Chill for several hours until firm. Unmold and serve cold with Vanilla Sauce.

VANILLA SAUCE:

1 cup milk
1 cup light cream
1 ½ tsp. vanilla extract
4 egg yolks
½ cup sugar
Pinch of salt

Scald the milk and cream. Then put into the top of a double boiler over gently simmering water and add the vanilla extract. Beat together the egg yolks, sugar, and salt. Gradually beat in the scalded milk and cream mixture and stir constantly until sauce thickens and coats the spoon. Strain the sauce through a fine sieve and let cool.

FRIED PUMPKIN RINGS WITH CINNAMON SYRUP
[South American]

SERVES 6

1 cup pumpkin purée, canned   *2 Tbs. Parmesan cheese, grated*
2 cups flour   *4 Tbs. butter, softened*
1 tsp. salt   *Oil for deep frying*
1 tsp. baking powder

Sift the flour, salt, and baking powder together. Add the Parmesan cheese and beat in the softened butter and pumpkin purée. On a floured board, roll out the dough ½ inch thick. Cut into strips 6 inches long by 1 inch wide, and shape into rings by moistening the ends and pinching them together. Deep fry in hot oil until they are brown on all sides. Drain on paper towels and serve with Cinnamon Syrup.

CINNAMON SYRUP:

> *2 cups dark brown sugar*
> *1 cup water*
> *One 1-inch piece cinnamon stick*

Mix all ingredients together and stir over medium heat until sugar is dissolved, about 8 minutes. Discard cinnamon and pour syrup over pumpkin rings.

COLD PUMPKIN SOUFFLÉ
[*United States*]

SERVES 8

1 cup pumpkin purée, canned	*½ tsp. ground ginger*
1 envelope unflavored gelatin	*¼ tsp. mace*
¼ cup rum	*¼ tsp. ground cloves*
4 eggs	*1 cup heavy cream*
⅔ cup sugar	*Candied fruits for decoration*
½ tsp. cinnamon	

Oil a 6-inch band of wax paper and tie it, oiled side in, around a 1-quart soufflé dish to form a collar. In the top of a double boiler over simmering water, sprinkle the gelatin into the rum; stir occasionally until gelatin is completely dissolved. Beat the eggs thoroughly and gradually add the sugar, and continue to beat until mixture has thickened. Stir in the pumpkin purée and all the spices, then the gelatin-rum mixture and stir all together. Whip cream until stiff and fold in. Spoon into prepared soufflé dish and chill until set. Remove the paper collar and decorate the edge of the soufflé with pieces of candied fruit.

FROZEN PUMPKIN ALASKA WITH WHEAT GERM
[*United States*]

SERVES 8

PUMPKIN MOLD:

¾ cup pumpkin purée, canned	½ tsp. salt
¼ cup wheat germ	¼ cup sugar
1 tsp. cinnamon	¼ cup light molasses
1 tsp. powdered ginger	3 eggs, separated
½ tsp. mace	1 cup heavy cream, whipped

In heavy saucepan mix together pumpkin, wheat germ, cinnamon, ginger, mace, salt, sugar, and molasses. Add the egg yolks and cook, stirring constantly over low heat until thickened. Let cool to room temperature. Beat egg whites until stiff and gently fold into the pumpkin mixture. Then fold in whipped cream. Spoon into dome-shaped metal mold and freeze overnight. Before serving, preheat oven to 475° and make meringue.

MERINGUE:

3 egg whites
¼ tsp. salt
3 Tbs. fine sugar
¼ tsp. cream of tartar

Beat egg whites with salt until foamy. Gradually add fine sugar and cream of tartar. Beat until very stiff, but not dry. Invert frozen pumpkin mold into ovenproof dish and spoon meringue over it with a spatula, making a pleasant design. Make sure no pumpkin shows. Put in very hot 475° oven for 3 to 4 minutes until meringue starts to brown lightly. Make sure the pumpkin mold is frozen solid, and work quickly putting on the meringue so that the heat of the oven will not melt the mold, but only brown the meringue. Serve immediately.

BAKED CHAYOTE STUFFED WITH RAISINS, ALMONDS, AND CAKE CRUMBS
[South American]

SERVES 6

3 large chayotes (about 1 lb. each)	*¾ cup sugar*
2 eggs, lightly beaten	*1 cup white seedless raisins*
½ cup sweet sherry	*3 cups cake, ladyfingers, or spongecake, crumbled*
1 tsp. cinnamon	*½ cup almonds, blanched and slivered*
½ tsp. ground nutmeg	

Cut chayotes in half, cover with cold water, and bring to a boil over high heat. Reduce heat to low, and simmer covered for 30 minutes. Drain on paper towels and cool before removing seeds with a spoon. Scoop out pulp, leaving ¼ inch near shell, and mash the pulp until smooth. Beat in eggs, sherry, spices, sugar, raisins, and cake crumbs. If filling seems too thin, add more cake crumbs until it is the consistency of mashed potatoes.

Preheat oven to 350°. Fill the shells with stuffing and stud with slivered almonds. Arrange in a buttered baking dish and bake 15 minutes until golden. Serve warm.

BREADS

ZUCCHINI PARMESAN BREAD   [United States]

MENNONITE PUMPKIN SPICE BREAD   [United States]

PUMPKIN BREAD WITH CANDIED FRUIT   [United States]

PUMPKIN OR SQUASH YEAST BREAD   [United States]

ZUCCHINI WALNUT BREAD   [United States]

PUMPKIN MUFFINS   [United States]

ZUCCHINI PARMESAN BREAD
[United States]

YIELD: 1 LOAF

1 medium zucchini (about ½ to ¾ lb.), shredded and unpeeled
3 cups flour, sifted
4 Tbs. sugar
4 Tbs. Parmesan cheese, grated
5 tsp. baking powder
½ tsp. baking soda
1½ tsp. salt
1 cup buttermilk
6 Tbs. butter, melted
2 eggs, beaten
3 Tbs. onion, grated

Preheat oven to 350°. Butter 9 × 5 × 3-inch loaf pan. Mix flour, sugar, cheese, baking powder, baking soda, salt, and grated zucchini. Mix buttermilk, melted butter, eggs, and onion until smooth. Then add the liquid mixture to the dry ingredients all at once and mix until just blended. Batter should be somewhat dry. Spread in pan and bake about 1 hour, until toothpick inserted in center comes out clean and bread pulls away from the sides of pan. Cool on rack before slicing.

MENNONITE PUMPKIN SPICE BREAD
[United States]

YIELD: 2 LOAVES

There is a motel in Lancaster County where I first tasted this pumpkin bread. It is baked daily by a charming Mennonite lady who delivers it to the motel's restaurant. After my first sample, I bought two dozen loaves as gifts and for the freezer until I could duplicate the recipe myself.

2½ cups pumpkin purée,   1¼ cups sugar
    canned or fresh   ½ tsp. ground allspice
3 cups flour   4 eggs, well beaten
2 tsp. baking soda   1 cup oil
2 tsp. baking powder   ½ cup walnuts, chopped
1 tsp. salt   ¼ cup raisins
2 tsp. cinnamon

Preheat oven to 350°. Butter two 9 × 5 × 3-inch loaf pans. Sift all dry ingredients together in large bowl; add walnuts and raisins. In another bowl, mix eggs, oil, and pumpkin purée. Combine the contents of both bowls and beat well. Spoon into loaf pans and bake 1 hour. When cool, remove from pans.

This bread is excellent served with cottage cheese and apple butter, the way it is served in Amish and Mennonite country in Lancaster County, Pennsylvania.

PUMPKIN BREAD WITH CANDIED FRUIT
[United States]

YIELD: 1 LOAF

¾ cup pumpkin purée, canned
  or fresh
¼ cup butter, softened
¾ cup light brown sugar
2 eggs

1⅔ cups flour
3 tsp. baking powder
½ tsp. salt
½ tsp. ground allspice
½ cup candied mixed fruits

Preheat oven to 350°. Cream butter and sugar. Add eggs one at a time and beat well. Stir in the pumpkin. Sift flour, baking powder, salt, and allspice, and stir into pumpkin mixture until smooth. Stir in candied fruits and spoon into 9 × 5 × 3-inch loaf pan. Bake 45 minutes. Cool on rack before inverting pan.

PUMPKIN OR SQUASH YEAST BREAD
[United States]

YIELD: 3 LOAVES

2 cups pumpkin or squash
  purée, canned or fresh
8½ cups flour
2 packages dry yeast
¼ cup lukewarm water

¼ cup sugar
1¾ cups milk, scalded
1 Tbs. salt
¼ cup butter, melted

Sift flour. Sprinkle yeast into lukewarm water and add 1 tsp. sugar. Let stand 10 minutes. Pour scalded milk into large mixing bowl. Add 2½ cups of the flour and beat until batter is smooth, then add pumpkin purée and cooled, melted butter. Add another 6 cups flour to make stiff dough. Turn out on board sprinkled with flour. Cover with cloth towel and let rest 10 minutes. Then knead for 10 minutes until smooth and elastic. Butter a large bowl and turn dough into it once to cover lightly with butter. Cover again and let rise in warm place until doubled in bulk, about 1 hour. Punch down, turn over in bowl again, and let rise for a second time until double in bulk, another 45 minutes. Turn out onto floured board and divide into three equal pieces. Cover and let rest 10 minutes. Shape into loaves and put into three 9 × 5 × 3-inch buttered pans. Cover and let rise again until double, another hour. Bake in a 400° oven for 40 minutes. Turn out and cool on racks before slicing.

Variation: Add 1½ cups scalded milk and ½ cup orange juice for the liquid, and mix 1 tsp. ginger, 2 tsps. cinnamon, ½ tsp. nutmeg, and 1 tsp. grated orange rind into the flour; follow the same directions above.

ZUCCHINI WALNUT BREAD
[*United States*]

YIELD: 2 LOAVES

*3 medium zucchini (about 2
  cups or 1½ lbs.), unpeeled
  and grated
3 eggs
¾ cup corn oil or peanut oil
1¼ cups sugar
Grated rind of 1 orange
Grated rind of 1 lemon*

*½ tsp. vanilla extract
2½ cups flour*
¾ tsp. salt
2 tsp. baking powder
1 tsp. baking soda
½ tsp. cinnamon
¾ cup walnuts, chopped*

Preheat oven to 350°. Beat eggs, add oil and sugar. Mix well. Add grated orange and lemon rinds, vanilla, and zucchini. Mix well again. In a separate bowl, mix together flour, salt, baking powder and baking soda, cinnamon, and walnuts. Combine with zucchini mixture and mix well. Oil thoroughly two 1-lb. coffee cans and

---

* Some zucchini may contain more moisture than others and, therefore, more flour may be needed. This bread freezes well, also.

pour bread batter into them. Bake for 1 hour. Let breads cool completely, loosen with a spatula, and remove. If difficult to remove, open the bottom of can with can opener and force the bread out.

PUMPKIN MUFFINS
[United States]

YIELD: I DOZEN

¾ cup pumpkin purée, canned
1 ½ cups flour
1 cup sugar
2 tsp. baking powder
½ tsp. salt
½ tsp. cinnamon

¼ tsp. ground allspice
¼ tsp. nutmeg
4 Tbs. butter, softened
1 egg, beaten
⅓ cup milk

Preheat oven to 400° and butter twelve 2½-inch muffin tins. Sift together flour, sugar, baking powder, salt, and spices. Add the butter and combine with the flour mixture until it looks mealy. Add the egg and pumpkin and then the milk. Stir until the mixture is combined. Pour into muffin tins and bake for 25 minutes or until a cake tester comes out clean.

TWO

Eggplant

HISTORY AND INTRODUCTION

THE EGGPLANT is a super-vegetable and one of the most adaptable. It can be an hors d'oeuvre, an accompanying side dish, a soup, or a main dish. It can even be a pickle, a salad, a preserve, or a dessert.

If there were to be an award given for excellent design in vegetables, surely the eggplant would be declared the winner. Its perfect ovoid shape, its royal-purple satin skin, crowned with its vibrant green cap, its heaviness in the hand, its sensual touch, makes it truly a visual and tactile delight. What's more, it is a work of art that is edible, economical, and nourishing as well.

The eggplant was first grown in Asia where it was considered mostly an ornamental plant and one that was highly poisonous as well since its botanical origin is the deadly nightshade family. It is also related to belladonna and tobacco. In India eggplant was first tried as food; it was then introduced to China as an edible plant and from there, in the fourth century, the Arabs first ate it.

At first it was called "egg fruit," because the early varieties were small and were usually white or brown, the color of hens' eggs. But today eggplant has many colors and varieties which are popular and are grown and eaten throughout the entire world.

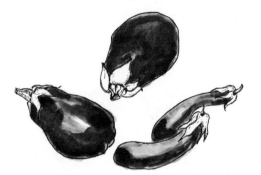

In Malagasy, for instance, there is a greenish-yellow variety called *"grasse anguine,"* which has a rather bitter taste. A small, white, delicate eggplant is grown in China that can now be purchased in the United States in Chinese markets.

There are many different varieties eaten in Europe and the Middle East, the most popular being the small, purple, elongated eggplant. Here in the United States, this clearly universal vegetable is large, purple, and ovoid in shape.

In medieval Europe, the eggplant was at first considered to be a highly effective love potion, and it was believed to have great aphrodisiac properties. Others called it "malainsana" or "mad apple," and they believed that eating the eggplant caused madness. Then again, there were some who thought that love was madness —so who knows.

About the fifth century, it became fashionable in China for Oriental ladies to make a black dye with eggplant skins. They then used it to stain and polish their teeth until they gleamed like shining metal.

About the thirteenth century, the eggplant made its debut in Pisa, Genoa, and Venice, and it was first brought into these ports on ships from the East, along with their cargoes of Indian spices and Chinese silks. Moving outward from these active trading ports, the strange purple fruit was then introduced into other European countries. Then, in 1806, it was shipped from Spain and Portugal to the American possessions in the Western hemisphere and grown in American gardens.

In each country, this universal vegetable has its own name, and in some countries it has been given a nickname. This leads me to believe that the eggplant has finally overcome its bad press. It is known as "Guinea squash," "Jew's apple," "egg fruit." In France it is called *"aubergine,"* in Bengal *"bringal,"* and a corruption of this word is known in the West Indies as "brown jolly." In Spanish it is *"alberengena,"* in Portuguese *"beringela,"* in Persian Pharsee *"badin-gan,"* in Sanskrit *"vatingana,"* in Italian *"melanzane,"* and in Greek *"melitzana."*

However, the eggplant has much more going for it than its physical beauty, euphonious names, and a need to overcome a bad reputation. It is *the* most versatile and adaptable of all vegetables. And in the United States, because of climactic differences throughout the country, it knows no special season.

Although the eggplant has no protein to speak of, it is often thought of as a meat substitute—and rightly so. In many dishes, it is truly a filling and satisfying main course, and a budget-stretcher as well. With the addition of a small amount of ground beef, lamb, poultry, fish, cheese, or seafood, there are any number of unusual and elegant recipes to be tried. If one uses only small amounts of oil, the eggplant is also excellent for diet-watchers, since it is low in calories.

It is probably written somewhere in Arabic that an Arabian bride can command a costly "bride-price" or dowery by the number of eggplant dishes she can prepare. One hundred separate dishes could bring her an enormously wealthy sultan as a husband. Fifty eggplant dishes and perhaps a wealthy businessman could afford her. Twenty-five could bring her a bride price that could be met by anyone.

This collection of eggplant recipes, which numbers over 100, will allow, if one is interested, a wedding with a sultan—but if you are a creative woman, you will no doubt invent or collect some more recipes of your own and thus also become the favorite concubine in the seraglio.

As for the man who cooks (and I find, personally, that most men who like to eat also like to cook) and is not interested in "bride prices," this sensual vegetable can certainly add a varied nuance to his repertoire. And finally, though this much maligned vegetable has never gotten its due, that is not why this book was written.

Why a whole half of a book on eggplant? It started with my husband's unfair prejudice about eggplant; I was determined to find a palatable way to present it to him and thus make him a convert. This I have done.

And besides—I just simply love the color.

An eggplant can be:
    Souffléed
    Stuffed
    Sautéed
    Fried
    Boiled
    Baked
    Broiled
It can become a:
    Soup
    Hors d'oeuvre
    Main dish
    Relish
    Accompanying vegetable
    Sauce
    Salad
    Preserve
It can also be served:
    Hot   With fish
    Cold   With poultry

Alone　　　　　　　　With beef
With other vegetables　With lamb
With seafood　　　　　With veal

TIPS ON SELECTION AND PREPARATION

When buying an eggplant, be sure the skin is taut, sleek, and shiny, and that its surface is unblemished and unwrinkled. Eggplants are generally picked before they are totally mature. When an eggplant ages, the flesh softens, the flavor turns somewhat bitter, and seeds get larger and tougher. So after you purchase the eggplant, make certain you keep it no longer than a few days before using it.

When an eggplant is cooked for a short time, it is necessary to peel it or the skin will be tough. When the recipe calls for cooking it in the oven for an hour or so, then the skin should be retained. It is edible and attractive and also helps to keep the shape of the eggplant intact.

The eggplant contains a great deal of liquid, which may at times make your recipe too watery. There is also a slight bitterness to this liquid which some people find objectionable. Therefore, when preparing the eggplant for cooking, it is necessary to pre-prepare it according to the form it will take in each dish.

Unsalted eggplant will drink up tremendous amounts of oil. Salting and draining the eggplant prevents this, so that less oil can be used in the recipe.

For some recipes, such as stuffed eggplant, it is necessary to parboil the vegetable first, unpeeled, in boiling, salted water. This method is used when the eggplant must retain its shape. In addition, the slight bitterness of the liquid will be released into the boiling, salted water. Remember to refresh the parboiled eggplant under gently running cold water before continuing the recipe.

For some dishes it is desirable to have a smoky taste. When this is called for, the eggplant must be salted and broiled until the skin is almost charcoal, then cooled, peeled, and drained so that the smoky-flavored pulp can be used in the preparation of the dish.

I have devised four simple methods for pre-preparing eggplant. Each recipe in the book begins with one of these methods, according to the requirements and the taste of the dish.

Method One

Wash the eggplant, dry it, and remove the green tip from the top of the vegetable, plus a small slice from the bottom. Split it into quarters lengthwise, and then slice to desired thickness. Do not peel. Cubes can also be made, if you desire.

Sprinkle the slices or cubes on both sides with 1 Tbs. salt. The amount of salt will vary, of course, with the size of the eggplant. Place salted slices or cubes in a colander or strainer that is *not* made of metal. (Plastic is fine.) Put a bowl underneath to catch the excess liquid.

Let stand for 30 minutes. Rinse the slices under cold water and dry thoroughly on paper towels. Proceed with recipe.

Method Two

To 3 quarts of boiling water, add 2 Tbs. salt. (If using fewer eggplants, use 1½ tsps. salt per quart of water.) According to the recipe directions, drop the unpeeled whole or halved eggplant into the boiling water. Let cook for 10 to 15 minutes, depending upon size of vegetable. Refresh under gently running cold water and dry on paper towels. Remove center part of pulp, leaving ½ inch near the skin. If eggplant loses its shape, which sometimes happens, place it in a preheated oven at 400° for a few minutes to crisp the skin and help it retain its shape. Proceed with recipe.

METHOD THREE

Split unpeeled eggplant lengthwise, and place it on a foil-lined cookie sheet with sides to catch the liquid, or on a wire rack. Or, if you prefer, use a disposable pan. Slip under moderate heat on the lowest rack of the broiler, skin side up. When the skin has charred, turn the eggplant carefully and broil on the other side. When skin is blackened and eggplant is soft (about 15 to 20 minutes, depending upon size of eggplant), remove from broiler and sprinkle with ½ tsp. salt. Let cool slightly. With the point of a knife, make an incision at several points in the blackened skin. Let the eggplant cool completely and this will drain off the excess fluid. Discard this liquid, then peel off the charred skin and proceed with the balance of the recipe, using the pulp only.

METHOD FOUR

In recipes requiring shorter cooking time, it is necessary to peel the eggplant first. Either slice it or cube it after it is peeled, and then cook in a small amount of boiling, salted water until tender but firm. (Between 5 and 10 minutes is usually sufficient.) Drain refresh under gently running cold water, and proceed with the recipe.

HOW TO GROW EGGPLANT

There are about ten varieties of eggplant that are now grown in the United States:

Golden Yellow	Black Hybrid
Golden Egg	Black Beauty

Apple Green   Black Magic
White Beauty   Morden Midget
White Long Italian   Early Long Purple

long purple

dwarf golden

black beauty

large round purple

white beauty

If you seek variety in your garden and wish to grow your own eggplant, you are in for a culinary delight. Its culture takes patience, since it requires four months to develop from seed to fruit, but it's worth growing just to sample a freshly picked baby fruit.

Four plants will yield about twenty-four eggplants. But if you want to cut the time for harvesting, buy a flat of seedling transplants which will be ready to harvest in about 80 days. Eggplants, like tomatoes, require daily temperature of about 70 degrees and require staking. Set plants out about 18 inches apart in a warm, loamy soil enriched with compost or well-rotted manure. Water weekly to a depth of 4 inches. Fertilize with a well-balanced fertilizer once a month in a circle at the base of the plant and scratch fertilizer in lightly. Although the flowers are very beautiful, do not allow more than six blossoms to develop on each plant. Pinch off the extras so that the remaining flowers will fruit well. Harvest by cutting, not pulling, from the plant when fruit is glossy and about 4 inches in diameter.

To freeze the surplus, peel, slice ⅓ inch thick, and drop into 1 quart of boiled water containing ¼ cup of salt to prevent discoloration. Let steep 1 minute and refresh under cold water. Freeze flat on a cookie sheet, then pack frozen slices in plastic bags.

EGGPLANT WEIGHTS

Since nothing in nature is regimentally precise, all eggplant sizes and weights are approximate. Each recipe states the recipe size and weight. In buying eggplant, perhaps this guide will help somewhat.

1 very small eggplant = about ¼ pound
1 small eggplant = about ½ to ¾ pound
1 medium eggplant = about 1 pound
1 large eggplant = about 1½ to 2 pounds

HORS D'OEUVRES

EGGPLANT BUTTER WITH GARLIC [*Greek*]

STUFFED EGGPLANTS WITH GARLIC [*Turkish*]

EGGPLANT WITH GARLIC AND WALNUTS [*Syrian*]

EGGPLANT CAPONATA [*Italian*]

EGGPLANT WITH SESAME OIL [*Lebanese*]

EGGPLANT WITH MINT [*Iraqi*]

EGGPLANT APPETIZER [*Armenian*]

EGGPLANT PUFFS WITH CUMIN AND GRUYÈRE CHEESE [*French*]

POOR MAN'S CAVIAR [*Turkish*]

EGGPLANT BUTTER WITH GARLIC
[*Greek*]

SERVES 6

3 medium eggplants   *2 cups water*
¾ cup butter, softened   *3 Tbs. parsley, chopped*
5 cloves garlic, minced   *Salt and pepper to taste*
1 Tbs. tomato paste   *Black olives*

[178]

Prepare eggplants, using Method 4, and cube eggplant. Heat butter and add eggplant cubes. Turn to brown on all sides. Add garlic, tomato paste diluted in 1 cup water, parsley, and the additional cup of water. Add salt and pepper. Cover and simmer until all the liquid is absorbed, about 45 minutes. Combine in a blender a few batches at a time and serve topped with black olives. Chill and serve with crackers as a spread.

STUFFED EGGPLANTS WITH GARLIC
[Turkish]

SERVES 10

20 very small eggplants	1 tsp. tomato paste
5 heads of garlic, or 60 cloves,	1½ tsp. salt
peeled*	½ tsp. pepper
1 cup olive oil	½ tsp. sugar
½ cup water	½ tsp. cinnamon
Juice of 1 lemon	

Prepare eggplants, using Method 4, but since they are small, leave them whole and do not peel them. Cook only for 5 minutes. Refresh under cold water. Drain and pierce each eggplant with tip of knife and insert a whole clove of peeled garlic in each incision. Then deep-fry eggplants in hot oil until golden and soft, about 5 to 7 minutes. Remove and place side by side in a flat casserole. Add water, lemon juice, tomato paste, salt and pepper, sugar and cinnamon. Preheat oven to 375°, cover casserole with foil, and bake 30 minutes; remove foil and bake 15 to 20 minutes more, if necessary, to evaporate excess liquid. Chill and serve cold.

* This recipe depends on a large quantity of garlic. Put a sprig of fresh parsley on each plate to be eaten afterward, so you can breathe easily. The parsley counteracts the garlic, as it contains chlorophyll, which is a breath freshener.

EGGPLANT WITH GARLIC AND WALNUTS
[Syrian]

SERVES 6

12 very small eggplants
2 cups shelled walnuts, ground
2 Tbs. salt
12 cloves garlic
Olive oil
Black pepper to taste

Prepare eggplants, using Method 2. However, these are small egg-plants and should be left whole. Cook in boiling water 25 minutes. Remove and refresh under cold water. Drain on paper towels, then slit each eggplant on one side. Press gently with palms of hands until all liquid is removed, and set aside for 20 minutes. Pour off any more accumulated liquid.

Mix together ground walnuts and salt. In the slit of each egg-plant, place 1 tsp. walnuts and 1 clove garlic. Press the opening together to close, sprinkle with pepper and place stuffed eggplants tightly in a jar. Cover jar and leave until the following day, then turn upside down and leave for 1 more day. If any liquid appears in jar, drain it off. Then fill jar halfway with olive oil. The oil will rise in the jar. Let stand for 3 or 4 days and check to see if the oil will spill over. If the oil decreases, add more to keep eggplants soaked. Keep jar covered. Eggplants are ready to eat in 1 week. Serve on bed of lettuce as a first course.

EGGPLANT CAPONATA
[Italian]

SERVES 6

1 large eggplant
¼ cup olive oil
Salt and pepper to taste
2 onions, sliced thin
2 cloves garlic, minced
2 stalks celery, diced
3 large, ripe tomatoes, cubed
10 large black olives, or 5 green
  and 5 black, pitted and cut in
  quarters

2 green peppers, seeded and cut
  in squares
2 tsp. capers, rinsed and drained
2 Tbs. vinegar
½ tsp. sugar
½ cup pine nuts (optional)

Prepare eggplant, using Method 1. Sauté drained eggplant quickly in hot oil for 2 or 3 minutes. Remove from pan with slotted spoon, season with salt and pepper, and set aside.

In the same pan, sauté onions (add more oil if necessary), and add garlic, celery, tomatoes, olives, and green peppers. Cook over low heat for 15 minutes.

Combine with sautéed eggplant, add capers and stir.

Heat vinegar and sugar; add more salt and pepper if necessary, and pine nuts if desired. Cook for 5 minutes more. Chill and serve cold as an appetizer.

Note: Almost every Southern Italian has a family recipe for Caponata. This is a good, basic one.

EGGPLANT WITH SESAME OIL
[Lebanese]

SERVES 8

3 large eggplants
1 cup tahini*
1 ¼ cups lemon juice
4 cloves garlic, minced

3 drops Tabasco sauce
2 tsp. salt
2 Tbs. parsley, chopped
1 Tbs. olive oil

Prepare eggplants, using Method 3. Place pulp in blender, and purée one-third at a time. Add tahini, lemon juice, garlic, Tabasco, and salt, and combine all together. Garnish with parsley and a trickle of olive oil. Serve cold and decorate with radish flowers and small scallions. Dip up with pieces of Arabic flat bread, called pita.

Variations: There is a Turkish, Romanian, Armenian and Israeli version of this Middle Eastern appetizer known as Baba Ghanouj in Lebanon. The ingredients vary slightly from country to country but rather than give 16 variations, we will use this as a base. For a Syrian version, one may add 2 Tbs. pine nuts and garnish with pomegranate seeds.

EGGPLANT WITH MINT

SERVES 6

[Iraqi]

1 large eggplant
Olive oil
8 oz. plain yogurt
¼ cup fresh mint leaves,
   chopped, or 1 Tbs. dried
   mint, crushed

1 clove garlic, minced
Salt and pepper to taste

* Tahini is a sesame seed paste that comes in a can. If it is too thick, it may be diluted with ½ cup water. The consistency varies with different brands. It can be purchased in any Oriental or Middle Eastern specialty store. (See Sources for Ingredients, page 289.)

Prepare eggplant, using Method 1. Fry quickly in hot olive oil on both sides. Drain on paper towels and chill.

Combine yogurt, mint, garlic, and salt and pepper. Add eggplant and serve cold with a sprig of fresh mint on top.

Good with Arabic bread, called pita, or sesame seed crackers.

EGGPLANT APPETIZER
[*Armenian*]

SERVES 6

1 large eggplant	*½ tsp. black pepper*
⅔ cup water	*1 clove garlic, minced*
⅓ cup olive oil	*½ tsp. thyme*
Juice of 1 large lemon	*2 sprigs parsley, minced*
½ tsp. salt	

Prepare eggplant, using Method 4; cube eggplant. Mix water, olive oil, lemon juice, salt, pepper, garlic, thyme, and parsley. Bring to a boil and let simmer 5 minutes.

Add eggplant cubes and cook an additional 10 minutes until tender. Allow to cool in this sauce. Serve chilled with Arabic bread, called pita.

Thyme

EGGPLANT PUFFS WITH CUMIN AND GRUYÈRE CHEESE
[French]

YIELD: ABOUT 2 DOZEN

2 *medium eggplants*	*1 egg, slightly beaten*
1 cup Gruyère cheese, grated	*Salt and pepper to taste*
8 Tbs. fine, dry bread crumbs	*Flour for dredging*
1 tsp. cumin	*Oil for frying*
2 cloves garlic, minced	

Prepare eggplants, using Method 4. Drain well on paper towels and purée. Add all other ingredients except flour and oil.

Shape into small balls and refrigerate for 1 hour.

Remove from refrigerator and, while still cold, roll in flour and fry in hot oil until crisp and golden brown. Serve hot on tooth-picks as hors d'oeuvres.

POOR MAN'S CAVIAR
[Turkish]

SERVES 6

2 *medium eggplants*	*½ cup fresh dill, snipped*
2 *cloves garlic, minced*	*1 Tbs. vinegar*
½ cup onion, minced	*2 Tbs. olive oil*
½ cup parsley, minced	*Salt and pepper to taste*

Prepare eggplants, using Method 3. Then chop peeled, cooked egg-plant fine. Mix with all other ingredients. Chill for 1 hour or more to blend flavors. Serve ringed with sliced tomato on a bed of lettuce.

Note: This recipe is a classic one found in most Middle Eastern countries, and with the price of fresh caviar, it is an excellent sub-stitute for tight food budgets.

SOUPS

SPICED EGGPLANT SOUP   [Indonesian]

EGGPLANT SOUP WITH BEEF AND PASTA SHELLS   [Italian]

EGGPLANT AND ZUCCHINI SOUP   [Moroccan]

EGGPLANT AND TOMATO SOUP   [United States]

EGGPLANT SOUR SOUP   [Armenian]

EGGPLANT, BEAN, AND TOMATO SOUP   [Italian]

SPICED EGGPLANT SOUP
[Indonesian]

SERVES 4 TO 6

3 small eggplants
¼ tsp. coriander seeds
¼ tsp. cumin seeds
¼ cup almonds
2 Tbs. peanut oil
1 medium onion, chopped
2 cloves garlic, minced
1 tsp. ground, dried red chili*
¼ tsp. ground turmeric

1 ¼-inch slice fresh ginger root,
   peeled and grated
2 Tbs. raw chicken, minced
Salt to taste
Chicken broth to cover
2 curry leaves**
2 cups coconut milk***
1 Tbs lime or lemon juice

Prepare eggplants, using Method 4, dice eggplant. In a blender, or with a mortar and pestle, pulverize the coriander seeds, cumin seeds, and the almonds. Use a 5-quart pot. Heat the oil and wilt the onion and garlic. Add the spices, including the chili, turmeric, and ginger root. Stir for 1 minute and then add the minced chicken. Cover with chicken broth and bring to a boil. Add salt to taste. Add the curry leaves and lower the heat. Simmer very slowly for 10 minutes. Add the coconut milk, and simmer uncovered for 10 more minutes. Finally, add the diced eggplant and continue cooking over very low heat until eggplant is tender, about 10 minutes more. Add the lime juice and stir.

* Ground, dried red chili can be purchased in Southeast Asia specialty stores. (See Sources for Ingredients, page 289.)
** Curry leaves: Not to be confused with curry powder. This spice is used as a flavoring throughout Southeast Asia and can be purchased here in the United States as well. (See Sources for Ingredients, page 289.)
*** See Method for Making Coconut Milk, page 285.

EGGPLANT SOUP WITH BEEF AND PASTA SHELLS
[*Italian*]

SERVES 8

1 medium eggplant
2 Tbs. butter
2 Tbs. olive oil
1 medium onion, chopped
2 cloves garlic, minced
1 lb. ground beef
1 small carrot, chopped
1 stalk celery, chopped
One 35-oz. can Italian plum
  tomatoes

Two 14-oz. cans beef broth
Salt and pepper to taste
1 tsp. sugar
½ tsp. nutmeg
½ cup small pasta shells
  (#23), uncooked
2 Tbs. parsley, minced
½ cup Parmesan cheese, grated

Prepare eggplant, using Method 4. Heat the butter and oil in a large pot with cover. Sauté onion and garlic until wilted and add the beef. Cook, stirring, until it loses its color. Add the eggplant, carrots, celery, tomatoes, beef broth, salt and pepper, sugar, and nutmeg. Cover and simmer for 30 minutes. Add the pasta shells and cook for 10 minutes more or until the shells are tender. Sprinkle with parsley and Parmesan cheese.

Note: This soup is somewhat like minestrone, and hearty enough for a one-dish meal if accompanied by a good, crusty Italian bread.

EGGPLANT AND ZUCCHINI SOUP
[Moroccan]

SERVES 4 TO 6

6 small eggplants, unpeeled and
    cut thick
4 zucchini, unpeeled and cut
    thick
1 cup olive oil
3 large tomatoes, peeled
1 large leek, white part only,
    minced

1 Tbs. fresh chervil, minced, or
    1 tsp. dried chervil
4 drops Tabasco sauce
1 tsp. cumin
3 cups chicken broth
Salt to taste

Prepare eggplants, using Method 1. Drain and fry in oil until soft, reserving 2 Tbs. of oil. Set aside.

In the same pan, cook and toss the zucchini for 5 minutes. Then add the tomatoes, and add the zucchini-tomato mixture to the eggplant, reserving several slices of eggplant to float on top of soup. Mix leek, chervil, Tabasco, cumin, and the reserved 2 Tbs. olive oil in a blender for 1 minute. Pour into a 5-quart saucepan. Add vegetables, chicken broth and salt to taste, mix and cook for 20 minutes.

Serve hot or cold, topped with reserved eggplant slices.

EGGPLANT AND TOMATO SOUP
[*United States*]

SERVES 4

1 large eggplant
4 Tbs. butter
2 garlic cloves, minced
¼ cup scallions, minced
2 stalks celery, coarsely chopped
1 green pepper, seeded and
coarsely chopped

½ tsp. thyme
1 cup fresh tomatoes, peeled
and chopped
Salt and pepper to taste
3 cups chicken broth
¼ cup Parmesan cheese

Prepare eggplant, using Method 4; cube eggplant. Using a 5-quart pot, melt butter and wilt garlic and scallions. Add celery, green pepper, eggplant cubes, and thyme. Sauté mixture for 5 minutes. Add tomatoes, salt and pepper, and simmer for an additional 5 minutes. Add chicken broth, bring to a boil, reduce heat, and simmer soup for 15 minutes more, or until vegetables are tender. Serve hot with grated Parmesan cheese sprinkled on top.

EGGPLANT SOUR SOUP
[*Armenian*]

SERVES 4 TO 6

1 large eggplant
*¼ cup dried chick peas**
½ cup lentils
2 cups canned tomatoes

2 cloves garlic, minced
½ cup lemon juice
1½ tsp. salt
2 Tbs. dried mint leaves, crushed

Soak chick peas overnight in ½ cup water. In the morning drain, add to 1½ cups water, and cook 15 minutes. Wash lentils, add to chick peas, and simmer 5 minutes.

* Small can drained and washed chick peas can be substituted, and added directly to lentils.

Prepare eggplant, using Method 4; cube eggplant. Set aside. Add undrained tomatoes, cubed eggplant, minced garlic, and lemon juice. Add water to just barely cover. Cook 45 minutes. Add salt and crushed mint leaves, mix, turn off heat and let stand for 10 minutes to blend flavors.

EGGPLANT, BEAN AND TOMATO SOUP
[Italian]

SERVES 6

1 large eggplant	2 medium onions, chopped
⅓ cup dried white beans (great	3 cups chicken broth*
Northern or small white)	1 tsp. oregano
1 qt. water	1 lb. Italian or Polish sausage,
6 Tbs. olive oil	cut in pieces
One 1-lb. can Italian plum	1 Tbs. fresh parsley, chopped
tomatoes	1 Tbs. fresh basil, chopped, or
4 cloves garlic, minced	1 tsp. dried basil
1 tsp. salt	½ tsp. thyme
½ tsp. black pepper	½ tsp. sage
4 leeks, chopped	½ bay leaf

Wash beans and drop into 1 quart boiling water. Let boil 2 minutes. Remove from heat. Cover pan and let soak in same water for 1 hour.

Prepare eggplant, using Method 1; slice. Dry well. Heat oil in 12-inch skillet and toss eggplant slices in oil until golden. Add undrained tomatoes, garlic, salt and pepper, and simmer slowly 15 minutes. Remove to bowl and set aside.

In same skillet, heat the remaining 3 Tbs. olive oil and sauté the chopped leeks and onions until wilted. Stir occasionally so they will not burn. Transfer to large 7-quart pot and add chicken broth

* Homemade, instant, or canned chicken broth can be used.

and soaked beans with their liquid, plus oregano and more salt and pepper to taste. Cover pot and simmer slowly for 1 hour, until beans are tender.

Add cut-up sausage. Cook 15 minutes and then add the eggplant and tomato mixture. Cook 15 minutes more. Add chopped fresh parsley and basil, thyme, sage, and bay leaf and simmer 5 more minutes to blend flavors. Taste to see if more salt and pepper are necessary. When served with crusty Italian bread, this soup can be, and is, a whole meal.

Oregano

SALADS

EGGPLANT SALAD WITH CORNICHONS [French]

EGGPLANT SALAD WITH GINGER ROOT [Chinese]

EGGPLANT SALAD WITH CUCUMBER, GREEN PEPPER, AND
   TOMATOES [Armenian]

EGGPLANT SALAD WITH RED AND GREEN PEPPER [Italian]

EGGPLANT SALAD WITH CORNICHONS
[French]

SERVES 4

1 large eggplant
3 Tbs. olive oil
1 Tbs. wine vinegar
2 cornichons, rinsed, and
   drained and minced*
1 tsp. fresh chervil, minced, or
   ½ tsp. dried chervil

1 tsp. fresh tarragon, minced,
   or ½ tsp. dried tarragon
Salt and pepper to taste
Lettuce leaves

* Cornichons are tiny French pickles which can be purchased at gourmet specialty stores. (See Sources for Ingredients, page 289.)

[192]

Prepare eggplant, using Method 4. However, *slice* thinly, rather than cube, before parboiling.

Mix oil, vinegar, cornichons, chervil, tarragon, and salt and pepper into a vinaigrette sauce and toss with sliced eggplant.

Serve cold, topped with an additional cornichon on lettuce leaves.

EGGPLANT SALAD WITH GINGER ROOT
[Chinese]

SERVES 4

1 large eggplant	*1 clove garlic, minced*
1 Tbs. vinegar (rice wine	*½ tsp. salt*
vinegar preferred) *	*2 thin slices fresh ginger root,*
1 Tbs. light brown sugar	*peeled and minced fine*
1 Tbs. peanut oil	*Scallions, slivered*

Prepare eggplant, using Method 3. Chop pulp coarsely with all other remaining ingredients, except scallions. Combine mixture well, and chill in covered bowl for at least 4 to 5 hours. Serve cold and garnish with slivers of scallions.

EGGPLANT SALAD WITH CUCUMBER, GREEN PEPPER, AND TOMATOES
[Armenian]

SERVES 6 TO 8

2 large eggplants	*1 Tbs. parsley, minced*
2 green peppers, seeded and	*3 Tbs. olive oil*
cut in halves	*1 Tbs. wine vinegar*
3 tomatoes, diced	*Salt and pepper to taste*
1 cucumber, peeled and diced	*Lettuce leaves*
1 small onion, grated	

* Rice wine vinegar is very mild and can be bought in Oriental food stores. (See Sources for Ingredients, page 289.)

Prepare eggplants, using Method 3, and add green peppers to same pan to broil for the last 10 minutes, so that skins are loosened for peeling. When green pepper has cooled, remove charred skin and dice fine.

Mash the eggplant pulp and add the tomatoes, green pepper, cucumber, grated onion, parsley, oil, vinegar, salt and pepper. Place mixture in the refrigerator and allow at least 1 hour, or preferably more, for flavors to blend.

Serve chilled on lettuce leaves topped with a black olive.

This is excellent as a salad with any kind of lamb.

EGGPLANT SALAD WITH RED AND GREEN PEPPER
[*Italian*]

SERVES 6 TO 8

2 medium eggplants
Juice of ½ lemon
8 peppers, diced fine (use 4 red and 4 green for color and variety in flavor)
2 cloves garlic, minced

1 Tbs. parsley, minced
2 to 3 drops Tabasco sauce
Salt to taste
1 Tbs. mayonnaise (or less)
Lettuce leaves

Prepare eggplants, using Method 3. Beat pulp and lemon juice with a wooden spoon. Add diced peppers and all other ingredients except mayonnaise and lettuce. Use only enough mayonnaise to bind ingredients together. Serve cold on lettuce leaves.

SIDE DISHES

EGGPLANT AND ONIONS IN COCONUT CREAM [*West Indian*]

EGGPLANT AND POTATO CURRY [*African*]

EGGPLANT WITH YOGURT, CARAWAY SEEDS, AND DILL
  [*Yugoslavian*]

EGGPLANT SANDWICHES WITH GINGER SOY SAUCE [*Japanese*]

EGGPLANT CURRY WITH SPICED RICE [*African*]

FRIED EGGPLANT WITH GARLIC SAUCE [*Greek*]

RATATOUILLE [*French*]

EGGPLANT RAYATHA [*Indian*]

BAKED EGGPLANT [*Armenian*]

EGGPLANT WITH SHERRY SAUCE, SCALLION, AND DAIKON
  [*Japanese*]

EGGPLANT WITH TOASTED SESAME SEED SAUCE [*Japanese*]

STIR-FRIED EGGPLANT WITH GARLIC [*Chinese*]

EGGPLANT IN TOMATO SAUCE [*Israeli*]

STEWED EGGPLANT WITH ZUCCHINI AND CHICK PEAS [*Syrian*]

EGGPLANT WITH MACADAMIA NUTS [*Hawaiian*]

EGGPLANT WITH GARLIC AND BLACK BEAN SAUCE [Chinese]

THE DERVISH'S ROSARY [Lebanese]

BROILED EGGPLANT WITH TARRAGON-LEMON BUTTER BALLS
[French]

EGGPLANT AND SPINACH WITH TOASTED PINE NUTS [Syrian]

EGGPLANT WITH YOGURT AND GARAM MASALA [Indian]

EGGPLANT AND TOMATOES WITH ANCHOVIES [Italian]

FRENCH-FRIED EGGPLANT STICKS [Italian]

EGGPLANT CREAM [Turkish]

FRIED EGGPLANT IN EGG BATTER [Armenian]

SWEET AND SOUR EGGPLANT [Italian]

EGGPLANT MELANGE [United States]

EGGPLANT AND TOMATOES BAKED IN CHEESE CUSTARD
[United States]

EGGPLANT AND ONIONS IN COCONUT CREAM
[West Indian]

SERVES 4 TO 6

> *1 large eggplant*
> *3 medium onions, sliced thin*
> *1 tsp. salt*
> *3 to 4 drops Tabasco sauce*
> *1½ cups coconut cream**

Prepare eggplant, using Method 1; slice eggplant. Preheat oven to
350°. In a large, flat, buttered casserole, layer eggplant slices. Place
sliced onions, separated into rings, over the eggplant slices. Sprinkle
with salt. Add Tabasco to coconut cream and pour over eggplant
and onions. Bake uncovered for 40 minutes.

* See Method for Making Coconut Cream, page 285.

EGGPLANT AND POTATO CURRY
[*African*]

SERVES 6

1 medium eggplant	*1 ½ cups boiling water*
¼ cup peanut oil	*3 Tbs. cornmeal*
3 medium onions, chopped	*2 Tbs. tomato sauce*
1 Tbs. curry powder	*1 egg, beaten*
½ tsp. salt	*3 to 4 drops Tabasco sauce*
4 large potatoes, peeled and	
cubed	

Prepare eggplant, using Method 4; cube eggplant. Heat oil and add onions. When onions are wilted, add eggplant cubes, curry powder, and salt. Cook slowly for 20 minutes. Add cubed potatoes and boiling water. Cook for 30 minutes more. Sprinkle with cornmeal, and stir, then cook 10 more minutes. Add tomato sauce, beaten egg, and Tabasco and cook 5 minutes more.

EGGPLANT WITH YOGURT, CARAWAY SEEDS, AND DILL
[*Yugoslavian*]

SERVES 4

3 small eggplants	*½ tsp. caraway seeds*
8 oz. plain yogurt	*3 Tbs. olive oil*
2 cloves garlic, minced	*2 sprigs fresh dill, snipped*
Salt to taste	

Prepare eggplants, using Method 1; slice eggplant. Mix the yogurt, garlic, salt, and caraway seeds together. Heat olive oil and brown slices of eggplant until soft on the insides and brown on the outsides. Arrange eggplant on a serving plate and pour yogurt sauce over them. Garnish with snipped dill.

EGGPLANT SANDWICHES WITH GINGER SOY SAUCE
[Japanese]

SERVES 6 TO 8

2 to 3 large eggplants
1 cup ground pork
1 egg
1 medium onion, chopped
1 Tbs. Japanese soy sauce
2 tsp. sugar

Prepare eggplants, using Method 1; however, cut slices across into ½-inch-thick rounds. Mix ground pork, egg, onion, soy sauce, and sugar together. Dust the surface of an eggplant slice with flour and place stuffing in the center of the slice. Top with another slice of eggplant, like a sandwich. Continue until all eggplant slices are used up.

BATTER:

1 egg
3 Tbs. water
5 Tbs. flour
¼ tsp. salt
Peanut oil for deep frying

Make the batter: Mix egg and water, then add flour and salt and mix well. Heat the oil. Dip sandwiches into batter on all sides and deep fry in oil until golden, turning once. Drain on paper towels.

DIPPING SAUCE:

3 Tbs. soy sauce
Pinch of sugar
One 1-inch piece ginger
  root, peeled and grated

Mix soy sauce, sugar, and ginger root together, and dip sandwich into sauce with each bite.

EGGPLANT CURRY WITH SPICED RICE
[African]

SERVES 4

CURRY:

4 small eggplants	1 Tbs. flour
2 Tbs. olive oil	1 cup chicken broth, fresh or
2 medium onions, sliced thin	canned
2 tsp. curry powder	Salt to taste

Heat oil and fry onions until golden brown. Add curry powder and flour, and then slowly add chicken broth. Prepare eggplants, using Method 4 (peel eggplants), and add to curry sauce. Add salt to taste. Simmer over low heat until soft, about 10 minutes. Serve over Spiced Rice.

SPICED RICE:

1½ cups coconut milk*
½ cup rice
2 whole cloves
1 stick cinnamon

Heat coconut milk over low heat. Add rice, cloves, and cinnamon. Cook over very low heat, uncovered, until liquid is absorbed, about 20 to 25 minutes. Remove cloves and cinnamon stick. Mound rice in a deep serving dish and pour eggplant curry over the rice.

Note: In Africa, each household has funnel-shaped, soft, woven straw baskets used especially for making coconut milk, which is a basic ingredient in African cuisine. I bought three of them on a trip to Kenya and they hang from my kitchen ceiling as a decoration and conversation piece. Hardly anyone can guess what these lovely baskets are used for. As for myself, I still use cheesecloth.

* See Method for Making Coconut Milk, page 285.

FRIED EGGPLANT WITH GARLIC SAUCE
[Greek]

SERVES 4

GARLIC SAUCE:

1 whole head of garlic (15 to 20 cloves), peeled
1 lb. boiled potatoes, peeled
2½ cups olive oil
½ cup white wine vinegar

Prepare Garlic Sauce first, so that eggplant may be served hot. Place peeled garlic in blender, adding cooked potatoes a few at a time. Alternately add the oil and vinegar. If sauce becomes too thick, add a small amount of water.

EGGPLANT:

1 large eggplant
¾ cup flour
½ tsp. salt
¼ tsp. pepper
½ cup melted butter
½ cup olive oil

Prepare eggplant, using Method 1; slice eggplant. Mix flour, salt, and pepper together and put in a small brown paper bag. Add slices of eggplant to bag and shake to coat evenly. Heat butter and oil and add a few slices of eggplant at a time to brown. Turn frequently to prevent scorching. Drain on paper towels and keep warm until all eggplant is fried.

Serve eggplant hot and pass Garlic Sauce to be served with it.

RATATOUILLE
[French]

There are as many versions of this recipe as there are people who have made it. I've tried several versions, and this one seems to be the easiest and the best.

2 *large eggplants, unpeeled*
3 *small zucchini, unpeeled,*
  and sliced 1 inch thick
2 *yellow squash, unpeeled and*
  sliced 1 inch thick
2 *green peppers, seeded and cut*
  into rings
2 *large Bermuda onions, sliced*
  and separated into rings
½ *lb. whole baby okra*

6 *cloves garlic, minced*
½ *cup parsley, minced fine*
1 *tsp. dried thyme*
9 *fresh basil leaves*
One 35-oz. can Italian plum
  tomatoes, drained
Salt and pepper to taste
½ *cup olive oil*
Lemon wedges

Prepare eggplants, using Method 1. In a large, 7½-quart casserole with cover, alternate layers of eggplant, sliced zucchini and yellow squash, sliced green pepper rings, onions, and half the okra. Sprinkle with minced garlic, parsley, thyme, half the basil and half the drained tomatoes, salt and pepper. Drizzle half the olive oil over this layer and then repeat until all herbs and vegetables are used up.

Cover and bake 1 hour at 350°. After about ¾ of an hour, if there is too much liquid, remove cover until liquid is evaporated. Or remove some liquid with a baster and continue cooking until vegetables are tender and sauce is not watery.

Serve hot or cold with lemon wedges as a first course. Ratatouille is also excellent as a sauce spooned over a whole fish and baked, or with any kind of lamb, and as the filling for an omelette or crêpes.

EGGPLANT RAYATHA
[Indian]

SERVES 6

1 large eggplant
1 Tbs. peanut oil or clarified
  butter
¼ tsp. mustard seeds
1 large onion, minced
1 tsp. fresh ginger root, peeled
  and grated

Pinch of asafoetida*
Salt and pepper to taste
1 large tomato, chopped fine
8 oz. plain yogurt
1 tsp. coriander leaves, chopped
  fine**

Prepare eggplant, using Method 4. Heat oil, add mustard seeds to skillet, and cook over medium heat until they pop. Add onion and sauté until wilted.

Add eggplant, ginger, asafoetida, salt and pepper. Cook 2 minutes.

Add tomato, cover skillet, and cook over medium heat 25 minutes. Let cool completely. Add yogurt and coriander. Serve warm or cold.

* Asafoetida is a spice that can be purchased in Indian or Middle Eastern groceries. (See Sources for Ingredients, page 289.)

** Coriander leaves can be purchased as cilantro in Spanish specialty food shops, or as Chinese parsley in Oriental specialty food shops that sell fresh vegetables.

BAKED EGGPLANT
[Armenian]

SERVES 6

2½ *lbs. small or 2 medium*   ¼ *cup parsley*
   eggplants   *1 cup canned tomatoes, drained*
½ *cup celery, sliced thin*   *2 Tbs. tomato paste*
2 large onions, chopped   ½ *tsp. salt*
1 large green pepper, seeded   ¼ *tsp. black pepper*
   and diced   ¼ *tsp. allspice*
⅔ *cup olive oil*   ½ *cup tomato juice*

Prepare eggplants, using Method 4. In a frying pan, sauté celery, onions, and green pepper in oil until wilted. Add parsley, tomatoes, tomato paste, salt, pepper, and allspice and cook 5 minutes.

Preheat oven to 400°. Arrange eggplant in a layer in large flat oval pan, spoon sauce over, then repeat layer. Pour tomato juice in corner of pan so as not to disturb. Bake, covered with foil, for 30 minutes.

Uncover after 30 minutes and continue cooking until all liquid is absorbed and vegetables are tender, or remove some liquid with a baster. Serve hot or cold.

This dish is even better if prepared 1 or 2 days before so that the flavors are allowed to blend.

EGGPLANT WITH SHERRY SAUCE, SCALLION, AND DAIKON
[Japanese]

SERVES 4 TO 6

8 very small, long eggplants 1 cup chicken broth
(about 6 x 2 inches) ¼ cup dry sherry
Peanut oil for frying 2 Tbs. scallion, minced
2 Tbs. soy sauce 2 Tbs. daikon, grated*
1 Tbs. cornstarch

Prepare eggplants, using Method 2. However, as these are small, leave them whole and do not remove pulp. Instead, after cooking slash the sides of the eggplants and allow the liquid to drain out on paper towels and the heat to penetrate. Wipe well before frying so oil does not spatter. Heat peanut oil and fry whole eggplants, turning several times, until soft, about 5 minutes. Lift out with slotted spoon, drain, and keep warm. In a small saucepan blend soy sauce and cornstarch until smooth; gradually add chicken broth and sherry. Cook, stirring over high heat until mixture thickens. Spoon sauce over eggplants and sprinkle with scallion and grated daikon.

* Daikon is the long Japanese radish that can be found in Japanese specialty food shops. (See Sources for Ingredients, page 289.)

EGGPLANT WITH TOASTED SESAME SEED SAUCE
[*Japanese*]

SERVES 4

> *8 very small eggplants*
> *Peanut oil for frying*
> *¼ cup chicken broth*
> *¼ cup soy sauce*
> *1 tsp. fresh ginger root, peeled and grated*
> *1 Tbs. sesame seeds, toasted**

Prepare eggplants, using Method 1. However, leave them whole and slash in several places before frying to allow heat to penetrate. Drain. Fry in oil, turning frequently until soft, about 5 minutes—depending on size of eggplants. Drain and keep warm.

Make sauce by stirring chicken broth and soy sauce, ginger root, and toasted sesame seeds. Serve sauce separately to be spooned over eggplants.

STIR-FRIED EGGPLANT WITH GARLIC
[*Chinese*]

SERVES 4

> *1 medium eggplant, cut into 1½-inch cubes*
> *5 Tbs. peanut oil for frying*
> *1 scallion, cut fine*
> *1 large onion, sliced into rings fine*
> *2 cloves garlic, minced*

SAUCE:

> *2 Tbs. soy sauce*
> *1 tsp. sugar*
> *⅛ tsp. M.S.G.*

---

* To toast seeds, place on flat cookie sheet in hot, 400° oven for a few minutes. Stir occasionally or shake pan so that the seeds toast evenly.

THICKENING:

½ cup chicken broth
1 tsp. cornstarch

Prepare eggplant, using Method 1. But peel it first, since this is a quick-fry cooked dish. Heat skillet or wok, add oil and heat again. Add scallion and cook 1 minute, stirring constantly. Add eggplant and onion and cook 3 minutes, stirring constantly. Mix together ingredients for sauce and thickening in 2 separate measuring cups. Add minced garlic, sauce, and thickening to eggplant mixture and stir-fry for 3 minutes more.

Serve as a vegetable course with other dishes.

EGGPLANT IN TOMATO SAUCE
[Israeli]

SERVES 6 TO 8

2 large eggplants   *Oil for frying*
2 eggs, beaten   *Salt and pepper to taste*
½ cup flour   *2 cloves garlic, minced*
½ cup water

Prepare eggplants, using Method 1; slice ½ inch thick. Make batter with eggs and flour, adding water slowly so batter will not be too thin. Less than ½ cup water may be necessary. Dip eggplant in batter and fry in hot oil, turning once, until golden. Drain on paper towels and then arrange slices in flat, oval casserole. Sprinkle liberally with salt, pepper, and minced garlic and cover with tomato sauce. Bake at 350° for 30 minutes. Serve hot or cold.

TOMATO SAUCE:

One 17-oz. can Italian plum tomatoes
2 to 3 drops Tabasco sauce
2 tsp. sugar
½ tsp. salt
1 clove garlic
1 tsp. oregano

To make tomato sauce: Put all ingredients into blender for a few seconds, then into a saucepan. Bring to boil, remove from heat, and let stand for 10 minutes before pouring over eggplant.

STEWED EGGPLANT WITH ZUCCHINI AND CHICK PEAS
[Syrian]

SERVES 6 TO 8

1 large eggplant
1 clove garlic, minced
1 onion, chopped
⅓ cup olive oil
1 cup canned chick peas,
drained
2 small zucchini squash,
unpeeled and cut into 1-inch
cubes

One 1 lb. 1 oz. can Italian
tomatoes, drained
½ tsp. oregano
Salt and pepper to taste

Prepare eggplant, using Method 1. In a 12-inch skillet with deep sides, sauté garlic and onion in hot olive oil until wilted. Add chick peas, cover, and simmer over low heat about 10 minutes. Add zucchini, eggplant, tomatoes, oregano, salt and pepper. Cover and cook over medium heat until vegetables are tender, about 30 minutes. Serve hot or cold.

EGGPLANT WITH MACADAMIA NUTS
[Hawaiian]

SERVES 6 TO 8

3 medium eggplants
⅓ cup olive oil
1 clove garlic, minced
1 onion, chopped
Salt and pepper to taste
1 large, fresh tomato, peeled
    and chopped
1 tsp. Worcestershire sauce

2 eggs, lightly beaten
⅔ cup canned Hawaiian
    macadamia nuts, chopped,
    plus several whole nuts for
    garnish
½ cup soft bread crumbs,
    buttered

Prepare eggplants, using Method 2. Reserve pulp and shells. Heat oil and wilt garlic and onion. Add chopped eggplant pulp from center of shell and cook slowly for 5 minutes. Season with salt and pepper. Add tomato and Worcestershire sauce, and simmer 3 minutes more. Remove from heat, add beaten eggs and nuts. Fill shells with this mixture. Top with bread crumbs. Set in shallow, oiled casserole. Bake for 20 minutes in 350° oven. Garnish with whole macadamia nuts.

EGGPLANT WITH GARLIC AND BLACK BEAN SAUCE
[*Chinese*]

SERVES 4

1 large or 4 small eggplants	*1 Tbs. black beans***
Peanut oil for frying	*2 Tbs. soy sauce*
8 cloves garlic, peeled and	*½ tsp. sugar*
*center buds removed**	*1 cup chicken broth*

Prepare eggplant, using Method 1. Heat oil in a wok or large skillet and brown in hot oil, a few pieces at a time. Make a paste of crushed garlic and black beans with a mortar and pestle. Stir this paste into the eggplant for 2 minutes, then mix together soy sauce, sugar, and chicken broth and add to eggplant. Reduce heat and simmer 10 minutes.

* Split each clove of garlic lengthwise and remove inner green bud for a more delicate taste.
** Black beans can be purchased in Chinese or Oriental specialty shops. They are salted and fermented and can be kept for long periods of time in a closed jar.

*THE DERVISH'S ROSARY**
[Lebanese]

SERVES 8

1 large eggplant
4 potatoes
2 lbs. small zucchini
1 lb. ground beef or lamb
2 large onions, minced
2 Tbs. olive oil
½ tsp. cinnamon
2 cups tomatoes, peeled and
  chopped

1 tsp. salt
½ tsp. black pepper
2 Tbs. pine nuts, toasted**
2 Tbs. flour
1 cup chicken broth, fresh or
  canned

Prepare eggplant, using Method 4. Preheat oven to 350°. Peel potatoes and cut into 1½-inch chunks. Cut unpeeled zucchini into 2-inch pieces and cut eggplant the same size. In a large bowl, mix eggplant, zucchini, and potatoes together with ground meat, onions, and olive oil and sprinkle with cinnamon. Add tomatoes, salt, pepper and pine nuts. Transfer to oiled baking dish. Sprinkle with flour and pour chicken broth over all. Bake for 1 hour until vegetables are tender and browned on top.

* Why this classic recipe has the poetic name of "The Dervish's Rosary" will probably always be one of the mysteries of the East.
** To toast pine nuts: Melt 1 tsp. butter in a pie tin and add pine nuts. Toast in 400° oven for 1 or 2 minutes, shaking pan occasionally until nuts are lightly browned.

BROILED EGGPLANT WITH TARRAGON-LEMON BUTTER BALLS
[French]

SERVES 4 TO 6

TARRAGON-LEMON BUTTER BALLS:
¼ cup butter, softened
1 Tbs. lemon juice
Salt and pepper
1 Tbs. fresh chopped Tarragon

Blend softened butter with lemon juice, salt, and tarragon. Form into ½-inch balls with the palms of your hands. Chill.

EGGPLANT:
1 medium eggplant
6 Tbs. soft butter
2 Tbs. onion, grated
½ tsp. salt
½ tsp. pepper

Prepare eggplant, using Method 1; cut eggplant into ½-inch thick round slices. Preheat broiler and place eggplant in flameproof dish in one layer. Broil slices under moderate flame, turning once when tender and browned, to brown the other side. Remove to heated oval serving plate. Mix soft butter with grated onion, salt and pepper. With spatula, smear thin layer on eggplant slices as if you were buttering a slice of bread. Top with chilled tarragon-lemon butter balls, which should retain their shape and melt at the table.

EGGPLANT AND SPINACH WITH
TOASTED PINE NUTS
[Syrian]

SERVES 8

2 large eggplants
⅓ cup olive oil
3 onions, sliced
2 cloves garlic, minced
1½ cups fresh or canned
   tomatoes, chopped
2 cups raw spinach, chopped

6 Tbs. celery leaves, chopped
3 Tbs. chives
1 tsp. oregano
1 tsp. black pepper
Salt to taste
3 Tbs. pine nuts, toasted*

Prepare eggplants, using Method 1; slice eggplant. In a heavy 12-inch skillet, heat oil, add onions and garlic, lower heat, and cook for 2 minutes until wilted. With a slotted spoon transfer to a bowl, and add tomatoes, spinach, celery leaves, chives, oregano, and pepper and salt to taste. Put the eggplant in the skillet and sauté the slices in batches, turning once until browned lightly. More oil may be necessary. Arrange one-third of the slices in the skillet, then one-third of the tomato mixture, and continue until all is used. Tomatoes should be on top. Cover skillet and cook over low heat for 10 minutes until flavors blend. Top with toasted pine nuts.

* To toast pine nuts: Melt 1 tsp. butter in a pie tin and add pine nuts. Toast in 400° oven for 1 or 2 minutes, shaking pan occasionally until nuts are lightly browned.

EGGPLANT WITH YOGURT AND GARAM MASALA
[Indian]

SERVES 6

2 *large eggplants*	1 *tsp. olive oil*
1 *small onion, chopped*	16 *oz. plain yogurt*
4 *to 6 drops Tabasco sauce*	*Salt to taste*
1 *tsp. garam masala**	

Prepare eggplants, using Method 3. Mash pulp with a potato masher or the back of a wooden spoon. Add chopped onion, Tabasco, garam masala, olive oil, yogurt, and salt to taste. Mix together and serve chilled.

This dish is good with lamb or chicken curry.

EGGPLANT AND TOMATOES WITH ANCHOVIES
[Italian]

SERVES 8

2 *large eggplants, or 2 to 3 lbs.*	1 *tsp. salt, or more to taste*
small eggplants	4 *anchovy fillets, rinsed and*
½ *cup olive oil*	*dried*
Two 1 lb. 1 oz. cans tomatoes,	1 *tsp. flour*
drained	¼ *cup milk*
3 *cloves garlic, minced*	

* Garam masala is an Indian mixed spice that can be bought in specialty food shops or that can be made at home in a blender or spice grinder.

For 3 tablespoons of Garam Masala use:

> 1 *Tbs. cardamom seed*
> 1 *tsp. cumin*
> 1 *tsp. black peppercorns*
> 1 *tsp. cloves*
> ½ *tsp. nutmeg*
> *One 2-inch cinnamon stick, broken into pieces*

Whirl all spices in blender until pulverized. Store in airtight glass bottle. It will keep its pungency for 2 to 3 weeks.

Prepare eggplants, using Method 4. Heat oil in a large skillet and brown eggplant. Add tomatoes, garlic, and salt to taste. Cover and simmer 20 minutes, then remove cover and cook until mixture thickens. In another small skillet, heat 1 Tbs. oil and add the anchovies. Press down with a wooden spoon while stirring until anchovies melt. Lower the heat, add flour to the anchovies, stirring until blended. Then slowly add milk and cook until mixture is thick. Add this sauce to the eggplant mixture and simmer for a few minutes to blend flavors.

This versatile dish is excellent with lamb or veal as a vegetable course, and also makes a fine omelette filling or, when mixed with eggs, a frittata.

FRENCH-FRIED EGGPLANT STICKS
[*Italian*]

SERVES 6

1 medium eggplant	Fine, dry bread crumbs
1 egg, beaten	Peanut oil for deep frying
2 Tbs. milk	Lemon wedges
Flour	Parsley

Prepare eggplant, using Method 1. Cut into ½-inch thick slices, and then across like French-fried potato sticks. Combine egg and milk. Dip pieces of eggplant into flour and then into egg and milk mixture, and roll in bread crumbs. Fry in deep, hot oil, turning once or twice with tongs, until golden brown. Drain on paper towels and sprinkle with salt and pepper. Serve with lemon wedges and a sprig of parsley.

Simple, delicious, and elegant, and a nice change from French-fried potatoes.

EGGPLANT CREAM
[Turkish]

SERVES 6 TO 8

3 large eggplants	*2 cloves garlic, minced*
2 Tbs. lemon juice	*¼ cup Parmesan cheese,*
4 Tbs. butter	*grated**
5 Tbs. hot milk	*Salt and pepper to taste*

Prepare eggplants, using Method 3. Place eggplant pulp into saucepan. Add lemon juice and simmer for 5 minutes.

Meanwhile, melt butter. Add flour and cook, stirring constantly until the color starts to turn pale golden. Add this butter and flour mixture to the eggplant pulp, beating with a wire whisk. Slowly add hot milk while continuing to beat until mixture has the consistency of mashed potatoes. Add minced garlic and grated cheese, salt and pepper, and cook 1 minute more. Serve immediately.

This is good served with any roasted beef, lamb, veal, fish, or poultry.

FRIED EGGPLANT IN EGG BATTER
[Armenian]

SERVES 4

1 large eggplant	*½ tsp. oregano*
3 large eggs, beaten	*½ tsp. garlic powder*
1 tsp. salt	*Oil for frying*
3 Tbs. flour	*1 lemon, cut in wedges*
½ tsp. black pepper	

---

* There is a soft, white, unsalted cheese that is used in Turkey, but it does not seem to be imported into the United States. Therefore, substitute Parmesan.

[215]

Prepare eggplant, using Method 1. However, do not quarter, cut into ¼-inch-thick round slices. Mix eggs and salt together and add flour and herbs to make a batter. Dip slice of eggplant into batter and fry, a few slices at a time, in hot oil until golden. Turn and fry other sides. Drain on paper towels and keep warm. Sprinkle with additional salt and pepper and serve with lemon wedges.

SWEET AND SOUR EGGPLANT
[Italian]

SERVES 6

1 large eggplant cut in half lengthwise and then cut across into ½-inch slices
4 Tbs. olive oil
Salt and pepper to taste
¼ cup wine vinegar

1 Tbs. honey
1 Tbs. fresh basil, chopped
1 Tbs. parsley, minced
1 tsp. fresh mint leaves, chopped
1 tsp. sugar

Prepare eggplant, using Method 1. Cut into ¼-inch-thick round oil and broil under medium heat until soft and lightly browned on both sides. Sprinkle with salt and pepper and put aside. In the meantime, blend remaining oil and vinegar, honey, herbs, and sugar in a bowl. In a serving bowl, layer the slices of eggplant. Pour some of the sauce over, then add another layer of eggplant, then more sauce until all ingredients are used up. Serve warm as a side dish, or cold as an hors d'oeuvre.

EGGPLANT MÉLANGE
[United States]

SERVES 6

1 medium eggplant	*½ tsp. dried oregano, crushed*
Salt and pepper to taste	*1 cup green peas, cooked*
6 Tbs. olive oil	*1 cup Italian plum tomatoes,*
1 lb. small mushrooms	*drained and crushed*
1 clove garlic, minced	

Prepare eggplant, using Method 1, and slicing the eggplant. Season slices with salt and pepper, and sauté in 4 Tbs. olive oil until golden on both sides. Set aside.

In another skillet, sauté mushrooms in 2 Tbs. olive oil, add garlic, oregano, and salt and pepper. Stir occasionally and cook over moderate heat for about 10 minutes. Add eggplant and tomatoes and simmer for 10 minutes. Then add cooked green peas and simmer for 5 minutes more to heat thoroughly.

This is a good accompaniment for roast beef or steak.

EGGPLANT AND TOMATOES BAKED IN CHEESE CUSTARD
[Italian]

SERVES 6

2 small eggplants	*1 small onion, minced*
½ cup olive oil	*2 egg yolks*
¼ cup parsley, chopped	*1 cup milk*
1 Tbs. fresh basil leaves, minced	*¾ lb. mozzarella cheese, sliced*
Salt and pepper to taste	
3 fresh tomatoes, peeled and	
sliced	

Prepare eggplants, using Method 1; slice eggplant. Heat olive oil and sauté eggplant slices on both sides until golden. Remove and set aside.

Preheat oven to 350°.

Oil the bottom of an ovenproof dish and arrange eggplant slices on bottom. Sprinkle with parsley, basil, salt, and pepper. Add slices of tomatoes and minced onion. Mix egg yolks with milk and pour over. Top with slices of mozzarella cheese and bake in top part of oven for 40 minutes until top is brown and melted.

MAIN DISHES

GHIVETCH   [*Rumanian*]

EGGPLANT AND ZUCCHINI FANS WITH RICE AND TOMATOES
  [*Italian*]

EGGPLANT STUFFED WITH HAM AND EGGS   [*Brazil*]

EGGPLANT STUFFED WITH GROUND PORK AND SCALLIONS
  [*Indonesian*]

STUFFED EGGPLANT WITH PARSNIP AND TOMATO SAUCE
  [*Yugoslavian*]

EGGPLANT WITH COTTAGE CHEESE AND EGGS   [*Israeli*]

EGGPLANT AND BACON   [*United States*]

STRIPED EGGPLANT AND GROUND BEEF   [*Japanese*]

EGGPLANT POCKETS STUFFED WITH SALAMI ROUNDS   [*Israeli*]

EGGPLANT STUFFED WITH MUSHROOMS   [*United States*]

STUFFED EGGPLANT CIRCLES WITH LAMB AND PINE NUTS
  [*Syrian*]

STUFFED EGGPLANT WITH BACON AND CORN   [*United States*]

STUFFED EGGPLANT WITH LAMB AND TOMATOES   [Lebanese]

MOUSSAKA À LA TURQUE   [Turkish]

IMAM BAYALDI   [Turkish]

EGGPLANT PARMIGIANA   [Italian]

EGGPLANT WITH SHRIMP AND HOISIN SAUCE   [Chinese]

STUFFED EGGPLANT WITH FETA CHEESE AND RICE   [Greek]

EGGPLANT WITH POTATOES AND GINGER ROOT IN COCONUT
MILK   [Indian]

STUFFED EGGPLANT SANDWICHES WITH PORK, BEEF, AND
SALAMI   [Italian]

EGGPLANT WITH RICE AND CHICKEN LIVERS   [United States]

RATATOUILLE ON PASTRY   [French]

VEGETARIAN HOT, SPICED EGGPLANT   [Indian]

EGGPLANT WITH CHICKEN AND MUSHROOMS   [Italian]

EGGPLANT STUFFED WITH CHICKEN, CHIVES, AND WALNUTS
[United States]

EGGPLANT WITH PORK, GINGER ROOT, AND RED BEAN SAUCE
[Chinese]

EGGPLANT AND GREEN PEPPERS WITH MINCED BEEF   [Japanese]

WHITE EGGPLANT AND CHICKEN WITH CHINESE RICE WINE
[Chinese]

EGGPLANT WITH CLAMS, THYME, AND GRUYÈRE CHEESE
[French]

FISH FILLETS WITH EGGPLANT, TARRAGON, AND CAPER SAUCE
[French]

EGGPLANT WITH COOKED FISH, DILL, AND CHEDDAR CHEESE
[United States]

BAKED EGGPLANT WITH LAMB, POTATOES, GREEN PEPPERS,
AND ROSEMARY   [Greek]

SKEWERED EGGPLANT WITH LAMB AND VEGETABLES (SHISH
KEBAB)   [Turkish]

MOUSSAKA   [Greek]

EGGPLANT AND VEAL SCALLOPS [*Italian*]

ROAST LAMB ROLL WITH EGGPLANT [*Turkish*]

STUFFED EGGPLANT BOWLS WITH CURRANTS AND BEEF
[*Iranian*]

STUFFED EGGPLANT ROLLS WITH THREE CHEESES [*Italian*]

EGGPLANT STUFFED WITH TUNA FISH, OLIVES, AND ANCHOVIES
[*Italian*]

STRIPED EGGPLANT AND LAMB DOLMAS WITH EGG AND
LEMON SAUCE [*Turkish*]

EGGPLANT AND PORK STEW [*West Indian*]

EGGPLANT CASSEROLE WITH CLAMS, HARD-BOILED EGGS, AND
GREEN PEPPER [*United States*]

STEAMED EGGPLANT STUFFED WITH GROUND PORK, GINGER,
AND BLACK MUSHROOMS [*Chinese*]

EGGPLANT, ZUCCHINI, AND PEPPERS À LA GRECQUE [*Greek*]

GHIVETCH
[*Rumanian*]

SERVES 6 TO 8

1 small eggplant
1 small yellow squash, sliced
thin
1 small zucchini, sliced thin
2 potatoes, peeled and diced
½ head cauliflower, separated
into flowerettes
2 medium onions, quartered
½ cup green peas
½ cup string beans, cut up

2 carrots, sliced thin
One 17-oz. can Italian plum
tomatoes, drained
1 green pepper, seeded and cut
into strips
Salt and pepper to taste
1 cup tomato juice
5 Tbs. olive oil
2 cloves garlic, minced
1 Tbs. fresh dill, snipped

Prepare eggplant, using Method 1, and cut into cubes. Preheat
oven to 350°. Arrange vegetables in layers in a 3- to 4-quart but-

tered casserole, and sprinkle each layer with salt and pepper. In a saucepan heat together the tomato juice, olive oil, and garlic. Pour over the vegetables in the casserole. Sprinkle dill over the top. Cover and bake about 1 hour until all vegetables are tender. Cool slightly before serving.

Note: This is the Rumanian equivalent of the French ratatouille and a marvelous way to use part of your vegetable harvest if you are a "grow-it-yourselfer." It is also an excellent dinner for a vegetarian when accompanied by a cooked grain such as bulgur wheat. or brown rice.

EGGPLANT AND ZUCCHINI FANS WITH RICE AND TOMATOES
[*Italian*]

SERVES 6

3 small eggplants	*1 Tbs. onion, minced*
½ cup olive oil	*½ tsp. oregano*
Salt and pepper to taste	*3 small zucchini*
5 tomatoes	*3 slices Gruyère cheese, sliced*
½ cup rice, cooked	*thin*
¼ cup green peas, cooked	

Prepare eggplants, using Method 1. However, cut both zucchini and eggplant into fan shapes lengthwise and do not cut all the way through. Preheat oven to 350°. Oil a large round baking dish. Spread eggplant fans on the outside of the dish leaving alternate space to tuck in the stuffed tomato halves which will be added later. Arrange these fans like the spoke of a wheel, with the small ends of the vegetables pointed toward the center of the dish. The center of the dish should be empty at this point. That is where the zucchini fans will be added later. Drizzle some oil and salt and pepper over. Bake for 10 minutes. While eggplant is baking, cut 2 tomatoes in half and scoop out the centers, reserving ¼ cup of the tomato pulp. Turn tomatoes upside down on paper towels to drain for five minutes. Combine rice, peas, onion, and oregano and tomato pulp. Turn tomato halves right side up, sprinkle with some salt and pepper and stuff the 4 halves with this rice and peas mixture. Remove eggplant from oven and add the stuffed tomatoes in the spaces next to the eggplant fans. In the center of the dish, place the zucchini fans, with the small ends of the zucchini pointed toward the center of the dish. Cut a tomato in half and place it in the very center of the dish. Slice the remaining 2½ tomatoes very thin and insert the slices in the slits of the vegetable fans. Drizzle

the remaining oil over the zucchini and tomatoes. Sprinkle with additional salt and pepper and top each vegetable with a part of the sliced cheese. Return to oven and bake for an additional 15 to 20 minutes until the zucchini and tomatoes are tender and the cheese has melted.*

This is a most delicious and decorative dish.

* Do not be intimidated by what seems like a complex recipe. Remember, if you love to eat well, you can cook well. There is no reason to be afraid of any recipe, no matter how elaborate it may seem. In every recipe there are certain standard things one must do to assemble every dish—fold, baste, cut, peel, drain, simmer, fry, broil, sift, measure.

Food, beautiful to the eye and imaginative to the palate, like well-cut clothing, is guided by basic simplicity.

EGGPLANT STUFFED WITH HAM AND EGGS
[*Brazilian*]

SERVES 4 TO 6

2 medium eggplants
3 eggs, hard-boiled and chopped
1 lb. cooked ham, chopped fine
Salt and pepper to taste

Two 8-oz. cans tomato sauce
1 clove garlic, minced
1 tsp. marjoram
¼ cup Parmesan cheese, grated

Prepare eggplants, using Method 2. Purée pulp. Mix eggs, ham, eggplant pulp, salt and pepper, and stuff back into shells. Preheat oven to 350°.

To a saucepan add tomato sauce, salt, pepper, garlic, and marjoram. Cook 5 minutes and then spoon over stuffed eggplant. Sprinkle with grated Parmesan cheese and bake in a shallow, oiled casserole for 25 minutes.

EGGPLANT STUFFED WITH GROUND PORK AND SCALLIONS
[*Indonesian*]

SERVES 4 TO 6

2 large eggplants
½ lb. ground pork
Salt and pepper to taste
3 small scallions, chopped
2 cloves garlic, minced
1 egg

Prepare eggplants, using Method 2. Mix pork, salt and pepper, scallions, garlic, and egg together. Cook, stirring, in skillet until meat loses color. Preheat oven to 350°. Put filling into eggplants and lay in flat casserole. Add 2 inches of water to bottom of pan. The water acts as moisture to the vegetables as they bake. Bake for 30 minutes.

STUFFED EGGPLANT WITH PARSNIP AND TOMATO SAUCE
[Yugoslavian]

SERVES 8

4 medium eggplants
3 Tbs. bread crumbs
2 eggs, beaten
2 Tbs. sour cream
1 medium onion, chopped
1 Tbs. parsley, minced
1 green pepper, seeded and
  chopped

Salt and pepper to taste
2 Tbs. olive oil
1 lb. fresh tomatoes, peeled and
  coarsely chopped
1 small parsnip, peeled and
  diced

Preheat oven to 325°. Prepare eggplant, using Method 2. Mix pulp with bread crumbs, eggs, sour cream, onion, parsley, and green pepper. Add salt and pepper to taste and 1 Tbs. olive oil. Fill the eggplant shells with this mixture. Place the eggplant halves together again to keep stuffing moist. Oil a deep casserole and place the eggplants in it.

In a saucepan cook the tomatoes and parsnip for about 15 to 20 minutes until soft. Force through a strainer and pour over eggplants. Bake for 45 minutes. If eggplants start to scorch, baste with pan juice.

EGGPLANT WITH COTTAGE CHEESE AND EGGS
[Israeli]

SERVES 4

1 large eggplant
1 Tbs. flour
¾ cup oil for frying
3 eggs

½ lb. cottage cheese
Salt and pepper to taste
1 tsp. parsley, minced
1 Tbs. lemon juice

Prepare eggplant, using Method 1. Cut into ¼-inch-thick round slices. Dip eggplant slices in flour and fry in oil until browned on both sides. Arrange slices on bottom of deep skillet, reserving some slices. Beat 2 of the eggs and mix with the cottage cheese, salt, pepper, and parsley and pour over slices of eggplant. Cover with reserved eggplant slices. Cover pan and cook for 5 minutes. Beat the remaining egg and pour over mixture in the pan. Uncover and cook slowly until egg is set. Garnish with parsley and pour lemon juice over all.

EGGPLANT AND BACON
[United States]

SERVES 4 TO 6

1 large eggplant	1 small onion, chopped
2 Tbs. butter	1½ cups fresh cherry tomatoes
½ cup bread crumbs	1 cup Cheddar cheese, grated
8 slices bacon, diced	½ tsp. black pepper

Prepare eggplant, using Method 4. Drain. Preheat oven to 350°. Melt 1 Tbs. butter and toss bread crumbs in it until well coated. Set aside. Fry bacon until golden, drain, and set aside. In the same pan in which bacon has been cooked, wilt the onion. Then add tomatoes, bacon, and cheese and toss gently. Butter 2-inch oval casserole with the remaining butter. Put eggplant in bottom of casserole and put bacon, cheese, and tomato mixture over it. Sprinkle with black pepper and top with buttered bread crumbs. Bake for 20 to 25 minutes.

STRIPED EGGPLANT AND GROUND BEEF
[*Japanese*]

SERVES 4

3 small eggplants
Peanut oil for deep frying
2 scallions, minced
5 Tbs. soy sauce
3 drops Tabasco sauce

2 cups water
7 Tbs. mirin*
1 lb. ground beef
½ fresh ginger root, peeled and
  slivered

Prepare eggplants, using Method 1. However, peel eggplants as illustrated. Then heat oil in a large saucepan and quickly fry egg-

plants, turning once. Remove from oil, cool, and drain on paper towels; cut lengthwise into 4 quarters. Set aside in a bowl. Mix scallions, 1 Tbs. soy sauce, ground beef and Tabasco together. Over a medium flame, in a large saucepan, put water, mirin, 4 Tbs. soy sauce, and ground-beef mixture with the quartered eggplants. Bring slowly to a boil, remove from heat, and serve over cooked rice topped with slivered ginger.

* Mirin is a sweet rice wine used in cooking; it is available in Oriental specialty stores. (See Sources for Ingredients, page 289.)

* Mirin is a sweet rice wine used in cooking; it is available in Oriental specialty stores. (See Sources for Ingredients, page 289.)

EGGPLANT POCKETS STUFFED WITH
SALAMI ROUNDS
[Israeli]

SERVES 3

1 medium eggplant	Oil for frying
6 thin slices salami	1 clove garlic, whole
2 Tbs. flour	Lemon wedges
Salt and pepper	

Prepare eggplant, using Method 1. Cut into circles 1 inch thick. Cut a pocket into center of eggplant slices. Do not cut all the way through. Insert a slice of salami into each slice of eggplant. Dip into flour. Sprinkle with salt and pepper. Heat oil and add garlic clove. Before garlic turns brown, remove it or it will be bitter. Fry eggplant slices, turning once, until nicely browned. Serve with lemon wedges.

EGGPLANT STUFFED WITH MUSHROOMS
[United States]

SERVES 4 TO 6

2 large eggplants	½ cup heavy cream
6 Tbs. butter	½ cup milk
1 cup onion, chopped	½ tsp. dry mustard
½ lb. mushrooms, chopped	2 drops Tabasco sauce
2 Tbs. parsley, minced	2 Tbs. Parmesan cheese
Salt and pepper to taste	¼ cup fresh bread crumbs
2 Tbs. flour	

Prepare eggplants, using Method 2. Chop and reserve pulp. Melt butter and sauté onion until soft. Add chopped mushrooms, parsley, salt and pepper, and cook mixture for 5 minutes.

Make white sauce: Melt 2 Tbs. butter and add flour. Stir constantly with wire whisk while adding milk and cream; stir until thickened. If too thick, add more milk. Stir in dry mustard and Tabasco, and then add sauce to mushroom mixture and reserved chopped eggplant pulp. Add 2 Tbs. Parmesan cheese and salt and pepper to taste. Preheat oven to 350°. Put stuffing into eggplant shells and place in a flat, buttered casserole. Sprinkle with bread crumbs mixed with remaining 1 Tbs. cheese, and dot with butter.

Bake for 15 minutes and then place under high heat in broiler for a few seconds until top is brown and crusty.

Variation: Add ½ lb. crumbled, well-seasoned pork sausage to the stuffing.

STUFFED EGGPLANT CIRCLES WITH LAMB AND PINE NUTS
[*Syrian*]

SERVES 6 TO 8

*3 large eggplants**	*¼ tsp. allspice*
1 lb. ground lamb	*⅛ tsp. nutmeg*
1 large onion, chopped	*¼ tsp. cinnamon*
¼ lb. butter	*Salt and pepper to taste*
½ cup pine nuts	*One 12-oz. can tomato juice*

Prepare eggplants, using Method 1; cut into round slices 1½ inches thick. Preheat oven to 350°. Sauté lamb and onion in butter until meat loses color. Remove from skillet and transfer to bowl. Add 1 tsp. butter to same skillet and sauté pine nuts until slightly tan. Mix nuts, allspice, nutmeg and cinnamon with lamb mixture. Slit each slice of eggplant, but not all the way through, making a pocket, and stuff with 1 Tbs. of the stuffing. Arrange in a flat, buttered baking dish. Pour tomato juice over all and sprinkle with salt and pepper. Bake in oven for 30 minutes.

* If small, cylindrical eggplants are obtainable, use 6 to 8 of these whole, making slits in the sides to receive the stuffing.

STUFFED EGGPLANT WITH BACON AND CORN
[*United States*]

SERVES 4

1 *large eggplant*	½ *cup soft bread crumbs*
1 *small onion, chopped*	1½ *cups canned corn kernels,*
3 *Tbs. butter*	*drained*
½ *tsp. salt*	4 *slices bacon, cooked and*
¼ *tsp. pepper*	*crumbled*

Prepare eggplant, using Method 2; chop and reserve pulp. Preheat oven to 375°. Brown onion in butter, add salt and pepper, chopped eggplant pulp, bread crumbs and corn. Cook 2 minutes. Fill eggplant shells with mixture. Place in buttered baking dish and bake in oven for 25 minutes. Sprinkle crumbled bacon on top for last 5 minutes to heat through.

STUFFED EGGPLANT WITH LAMB
AND TOMATOES
[*Lebanese*]

SERVES 4 TO 6

2 *large eggplants*	½ *tsp. black pepper*
3 *Tbs. olive oil*	¼ *tsp. allspice*
3 *onions, chopped*	¼ *tsp. cinnamon*
¾ *lb. ground lamb*	⅛ *tsp. nutmeg*
3 *Tbs. pine nuts*	*One 1 lb. 1 oz. can tomatoes,*
1 *tsp. salt*	*drained and liquid reserved*

Prepare eggplants, using Method 2; reserve pulp. In hot olive oil, wilt onions, then crumble meat and cook, stirring for 5 minutes. Preheat oven to 350°. Add pine nuts, half the salt and pepper, allspice, cinnamon, nutmeg, and the eggplant pulp. Stuff mixture into eggplant shells. There should be some stuffing left. Mix with the tomatoes, salt and pepper and pour over the eggplant. Cover and bake in oven for 20 minutes. Remove cover and continue baking for another 20 minutes. If there is not enough liquid after second 20 minutes of baking, add the reserved liquid from the tomatoes. Serve on bed of cooked rice.

MOUSSAKA À LA TURQUE
[*Turkish*]
SERVES 6 TO 8

This is a most elegant and colorful dish. It is tricky to make only for the first time, but well worth the effort, because it will surely be the *pièce de résistance* of any table upon which it is placed.

2 large eggplants	*2 tsp. salt*
2 large onions, chopped	*½ tsp. pepper*
2 cloves garlic, minced	*1 tsp. oregano*
4 Tbs. olive oil	*3 eggs*
½ lb. fresh mushrooms,	*2 cups soft, white bread crumbs*
chopped	*(4 slices bread)*
2 cups cooked, ground lamb	*Parsley, chopped*

Prepare eggplants, using Method 2; reserve pulp. Sauté onion and garlic in oil in a large skillet. Add mushrooms and cook for 3 minutes, then add eggplant pulp and cook until liquid evaporates. Add lamb, salt and pepper, oregano, and cook 3 minutes more. Beat eggs in large bowl, add bread crumbs, then eggplant-lamb mixture, and stir until well blended.

Line a buttered, straight-sided, 8-cup mold with the eggplant skins, skin side out with part of the skin hanging over the top. Spoon eggplant-lamb mixture into skin-lined mold. Fold top of skins over mixture. Cover mold with heavy aluminum foil. Place mold on rack or trivet in a large pot. Pour boiling water into pot half the depth of the mold.

Bake in a 375° oven for 1½ hours. Remove mold from water and take off foil cover. Allow to stand on rack for 10 minutes. Unmold carefully onto heated serving platter.

If there is excess moisture on platter, blot edges with absorbent paper towels. Ring the mold with tomatoes and onions that have been sautéed with garlic and oil (optional but colorful) and sprinkle with chopped parsley.

IMAM BAYALDI
[Turkish]

SERVES 8

There are as many versions and stories of the dish called Imam Bayaldi as there have been Turkish sultans. "Imam Bayaldi" translates loosely into "The Sultan or Imam Fainted." The legend has it that upon being presented with this dish, the aroma was so sensational that he fainted out of pleasure and anticipation. Another legend states that, at the price of olive oil, he fainted when his bride told him how much it contained. This version has less olive oil in it than the authentic Turkish one. First, to please Western palates and digestive tracts, and second, so *your* Imam will not faint —except for more pleasurable reasons.

3 large eggplants	*1 tsp. ground coriander*
One 35-oz. can Italian-style	*1 tsp. salt*
tomatoes, drained and with	*½ tsp. pepper*
the juice reserved	*1 tsp. sugar*
6 to 8 cloves garlic, minced	*¼ cup pine nuts*
5 large onions, chopped	*2 Tbs. lemon juice*
2 Tbs. parsley, minced	*½ cup olive oil*

Prepare eggplants, using Method 1. However, cut the whole eggplants horizontally into 1½-inch thick round slices. Then slit a pocket into each slice of eggplant by piercing the skin and then the flesh of the eggplant. Chop tomatoes into small pieces and add the garlic and onions, parsley, half the coriander, salt, pepper, and sugar. Add pine nuts and lemon juice. Stuff this filling gently into the eggplant pockets. Arrange the eggplant-stuffed slices in a casserole that has been oiled with ¼ cup of olive oil. Preheat oven to 350°. Sprinkle with remainder of salt, pepper, and sugar and rest of coriander. Drizzle the remaining ¼ cup of olive oil over the eggplant, and add the reserved tomato juice from the drained tomatoes. Cover the casserole and bake for 30 minutes, then lower heat to 325° and bake for 30 minutes more.

Serving suggestion: Accompany this dish with a small bottle of reviving "lavender-brand smelling salts"—just in case.

EGGPLANT PARMIGIANA
[*Italian*]

SERVES 6 TO 8

2 *large eggplants*
Olive oil for frying
1 cup onion, minced
2 cloves garlic, minced
One 35-oz. can Italian plum
   tomatoes

3 to 4 sprigs fresh basil, chopped
Salt and pepper to taste
1 tsp. oregano
½ lb. mozzarella cheese, sliced
1¼ cups Parmesan cheese,
   grated

Prepare eggplants, using Method 1. Slice eggplant, dry slices, and fry them in hot olive oil until golden. Drain on paper towels.

Heat 4 Tbs. olive oil in a deep pan. Add the onion and garlic and wilt them, then add tomatoes and basil and cook for about 30 minutes over low heat until sauce has thickened. Season with salt, pepper, and oregano.

Preheat oven to 375°. Oil a shallow baking dish and arrange the eggplant slices with the tomato sauce and mozzarella cheese. Sprinkle with Parmesan cheese and bake for 40 minutes.

EGGPLANT WITH SHRIMP AND HOISIN SAUCE
[Chinese]

SERVES 4 TO 6

2 *medium eggplants*	*1 Tbs. soy sauce*
1½ cups peanut oil	*½ tsp. sugar*
½ lb. shrimp, cleaned and	*1 Tbs. hoisin sauce**
chopped fine	*Salt to taste*
2 *cloves garlic, minced*	

Prepare eggplants, using Method 4. Heat the oil in a skillet or wok. Add eggplant to hot oil and sauté until tender and lightly brown. When eggplant is cooked and before removing from pot, mash against the side of wok with a spatula. Then drain in a colander and press out as much of the oil as possible with the spatula. Discard oil. Transfer to large bowl and add chopped shrimp, garlic, soy sauce, sugar, hoisin sauce, and salt.

Moisten wok with 1 Tbs. fresh peanut oil and heat oil. When oil is hot, return eggplant mixture to wok and simmer ingredients over low flame for 2 minutes, just long enough to have the minced shrimp turn color and cook through.

Serve with wedges of lemon and chopped parsley (Chinese parsley, if available, which is another name for coriander or, in Spanish, cilantro).

---

* Hoisin is a Chinese sauce that can be bought in any Oriental specialty food shop. It is an excellent sauce that can be used with pork, fish, chicken—almost anything.

STUFFED EGGPLANT WITH FETA CHEESE AND RICE
[Greek]

SERVES 4

2 medium eggplants
½ cup olive oil
1 cup onion, chopped
2 cloves garlic, chopped
1 cup cooked rice
½ lb. Greek feta cheese*
½ tsp. thyme

¼ cup parsley, chopped
¼ cup scallion tops, cut fine
2 tomatoes, peeled and chopped
½ tsp. thyme
Salt and pepper
1 cup dry, fine bread crumbs

Prepare eggplants, using Method 2, and reserve pulp. Then heat olive oil in a skillet and add onion, garlic, and eggplant pulp. Sauté, stirring for 5 minutes. Add cooked rice, crumbled feta cheese, oregano, parsley, and scallions, tomatoes, thyme, salt and pepper to taste. Mix together in skillet for 2 minutes. Stuff into eggplant shells and sprinkle with bread crumbs. Preheat oven to 350°. Place stuffed eggplants in shallow pan, and add 1 inch boiling water to the pan to receive moisture while it bakes. Bake 35 minutes, until the top of the eggplants are nicely browned.

* Feta cheese can be purchased in Middle Eastern specialty food shops. (See Sources for Ingredients, page 289.)

EGGPLANT WITH POTATOES AND GINGER ROOT IN COCONUT MILK
[*Indian*]

SERVES 8

4 medium eggplants	1 clove garlic, minced
4 medium potatoes, peeled and quartered	One 1-inch piece fresh ginger root, peeled and minced
2 Tbs. clarified butter*	1 cup coconut milk**
2 medium onions, chopped	Salt to taste
½ tsp. turmeric	6 drops Tabasco sauce
½ cup unsweetened, grated coconut	2 Tbs. white vinegar

Prepare eggplants, using Method 4. Cook potatoes in boiling, salted water for 20 minutes. Drain. Heat clarified butter in a large skillet. Fry onions until golden and add turmeric, grated coconut, garlic, and ginger root. Stir and cook for 3 minutes. Lower heat and gradually add coconut milk, stirring constantly so it won't curdle. Add potatoes, eggplant, salt, Tabasco, and let simmer 5 to 10 minutes. Remove from heat and stir in vinegar.

* Clarified butter does not burn as easily as regular butter, and will keep for weeks in the refrigerator. It is used widely in India, where it is called "ghee." (See Method for Clarifying Butter, page 287.)
* * See Method for Making Coconut Milk, page 285.

STUFFED EGGPLANT SANDWICHES WITH PORK, BEEF, AND SALAMI
[*Italian*]

SERVES 6 TO 8

1 large eggplant
6 Tbs. olive oil
1 cup onion, chopped
3 cups fresh tomatoes, peeled
and chopped, or one 17-oz.
can Italian plum tomatoes,
drained and chopped
1 tsp. dried oregano, crushed
Salt and black pepper to taste
6 to 8 slices salami, diced small

¼ lb. ground beef
¼ lb. ground lean pork
1 egg, slightly beaten
3 Tbs. heavy cream
⅓ cup toasted bread crumbs
2 cloves garlic, chopped fine
¼ cup parsley, minced
¼ tsp. ground nutmeg
½ cup Parmesan cheese, grated

Prepare eggplant, using Method 1. Slice into ½-inch circles. Preheat oven to 400°. Heat 1 Tbs. olive oil in a large skillet and add the onion. Cook, stirring, until wilted. Add the drained, chopped tomatoes and oregano, and cook, stirring frequently. Add salt and pepper to taste and continue cooking about 10 minutes. Set sauce aside. Heat a small amount of the oil at a time, and when very hot, add the eggplant slices. Brown and turn slices, adding more oil when needed to prevent sticking or burning. Drain slices.

Stack the slices of salami and dice. In a mixing bowl, with your fingers combine diced salami, ground beef, pork, egg, cream, bread crumbs, garlic, parsley, nutmeg, and ¼ cup Parmesan cheese. Divide meat mixture in such a way that there are 2 eggplant slices for each meat patty. Brown the meat patties on both sides in a little olive oil. Make eggplant sandwiches with meat in center. Pour ½ cup tomato sauce in bottom of 14-inch oval flat casserole, add "sandwiches," and cover with remaining sauce. Cover with a lid or aluminum foil and bake for 1 hour. Sprinkle with rest of Parmesan cheese and slip under broiler for 1 minute.

EGGPLANT WITH RICE AND CHICKEN LIVERS
[United States]

SERVES 4 TO 6

1 large eggplant
2 Tbs. butter
¾ lb. chicken livers, cut into
small pieces
1 small onion, minced
1 tsp. ground cumin
1 small green pepper, seeded
and diced

2 stalks celery, diced
1 cup rice, uncooked
2 cups hot chicken broth
1 tsp. Worcestershire sauce
Salt and pepper to taste
2 Tbs. parsley, chopped

Prepare eggplant, using Method 4. Heat butter in a large skillet and quickly brown livers on all sides, turning them while they brown; add cumin. Remove and set aside. In the same skillet, add onion, green pepper, and celery; add another small piece of butter, if necessary, and cook until tender. Add the eggplant, rice, and chicken broth to the vegetables. Stir and add the Worcestershire sauce, salt and pepper.

Preheat oven to 350°. Butter a 2-quart flat baking pan. Stir chicken livers and parsley into the mixture in the skillet and then transfer to the buttered baking pan. Bake for 20 minutes and then turn the oven heat off. Let dish stay in the oven for 10 more minutes. This will allow the rice to absorb some more of the liquid and not have the chicken livers be tough and overcooked.

RATATOUILLE ON PASTRY
[French]

SERVES 12

1 large eggplant, peeled	*2 medium zucchini, unpeeled*
3 Tbs. olive oil	*3 medium onions*
4 cloves garlic, minced	*4 basil leaves, minced*
4 large, ripe tomatoes	*2 tsp. salt*
2 peppers (1 green and 1 red),	
* seeded*	

Prepare eggplant, using Method 4. Heat oil in a heavy skillet. Add garlic and cook 1 minute. Cut tomatoes into 2-inch chunks and toss in hot oil. Cut peppers, zucchini, and onions into 2-inch pieces, and add to tomatoes when they are soft. Then add eggplant, basil, and salt. Mix and simmer uncovered until mixture has become a purée; it should be very dry before spreading on pastry. If it is too watery, remove some liquid with a baster. While this cooks, prepare the pastry.

PASTRY:

½ lb. sweet butter, softened
8 oz. cream cheese, softened
½ tsp. salt
2 cups flour

Cream butter and cream cheese together in electric mixer. Add salt. Sift flour over mixture and work into a ball with pastry blender or fork. Put ball in plastic bag and chill for 1 hour until firm. Then bring pastry to room temperature and roll out dough to fit a buttered cookie sheet. Dough should be about ½ inch thick. Bake 15 to 20 minutes in 375° oven. When done, butter the baked pastry shell and keep warm.

Spread vegetable mixture over pastry evenly and place briefly under broiler to heat. Cut into squares to serve.

VEGETARIAN HOT, SPICED EGGPLANT
[*Indian*]

SERVES 6 TO 8

2 *large eggplants*
8 *Tbs. clarified butter**
2 *large onions, chopped fine*
Salt
1 *large fresh tomato, cut in*
    wedges

1 *tsp. paprika*
½ *cup fresh ginger, peeled and*
    cut into matchstick slices
Hot red pepper flakes to taste
3 *Tbs. fresh coriander,*
    *chopped***

Prepare eggplants, using Method 3. Melt clarified butter in saucepan and add the eggplant pulp, discarding the skins. Add onion and cook, stirring, about 10 minutes. Add salt, tomato, paprika, ginger, and hot pepper flakes. Stir and cook 15 minutes more. Sprinkle with chopped coriander before serving.

Coriander

* See Method for Clarifying Butter, page 287.
* * Coriander, also known as Chinese parsley, can be purchased in Chinese markets, or, as cilantro, in Spanish specialty food shops. (See Sources for Ingredients, page 289.)

EGGPLANT WITH CHICKEN AND MUSHROOMS
[Italian]

SERVES 6 TO 8

1 *large eggplant*
2 *Tbs. butter*
2 *Tbs. olive oil*
1 *chicken, cut into 8 pieces*
Salt and pepper to taste
¼ *lb. mushrooms, sliced*
2 *tomatoes, peeled and chopped*
½ *green pepper, seeded and diced*

1 *doz. small, white onions, peeled*
½ *tsp. dried basil, or 2 leaves fresh basil, chopped*
½ *tsp. dried thyme*
1 *cup dry white wine*

In a deep casserole, heat butter and oil and brown chicken seasoned with salt and pepper. Prepare eggplant, using Method 4. Preheat oven to 350°. Add eggplant, mushrooms, tomatoes, green pepper, and white onions to casserole. Sprinkle with additional salt and pepper, basil and thyme. Pour wine over all, cover, and bake for 1 hour in oven.

This recipe is good served over the tiny rice-shaped pasta called orzo.

EGGPLANT STUFFED WITH CHICKEN, CHIVES, AND WALNUTS
[United States]

SERVES 4

1 *large eggplant*
4 *Tbs. chives, minced*
3 *Tbs. parsley, minced*
1 *cup fresh, toasted bread crumbs*

1 *cup cooked chicken, cubed*
½ *cup walnuts, broken*
Salt and pepper
Butter

Prepare eggplant, using Method 2 and reserving pulp. Mix chives, parsley, half the bread crumbs, chicken, walnuts, salt and pepper, and eggplant pulp. Preheat oven to 375°. Fill the shells with mixture, top with remaining half of bread crumbs, and dot heavily with butter. Bake in oiled, flat casserole for 25 minutes.

Chives

EGGPLANT WITH PORK, GINGER ROOT, AND RED BEAN SAUCE
[*Chinese*]

SERVES 3

1 medium eggplant	*2 Tbs. saong see jeung sauce**
½ lb. pork, cut into thin strips	*2 tsp. cornstarch*
2 cloves garlic, crushed	*2 Tbs. peanut oil*
1 tsp. soy sauce	*1 slice fresh ginger root, peeled*
½ tsp. sugar	*and minced*
½ tsp. salt	*½ cup boiling chicken broth*
¼ tsp. black pepper	

Mix pork strips with crushed garlic, soy sauce, sugar, salt, pepper, saong see jeung sauce, and 1 tsp. cornstarch and let marinate for 30 minutes.

Prepare eggplant, using Method 1. However, for quick Chi-

---

* Saong see jeung is an aromatic red bean sauce. It can be purchased in tins or jars in Chinese specialty food shops. (See Sources for Ingredients, page 289.)

nese stir-fry method of cooking, peel the eggplant first. Heat 1 Tbs. peanut oil in skillet or wok and add minced ginger, eggplant, and salt to taste. Cook, stir-frying for 2 minutes over high heat. Remove eggplant and ginger mixture to dish and reserve.

Heat the other tablespoon of peanut oil and stir-fry pork mixture for 1 minute. Add boiling chicken broth and 1 tsp. cornstarch dissolved in 1 Tbs. water. Cover pan and cook for 10 minutes, lowering heat slightly. Then add eggplant to pork mixture and cook an additional 5 minutes.

EGGPLANT AND GREEN PEPPERS WITH MINCED BEEF
[Japanese]

SERVES 4 TO 5

*1 large eggplant, or 8 small,
  long, Oriental eggplants
½ cup peanut oil
1 large green pepper, seeded
  and cut into strips
¾ lb. chuck, minced fine
1 Tbs. cornstarch
1 Tbs. soy sauce*

*⅓ cup sherry
⅓ cup beef broth (MBT can be
  used)
1 tsp. sugar
1 tsp. fresh ginger root, peeled
  and grated
1 Tbs. parsley, minced*

Prepare eggplant, using Method 1; slice eggplant and then fry slices in peanut oil until soft, about 5 minutes, turning to cook both sides. Add pepper and fry until wilted, about 1 minute more. Lift out, drain, and keep warm.

In same frying pan, brown the meat. Add the meat and cornstarch mixed with soy sauce. Stir to coat, then add sherry and beef broth, sugar and ginger root. Stir all together until thickened. Remove from heat and keep warm.

Arrange the eggplant and pepper in a shallow serving bowl. Spoon over the meat mixture and sprinkle with minced parsley. Serve with rice.

WHITE EGGPLANT AND CHICKEN WITH CHINESE RICE WINE
[Chinese]

SERVES 4

3 small, white eggplants*	*8 thin slices fresh ginger root,*
1 chicken breast, boned	*grated*
1 Tbs. cornstarch	*2 cloves garlic, minced*
1 Tbs. Chinese rice wine**	*¼ cup chicken broth*
1 Tbs. soy sauce	*4 drops Tabasco sauce*
4 Tbs. peanut oil	

Peel and prepare eggplants, using Method 4. However, cut into lengthwise strips before parboiling. Cut the skinned and boned chicken breast into thin strips. Combine cornstarch, rice wine, and soy sauce. Add to strips of chicken and toss to coat. Let marinate 10 minutes.

Heat oil in wok or skillet, add chicken, and cook 1 minute. Add ginger and garlic and stir-fry 1 minute more. Add chicken broth, eggplant, and Tabasco. Cook 2 minutes more, stir-frying constantly, until flavors are blended.

* White eggplant can be purchased in Chinese markets. It is smaller in size, has less pulp, and is more delicate in flavor. In fact, it is the size and shape of a small cucumber.

** Use sherry if you cannot get rice wine in your liquor store.

EGGPLANT WITH CLAMS, THYME, AND GRUYÈRE CHEESE
[*French*]

SERVES 6 TO 8

2 *large eggplants*
2 *cups soft bread crumbs*
1 *egg, beaten*
24 *small clams, chopped, or* 1
   can minced clams, undrained
1 *tsp. thyme*

3 *Tbs. parsley, chopped*
Salt and pepper to taste
1 *medium onion, chopped*
3 *Tbs. butter*
1 *cup Gruyère, grated*

Prepare eggplants, using Method 4. Put cooked, drained eggplant in bowl. Add 1 cup of the bread crumbs, beaten egg, minced clams and juice, thyme, parsley, salt and pepper, and mix well. Sauté onion in butter until wilted. Add to mixture and cook for 3 minutes. Preheat oven to 350°. Put into buttered, shallow casserole, top with additional cup of bread crumbs, butter, and cheese. Bake for 25 minutes.

FISH FILLETS WITH EGGPLANT, TARRAGON, AND CAPER SAUCE
[*French*]

SERVES 4

S A U C E :

1 *medium eggplant*
¼ *cup butter*
1 *onion, sliced thin*
1 *green pepper, seeded and cut*
   into thin strips
3 *tomatoes, peeled and cut in*
   wedges

1 *Tbs. capers, drained and rinsed*
Salt and pepper to taste
¼ *tsp. dried tarragon, or* 1 *tsp.*
   fresh tarragon, minced

Make sauce first. Prepare eggplant, using Method 4. Melt butter and sauté onion until golden. Add eggplant and green pepper, and sauté 5 minutes. Add tomatoes, capers, salt and pepper, and tarragon and simmer for 10 to 15 minutes until vegetables are soft.

FISH

4 fish fillets (flounder, fluke, sole, or any white-fleshed fish)
Flour for dredging
Salt and pepper
¼ cup butter and ¼ cup oil for frying

While sauce is cooking, prepare fish. Dredge in flour, salt, and pepper. Heat oil and butter in a large, heavy skillet and fry on each side about 3 minutes.

Transfer to heated platter and spoon eggplant sauce over fish.

EGGPLANT WITH COOKED FISH, DILL, AND CHEDDAR CHEESE
[*United States*]

SERVES 6 TO 8

3 medium eggplants	*½ cup toasted bread crumbs*
4 Tbs. oil	*1 Tbs. dill, snipped*
2 medium onions, chopped	*3 cups cooked fish, boned and*
1 Tbs. parsley, minced	*flaked*
1 Tbs. tomato paste	*4 Tbs. butter*
1 cup water	*3 Tbs. flour*
Salt and pepper to taste	*2 cups milk, scalded*
2 eggs, separated	*1 cup Cheddar cheese, grated*

Prepare eggplants, using Method 1, and fry lightly in oil on both sides. Drain on paper towels. Add onions to oil in same skillet and wilt. Add parsley, tomato paste, water, salt, and pepper. Bring to boil and then remove from stove and let cool. Beat the egg whites and add with the bread crumbs and dill. Preheat oven to 350°. In a buttered casserole, alternate layers of eggplant, fish, and crumb mixture, ending with a layer of eggplant. Then melt butter, add flour, and stir with a wooden spoon. Cook, stirring, until mixture bubbles. Slowly add scalded milk and stir constantly with wire whisk until sauce is thick. Remove from heat and add grated cheese. Beat egg yolks and add with salt and pepper. Pour this sauce over the casserole. Bake for 30 minutes until a crust, formed by the sauce, is golden.

BAKED EGGPLANT WITH LAMB, POTATOES, GREEN PEPPERS, AND ROSEMARY
[Greek]

SERVES 8

1 large eggplant
2 lbs. lamb, cut into 1-inch
  cubes
¼ cup olive oil
4 Tbs. sweet butter
1 tsp. salt
½ tsp. black pepper
2 cloves garlic, minced
2 medium potatoes, cut into
  1-inch cubes

2 small green peppers, cut into
  1-inch cubes
3 onions, cut into ½-inch cubes
One 17-oz. can Italian plum
  tomatoes, drained, and juice
  reserved
1 tsp. dried rosemary, crushed

Prepare eggplant, using Method 1; cube eggplant. Brown cubes of meat in mixture of hot olive oil and butter. Add salt and pepper, garlic, and all cubed vegetables, except tomatoes, and toss with the meat until coated with the butter and oil. Preheat oven to 350°. Add tomatoes and stir for 1 more minute. Add rosemary and, if too dry, juice from canned tomatoes. Transfer to buttered baking dish. Cover and bake in oven for 1 hour or until meat is tender.

Rosemary

SKEWERED EGGPLANT WITH LAMB AND VEGETABLES (SHISH KEBAB)
[*Turkish*]

SERVES 6 TO

MARINADE:

1 large onion, sliced thin
3 cloves garlic, slivered
1 cup olive oil
Juice of 2 lemons
1 tsp. salt
½ tsp. black pepper

Prepare marinade. Add onion and garlic to olive oil and lemon juice. Add salt and pepper. Place cubes of lamb in any nonmetallic dish (glass, Pyrex, etc.) or in a large plastic bag in a bowl. Pour marinade over and refrigerate, turning several times, for 3 to 4 hours, or preferably overnight.

EGGPLANT:

1 large eggplant
2 lbs. boned leg of lamb, cut into 2-inch cubes
2 large green peppers, seeded and cut into 1½-inch cubes

8 small white onions, peeled
8 small tomatoes, left whole
2½ cups cooked rice

Prepare eggplant, using Method 1. Skewer cubed eggplant, green peppers, whole onions, tomatoes, and mushrooms, alternating vegetables for color, on separate skewers and roll in marinade to coat. Spear meat on separate skewers, not too close together to allow room for even cooking. Pour marinade, including onions and garlic, over lamb in large flat cookie pan with sides. Broil under high heat, turning and basting with marinade for about 5 minutes. Add skewers of vegetables and keep basting and turning until meat is brown outside but pink inside, approximately 10 to 15 minutes, and vegetables are cooked and slightly brown.

Serve with rice pilaf: Pour marinade and grilled onions remaining in pan over 2½ cups cooked rice and serve as an accompanying pilaf. Two Tbs. pine nuts sautéed until tan in a small amount of butter can be added to the rice as well.

Almost all Middle Eastern countries have some version of this recipe. This one is colorful as well as delicious.

MOUSSAKA
[Greek]

SERVES 8 TO 10

3 large eggplants	¼ tsp. cinnamon
½ cup olive oil	4 Tbs. flour
8 Tbs. butter	3 cups hot milk
3 large onions, chopped fine	4 eggs, beaten
2 lbs. ground lamb	Pinch nutmeg
Salt and pepper to taste	2 cups ricotta cheese
One 35-oz. can Italian-plum	1 cup fine bread crumbs
tomatoes	½ cup Parmesan cheese, freshly
½ cup parsley, chopped	grated

Prepare eggplants, using Method 1, and cutting into ½-inch-thick slices. Brown quickly in olive oil on both sides, and set aside. Heat 4 Tbs. butter in same pan and sauté chopped onions until wilted.

Add the meat, salt, and pepper, and stir until the color is lost. Drain the tomatoes and add them with the chopped parsley and cinnamon to the meat mixture. Set aside.

Make white sauce by melting 4 Tbs. butter and adding flour. Stir constantly with a wire whisk until just before it turns color, then add the milk and stir constantly until sauce is thick. Remove from fire and let cool. When cool, add beaten eggs, nutmeg, and ricotta cheese that have been mixed together. Taste for additional salt and pepper. Preheat oven to 375°.

Butter an 11 × 16-inch pan and sprinkle it with half the bread crumbs. Arrange alternate layers of eggplant and meat and tomato sauce; sprinkle with Parmesan cheese and remainder of bread crumbs. Pour riccotta cheese sauce over the top and bake 1 hour. Remove and cool for ½ hour before serving. Cut into squares to serve.

The flavor improves upon standing 1 day in the refrigerator. Reheat before serving.

This is a classic Greek dish, although some versions of it can be found in Yugoslavia as well as in Middle Eastern countries.

EGGPLANT AND VEAL SCALLOPS
[Italian]

SERVES 4 TO 6

1 medium eggplant	*1 cup dry white wine*
8 thin veal scallops	*1 cup canned tomato sauce*
Salt and pepper to taste	*8 thin slices prosciutto*
3 Tbs. flour	*8 sage leaves, left whole*
2 eggs, slightly beaten	*8 thin slices mozzarella cheese*
¾ cup olive oil	*⅓ cup Parmesan cheese, grated*
4 Tbs. butter	

Prepare eggplant, using Method 1. Slice eggplant across into ¼-inch slices. Between two sheets of waxed paper, flatten veal with side of heavy cleaver or meat pounder until thin. Season with salt and pepper, dust with flour, dip in lightly beaten egg and then in flour again. In large skillet heat 3 Tbs. olive oil and brown the scallops on both sides over high heat. Remove to plate and pour off any remaining oil in the skillet and then add the butter and the wine, stirring any brown bits clinging to the pan. Reduce the heat, return the veal scallops to this sauce, and cook for 3 minutes. Arrange the scallops in a buttered baking dish and pour the pan juices and the tomato sauce over them.

Preheat oven to 375°. Dust eggplant slices with flour, and dip in remaining egg. In another skillet heat the rest of the olive oil over moderately high heat and brown the eggplant slices on both sides. Drain on paper towels. Then top each veal scallop with a slice of eggplant, and over the eggplant a slice of prosciutto, a leaf of sage, and a slice of mozzarella on top. Sprinkle with the Parmesan cheese and bake for 10 minutes until the cheese is melted and slightly brown.

ROAST LAMB ROLL WITH EGGPLANT
[Turkish]

SERVES 8 TO 9

1 large eggplant	*1 Tbs. fresh dill, snipped*
5–7 lbs. leg of lamb, boned,	*2 cloves garlic, slivered*
rolled, and then cut into	*3 Tbs. olive oil*
¾-inch-thick slices	*½ cup Emmenthal cheese,*
Salt and pepper to taste	*grated*
2 Tbs. parsley, minced	

Prepare eggplant, using Method 1; cut across into ¾-inch-thick slices. Preheat oven to 325°. Open the slices of meat carefully and season with salt and pepper. Sprinkle with the parsley, dill, and garlic. Reroll the slices, and between each 2 slices of lamb, insert a slice of eggplant and reassemble the meat and eggplant into a roll.

Tie the roll lengthwise with string. Brush with the olive oil and roast for about 1½ hours or until the lamb is tender, basting occasionally with more oil or ½ cup of water. About 10 minutes before finished, remove lamb from oven, let cool, and remove strings. Sprinkle with cheese and return to oven for 10 more minutes to let it melt.

STUFFED EGGPLANT BOWLS WITH CURRANTS AND BEEF
[Iranian]

SERVES 4

4 small eggplants	¼ cup dried currants
Salt and pepper to taste	3 Tbs. parsley, chopped
6 Tbs. olive oil	1½ cups boiling water
½ cup rice	1 tsp. cinnamon
1½ cups ground beef	

Prepare eggplants, using Method 1. However, cut the stem end off the top and design a sawtooth edge (see illustration). Remove pulp from center and chop, salt, and drain; salt the eggplant bowls, invert, and drain.

Heat the oil in a large skillet and stir the rice into it for 3 minutes to coat the grains. Add the beef, currants, parsley, salt, and boiling water. Simmer covered for 20 minutes until liquid is absorbed and rice is tender. Squeeze the eggplant pulp between the palms of the hands to drain, and combine with rice and meat mixture. Add cinnamon, salt, and pepper to taste. Stuff the eggplant bowls with the mixture, and stand the eggplants upright in a large pot with water reaching halfway up the sides of the eggplants. Simmer covered for 1 hour until most of the liquid is absorbed.

Serve hot with a ring of parsley leaves.

STUFFED EGGPLANT ROLLS WITH
THREE CHEESES
[Italian]

SERVES 8

1 large eggplant, or 2 medium eggplants*

Prepare eggplant, using Method 1. However, cut the eggplant or eggplants in half lengthwise, and then from each half, starting near the center cut, slice $\frac{1}{16}$-inch slices for the rolls.

BATTER:

1 egg, beaten	*½ tsp. baking powder*
⅓ cup milk	*Salt and pepper*
1 Tbs. olive oil	*¼ cup olive oil and 2 Tbs.*
2 Tbs. flour, plus flour for	*butter for frying*
coating eggplant	

Prepare the batter by adding the beaten egg, milk, and olive oil to the dry ingredients and beat until batter is smooth. Dip the eggplant slices first in flour, then in the batter, coating evenly but lightly with the batter, and sauté the slices in the oil and butter mixture until light brown on both sides. Drain on paper towels.

* This dish depends on the longest, narrowest eggplants you can find to make lengthwise slices for the eggplant rolls.

FILLING:

1 cup mozzarella cheese, grated *1 Tbs. prosciutto, chopped fine*
½ cup Parmesan cheese, grated *1 Tbs. parsley, chopped fine*
⅓ cup ricotta cheese *Salt and black pepper to taste*
1 whole egg, slightly beaten *1 egg white, beaten stiff*

Preheat oven to 375°, and prepare the filling for the eggplant rolls. Add all ingredients together except the stiffly beaten egg white. Work the ingredients into a smooth paste, pressing against the mixing bowl with a wooden spoon. Then add the stiffly beaten egg white and chill mixture thoroughly. To assemble, butter a baking pan, place 2 Tbs. of the three-cheese mixture on each slice of sautéed eggplant, and roll the slices loosely into a roll. Put them seam sides down in the pan and bake for 15 minutes, until the cheese is melted and the eggplant heated through. Sprinkle the rolls with chopped parsley and serve hot.

EGGPLANT STUFFED WITH TUNA FISH, OLIVES, AND ANCHOVIES
[Italian]

SERVES 6

3 medium eggplants *1 clove garlic, minced*
3 slices white bread, trimmed of *3 anchovy filets, rinsed and*
crusts *coarsely chopped*
1 can tuna fish, drained and *Salt and pepper to taste*
mashed *2 Tbs. olive oil*
10 black olives, pitted and
coarsely chopped

Prepare eggplants, using Method 1. However, split in half lengthwise, scoop out pulp, and chop it fine. Preheat oven to 300°. Soak bread in water and squeeze dry. Add the bread to the eggplant pulp, then add tuna fish, olives, garlic, anchovies, salt and pepper to taste. Fill the eggplant shells with this mixture. Oil a shallow baking dish and place the eggplants in it side by side. Drizzle olive oil over them and bake for 1 hour. Serve hot.

Variation: Instead of tuna fish and anchovies, substitute 1½ cups chopped, raw shrimp, 1½ Tbs. lemon juice, and 3 to 4 drops Tabasco sauce.

STRIPED EGGPLANT AND LAMB DOLMAS WITH EGG AND LEMON SAUCE
[*Turkish*]

SERVES 6

6 very small eggplants	*1 cup parsley, chopped*
½ cup safflower oil	*Salt and pepper to taste*
1 lb. ground lamb	*1½ cups water*
1 large onion, grated	*3 Tbs. butter, softened*
¼ cup raw rice	

Before using Method 2 to prepare the eggplants, stripe the skins lengthwise with a potato peeler, leave the eggplants whole. After

draining and cooling, cut off top tip of eggplant, and with a small spoon, scoop out pulp from the centers and discard. Heat oil until very hot and sauté the small, striped eggplants for 3 minutes on each side. Remove and set aside. In a bowl, thoroughly mix the ground lamb, onion, rice, parsley, and salt and pepper together. Stuff the eggplants with this mixture, using a small spoon and forcing the filling into the eggplants with the end of the spoon. If there is any filling left, shape it into 1-inch balls and put them between the eggplants.

Put a wire rack in a large pot and pour in the 1½ cups of water. Lay the eggplants and the little meatballs on the rack, dot with the butter, cover the pot, and cook over moderate heat for 1 hour. If more water is necessary, add it during cooking. Serve hot with Egg and Lemon Sauce.

EGG AND LEMON SAUCE (makes 1 cup):

> *2 eggs*
> *3 Tbs. lemon juice*
> *1 cup chicken broth*

In the top of a double boiler over simmering water, beat the eggs until they are frothy, add the lemon juice, and beat again. Slowly add the chicken broth and cook, stirring constantly, for 10 to 15 minutes or until the sauce thickens.

EGGPLANT AND PORK STEW
[*West Indian*]

SERVES 8

3 medium eggplants	*2 bay leaves*
One 3-lb. pork roast, end of loin, boned and rolled	*½ tsp. dried sage, or 1 tsp. fresh leaf sage*
2 cloves garlic, slivered	*½ tsp. dried thyme*
Flour, to dust	*Salt and pepper to taste*
1 cup water	*2 scallions, chopped*
2 Tbs. peanut oil	

Prepare eggplants, using Method 4. Insert garlic slivers into pork, dust the pork with flour, and heat the peanut oil in a heavy casserole. Brown the meat on all sides. Add the water, bay leaves, sage, thyme, salt and pepper. Cover and simmer for 2 hours or until the pork is tender. Add the eggplant cubes and cook covered 15 minutes more. Remove the strings from the pork and slice. Arrange on a heated platter surrounded by the eggplant, and sprinkled with chopped scallions.

EGGPLANT CASSEROLE WITH CLAMS, HARD-BOILED EGGS, AND GREEN PEPPER
[United States]

SERVES 6

1 large eggplant
24 clams, opened and chopped, or 1 can minced clams, undrained
4 scallions, chopped
1 egg, beaten
1 clove garlic, crushed
Salt to taste

3 drops Tabasco sauce
1 cup bread crumbs
6 eggs, hard-boiled and sliced across
1 green pepper, seeded and sliced
4 Tbs. butter

Prepare eggplant, using Method 4, and cubing eggplant. In a large bowl, mix eggplant cubes, clams, scallions, egg, garlic, salt, Tabasco, and ½ cup bread crumbs. Preheat oven to 375°. Butter a casserole and arrange the eggplant mixture in alternate layers with the slices of hard-boiled egg and green pepper, beginning and ending with the eggplant mixture. Sprinkle with the remaining ½ cup bread crumbs and dot with butter. Bake for 45 minutes.

STEAMED EGGPLANT STUFFED WITH GROUND PORK, GINGER, AND BLACK MUSHROOMS
[*Chinese*]

SERVES 6

2 small eggplants
2 large Chinese dried mush-
    rooms*
½ lb. ground pork
2 scallions, minced
1 slice fresh ginger root, peeled
    and minced

5 canned water chestnuts,
    minced
2 Tbs. soy sauce
½ tsp. sugar
1 Tbs. rice wine*

Prepare eggplants, using Method 4. However, split in half and leave skins on. Remove pulp from center, remove some of the seeds, and chop pulp finely. Drain pulp in strainer, pressing out the excess liquid. Soak mushrooms in hot water for ½ hour. When soft, remove center stems and discard; chop mushrooms coarsely. Mix ground pork with scallions, mushrooms, ginger, water chestnuts, soy sauce, sugar, rice wine, and eggplant pulp and stuff into eggplant halves. If there is too much stuffing, make remainder into 3-inch balls. Put on plate and then on rack in a wok and pour boiling water into bottom of wok. Cover tightly and steam for 40 minutes. After 20 to 25 minutes, check to see if there is enough water.

    * Rice wine and black mushrooms can be bought in Oriental food shops. (See Sources for Ingredients, page 289.)

EGGPLANT, ZUCCHINI, AND PEPPERS
À LA GRECQUE
[*Greek*]

SERVES 6 TO 8

2 very small eggplants
¼ cup olive oil
Juice of 1 lemon
1 clove garlic, split in half
½ tsp. salt
6 whole black peppercorns
Herb bouquet: 4 parsley sprigs,
   3 sprigs tarragon, 1 bay leaf
½ cup canned chicken broth

2 small zucchini, unpeeled and
   sliced ¼ inch thick
2 small green peppers, seeded
   and cut into 1-inch strips
1 small red pepper, seeded and
   cut into ½-inch strips
4 scallions, cut into 2-inch
   pieces

Prepare eggplants, using Method 1. Slice very thin. In a saucepan, combine oil, lemon juice, garlic, salt, peppercorns, herb bouquet, and chicken broth. Bring to a boil and then lower heat to simmer. Add all the vegetables and cook over low heat until tender-crisp. Remove them from liquid with a slotted spoon and put on a serving dish. Then boil the liquid in the pan until it is reduced to one-half the amount. Pour hot liquid over the vegetables and chill.

Serve cold. Good as a vegetarian summer main course.

PASTA, EGGS, SAUCES, FRITTERS, CROQUETTES, SOUFFLÉS, AND PANCAKES

EGGPLANT STUFFED WITH SAUSAGE, SAGE, AND MACARONI
   [Italian]
EGGPLANT AND TOMATO FRITTATA *[Italian]*
EGGPLANT SAUCE *[Lebanese]*
EGGPLANT FRITTERS *[French]*
EGGPLANT CROQUETTES *[United States]*
EGGPLANT PANCAKES WITH ONION AND CINNAMON *[Turkish]*
EGGPLANT SOUFFLÉ WITH PROSCIUTTO *[Italian]*
EGGPLANT AND CHICK PEAS STUFFED IN PASTA SHELLS
   [Italian]
SPAGHETTI WITH EGGPLANT SAUCE *[Syrian]*
EGGPLANT WITH LINGUINE AND BASIL *[Italian]*
LINGUINE WITH EGGPLANT AND CHICKEN *[United States]*
EGGPLANT AND VEGETABLE PAKORIS *[Indian]*

EGGPLANT STUFFED WITH SAUSAGE, SAGE, AND MACARONI
[Italian]

SERVES 8

2 *large eggplants*
1 *lb. hot Italian sausage, removed from casing*
1 *medium onion, chopped*
2 *cloves garlic, minced*
1 *tsp. fresh sage, chopped, or ½ tsp. dried sage*

1 *cup elbow macaroni, cooked*
¾ *cup Parmesan cheese, grated*
3 *cups canned Italian tomatoes, drained and juice reserved*
Salt and pepper to taste

Preheat oven to 400°. Prepare eggplants, using Method 2; halve eggplants, chop and reserve pulp. Butter an ovenproof flat casserole, large enough to accommodate the 4 eggplant halves. In a large pan, break up sausage and sauté slowly with onion and garlic and sage. When lightly browned, drain the excess fat and reserve. Add the chopped eggplant pulp to the onion-sausage mixture and cook until tender, about 10 minutes. Mix the macaroni, ¼ cup of the cheese, half the sausage mixture, and 1 cup of the tomatoes, reserving the

Sage

remaining half of the sausage mixture and 2 cups tomatoes. Sprinkle with salt and pepper and fill the eggplant shells. Sprinkle the rest of the cheese on top and brush the sides of the eggplant with some of the remaining fat. Mix the remaining sausage mixture and tomatoes and put in the empty spaces in the casserole. Bake 15 minutes.

EGGPLANT AND TOMATO FRITTATA
[Italian]

SERVES 8

3 medium eggplants	Salt and pepper to taste
1 cup olive oil	½ tsp. oregano
1 onion, sliced thin	3 eggs
3 large tomatoes, peeled and cut in quarters	

Prepare eggplants, using Method 1; slice eggplant. Heat the oil and wilt the onion. Add eggplant slices to the oil and onion and cook for 5 minutes. Turn once and cook for another 2 minutes. Most of the oil will be absorbed. Then add the tomatoes, salt, pepper, and oregano. Cover the pan and cook for 20 minutes over medium heat until the eggplant is soft.

Beat the eggs. Pour mixture into same pan on top of eggplant and vegetables and continue cooking in covered pan without stirring until the eggs are set. Then slip under broiler for 1 minute. Cut into pie-shaped wedges and serve at once.

EGGPLANT SAUCE
[Lebanese]

YIELD: 2 CUPS

1 large eggplant	*3 cloves garlic, crushed*
2 Tbs. butter	*⅛ tsp. coriander*
1 medium onion, minced	*⅛ tsp. turmeric*
1 cup water	*⅛ tsp. paprika*
2 Tbs. tomato purée	*Salt and pepper to taste*

Prepare eggplant, using Method 1. Drain and fry in butter until brown and soft. Add minced onion. Add water, cover pan, and cook for 15 minutes until soft and mushy. Add tomato purée, garlic, spices, and salt and pepper. Simmer 20 minutes more, stirring frequently. Purée through a sieve and keep warm.

This sauce is used over fried chicken or sliced, roasted lamb.

EGGPLANT FRITTERS
[French]

SERVES 6

1 large eggplant	*1 tsp. baking powder*
1 Tbs. olive oil	*1 tsp. salt*
1 large onion, chopped	*½ tsp. black pepper*
1 clove garlic, minced	*1 tsp. sugar*
2 stalks celery, chopped	*Flour*
1 egg, beaten	*Oil for frying*

Prepare eggplant, using Method 4. Heat oil and wilt onion and garlic, add celery and eggplant, stir, cover, and cook over low heat until vegetables are soft. Mash together and then purée to eliminate eggplant seeds and celery strings. To this purée, add egg, baking powder, salt, pepper, sugar, and enough flour to make batter hold its shape. Drop from spoon into hot oil and cook, turning once to brown on both sides.

EGGPLANT CROQUETTES
[*United States*]

SERVES 6 TO 8

3 medium eggplants	*2 Tbs. parsley, chopped*
2 eggs, beaten	*1½ cups fresh bread crumbs*
1 small onion, chopped	*Salt and pepper to taste*
½ cup Parmesan cheese, grated	*Cracker meal*
1 tsp. baking powder	*Oil for frying*

Prepare eggplants, using Method 3. Mash eggplants and add eggs, chopped onion, Parmesan cheese, baking powder, parsley, bread crumbs, salt and pepper. Mix well, shape into patties, and roll in cracker meal. Fry in hot oil, turning once, until golden.

EGGPLANT PANCAKES WITH ONION AND CINNAMON
[*Turkish*]

SERVES 4 TO 5

1 large eggplant	*1 Tbs. flour*
3 medium onions, chopped	*½ tsp. black pepper*
1 tsp. salt	*½ tsp. cinnamon*
4 eggs, beaten	*½ cup olive oil*

Prepare eggplant, using Method 4. Chop eggplant pulp and add onions. Add ½ tsp. salt and let stand 15 minutes. Then squeeze moisture out of eggplant and onion mixture, a handful at a time, and put drained mixture into a bowl. In a separate bowl, add beaten eggs and combine with flour, pepper, and cinnamon. Add eggplant-onion mixture and drop by tablespoonfuls into hot oil. Turn once while cooking, when golden, and cook on the other side. Remove with slotted spoon and drain on paper towels. Sprinkle with remaining salt.

EGGPLANT SOUFFLÉ WITH PROSCIUTTO
[*Italian*]

SERVES 4

2 *medium eggplants*
1 *cup fresh bread crumbs*
Salt and pepper to taste
4 *eggs, separated*
2 *Tbs. butter*
2 *Tbs. flour*

1 *cup light cream, scalded*
½ *cup ham or prosciutto,*
   minced
4 *Tbs. Parmesan cheese, grated*
Pinch cream of tartar

Prepare eggplants, using Method 3. Chop pulp and add fresh bread crumbs, salt and pepper, and 3 slightly beaten egg yolks (reserve 1 egg yolk).

In a saucepan, melt butter, add flour, and stir constantly. Add cream and cook over moderate heat, stirring constantly until sauce is thickened. Add ham and 2 Tbs. cheese and eggplant mixture. Then beat 4 egg whites with pinch of cream of tartar and salt, until they form stiff peaks, and fold into eggplant mixture.

Preheat oven to 400°. Butter a 1½-quart soufflé dish and sprinkle with 2 Tbs. cheese. Make a 6-inch band of silver foil, doubled and buttered, and secured with string to make a collar for soufflé dish to allow for any extra rising. Pour in eggplant mixture and place in oven. After 5 minutes reduce heat to 375° and bake for 50 minutes until puffed and lightly browned. Remove collar and serve at once.

EGGPLANT AND CHICK PEAS STUFFED
IN PASTA SHELLS
[*Italian*]

SERVES 6

1 large eggplant	*½ tsp. black pepper*
¼ cup olive oil	*6 leaves fresh basil, chopped,*
1 large onion, chopped	*or 1 tsp. dried basil*
2 cloves garlic, minced	*One 12-oz. box jumbo macaroni*
2 hard-boiled eggs, chopped	*shells, cooked according to*
One 20-oz. can chick peas,	*package directions*
rinsed, drained, and coarsely	*2 jars prepared tomato sauce*
chopped	*8 oz. mozzarella cheese,*
1 tsp. salt	*shredded*

Prepare eggplant, using Method 4. Heat oil in large skillet until hot. Add onion, garlic, and eggplant. Cook, stirring until lightly browned and soft. Remove from heat, let cool slightly, and add chopped eggs, chick peas, salt, pepper, and basil.

Preheat oven to 350°. When macaroni shells are removed from cooking water, rinse gently with cold water, place in a buttered dish, and roll them to coat with butter so they won't stick and will be easier to handle, as they are very fragile. Stuff the cooked shells with eggplant mixture and place in buttered, flat baking dish, stuffed side down. Spoon tomato sauce over stuffed shells and bake uncovered for 35 minutes. Remove and sprinkle with shredded mozzarella cheese, and return to bake for a few minutes to melt cheese.

SPAGHETTI WITH EGGPLANT SAUCE
[*Syrian*]

SERVES 6

3 medium eggplants
1 lb. spaghetti, cooked and
    drained
One 20-oz. can Italian tomatoes,
    drained
2 small green peppers, seeded
    and diced
Salt and pepper to taste

2 Tbs. flour
1 cup chicken broth
4 oz. plain yogurt
¾ cup Parmesan cheese,
    grated
1 cup bread crumbs, toasted
3 Tbs. butter

Preheat oven to 350°. Prepare eggplants, using Method 4. Butter thoroughly a large, flat casserole. Add drained and buttered spaghetti, tomatoes, and green peppers in layers. Sprinkle with salt and pepper and the flour. Place prepared eggplant on top layer. Add chicken broth to the yogurt and whisk together to combine. Pour over layered casserole. Sprinkle with cheese, bread crumbs, and dot with butter. Bake for 45 minutes to 1 hour until top is browned.

EGGPLANT WITH LINGUINE AND BASIL
[*Italian*]

SERVES 6

1 large eggplant
5 Tbs. olive oil
Salt and pepper to taste
2 cloves garlic, minced fine
Two 17-oz. cans tomatoes in
    tomato paste
1 tsp. sugar

½ cup parsley, chopped
1 Tbs. fresh basil, chopped
    fine, or ½ Tbs. dried basil
One 1-lb. box linguine
1 Tbs. butter
¾ cup Parmesan cheese, grated

Prepare eggplant, using Method 4. Heat 4 Tbs. olive oil and when very hot, add cubed eggplant and salt, and toss in oil until tender and browned. Set aside.

Heat 1 Tbs. oil in saucepan and wilt garlic; add tomatoes, sugar, salt and pepper, parsley, and basil. Simmer about 25 minutes, stirring frequently. Add the eggplant and cook another 25 minutes until it blends with the sauce. Cook linguine in salted water, drain, and toss with butter. Pour sauce over, and top with grated Parmesan cheese and more black pepper.

LINGUINE WITH EGGPLANT AND CHICKEN
[United States]

SERVES 6

1 small eggplant	*1 clove garlic, minced*
One 6-oz. can tomato paste	*3 drops Tabasco sauce*
1 cup water	*2 chicken breasts, cooked and*
½ tsp. oregano	*shredded*
1 basil leaf, left whole	*1 lb. linguine*
Salt to taste	*1 Tbs. butter*
1 small onion, chopped	*¼ cup Pecorino cheese, grated*

Prepare eggplant, using Method 4. Chop fine. In a 4-quart saucepan, mix tomato paste, water, herbs, salt, onion, garlic, and Tabasco. Add eggplant. Cover and simmer ½ hour. Add shredded chicken to eggplant sauce. Cook linguine according to package directions. Drain, and toss with butter. Pour sauce over linguine and serve with grated Pecorino cheese.

EGGPLANT AND VEGETABLE PAKORIS
[Indian]

SERVES 4

1 small eggplant
2 cups chick pea flour, sifted*
½ tsp. turmeric
½ tsp. ground cumin
Cayenne pepper to taste
½ tsp. salt
½ tsp. baking soda
1¾ cups water

1 small potato, peeled and
  sliced thin
1 small green pepper, seeded
  and cut into ½-inch strips
¼ lb. spinach, washed and
  stems left on
Oil for frying

Prepare eggplant, using Method 4. However, cut into circles ¼ inch thick. Make batter with chick pea flour, all the spices, salt, and baking soda. Add water, but reserve some; batter should be thick, so be cautious with the water, adding a bit at a time while stirring. Then dip each slice of vegetable into the batter and fry in very hot oil, a few pieces at a time, turning vegetables occasionally so they brown evenly. Drain on paper towels and sprinkle with additional salt. Use the stems of the fresh spinach leaves as a handle when dipping into the batter and cook these last.

* Chick pea flour is available at Indian specialty food shops. (See Sources for Ingredients, page 289.)

PICKLES AND RELISHES

EGGPLANT AND CARROT PICKLES [*Turkish*]
HOT EGGPLANT RELISH [*United States*]
PICKLED EGGPLANT [*Italian*]
EGGPLANT RELISH PROVENÇAL [*French*]
EGGPLANT CHUTNEY [*United States*]
EGGPLANT PICKLES WITH CHILI PEPPER [*Mexican*]
EGGPLANT PICKLES [*Syrian*]
SOUR EGGPLANT PICKLES STUFFED WITH PEPPERS [*Armenian*]

EGGPLANT AND CARROT PICKLES
[*Turkish*]

YIELD: ABOUT ½ GALLON

2 lbs. very small eggplants,
  unpeeled
4 carrots, cut into 1-inch pieces
1 stalk celery, cut into 1-inch
  pieces

6 cloves garlic
10 sprigs parsley, roughly cut
2 fresh, hot, red chili peppers
Vinegar
Salt

Prepare eggplants, using Method 4. However, keep whole and do not peel. Remove, let cool, and press out as much liquid as possible between the palms of the hands. Cut eggplants into quarters and add the carrots and celery, garlic and parsley. Split the chili peppers in half and remove seeds.* Put everything into large jar and cover with vinegar and a generous amount of salt. Let stand in a cool place for 2 weeks, when the pickles will be ready to eat.

HOT EGGPLANT RELISH
[*United States*]

YIELD: ABOUT 2 CUPS

1 large eggplant	*2 Tbs. ketchup*
3 Tbs. olive oil	*1½ tsp. salt*
1 cup onion, minced	*½ tsp. sugar*
2 cloves garlic, minced	*1 tsp. black pepper*
5 or 6 red pimientos, diced	*½ tsp. dried or fresh tarragon*
2 Tbs. lemon juice	*½ tsp. paprika*
2 Tbs. horseradish	

Prepare eggplant, using Method 4. Heat olive oil in large skillet, add onion, wilt, and then add minced garlic. Stir and cook 1 minute. Do not let garlic brown or it will be bitter. Add all other ingredients and cook, stirring over moderate heat for 15 minutes or until eggplant is tender and flavors have blended. Serve hot with beef, veal, fish, or poultry.

* When using fresh chilies, do not handle the seeds, as they will burn your hands.

PICKLED EGGPLANT
[Italian]

SERVES 6

1 large eggplant	*2 tsp. fresh basil, chopped*
2 cloves garlic, mashed	*½ tsp. dried oregano*
1 tsp. salt	*½ tsp. black pepper*
½ cup white wine vinegar	*¼ cup olive oil*

Prepare eggplant, using Method 4, but do not peel. Mash garlic with salt and add eggplant cubes, vinegar, basil, oregano, and black pepper. Refrigerate overnight or longer. Just before serving pour olive oil over and stir. This will keep for at least a week in the refrigerator and gets better as it stands.

EGGPLANT RELISH PROVENÇAL
[French]

YIELD: FOUR ½-PINT JARS

1 large eggplant	*1 large bunch parsley, minced*
½ cup olive oil	*1 cup apple cider vinegar*
3 cloves garlic, minced	*6 whole peppercorns*
3 ripe tomatoes, or about 3 cups	*1 bay leaf*
canned tomatoes, drained and	*1 Tbs. mustard seed*
chopped	*4 tsp. salt*
4 onions, sliced thin	*1 tsp. celery seed*
3 medium zucchini, sliced thin	*1 Tbs. dried basil*
1 green pepper, seeded and	
chopped	

Prepare eggplant, using Method 4. Heat oil in a large, heavy pot. Add eggplant and sauté 10 minutes, stirring occasionally. The last 2 minutes add garlic, taking care that it doesn't brown or it will be bitter. Add all other remaining ingredients and simmer, uncovered,

[273]

for 1 hour. While still hot, pour into sterilized jars, leaving ⅛ inch head space. Seal at once with paraffin. (See To Preserve with Paraffin, page 286.) Cool and label.

EGGPLANT CHUTNEY
[*United States*]

YIELD: 3 PINTS

2 *large eggplants*
½ *cup olive oil*
1 *cup green pepper, seeded and chopped*
1 *cup sweet red pepper, chopped*
1 *cup chopped onions*
1 *cup celery, chopped*
6 *black olives, chopped*
6 *green olives, chopped*

2 *cups fresh tomatoes, or canned tomatoes, drained*
1 *Tbs. pine nuts*
2 *Tbs. capers*
2 *Tbs. sugar*
½ *cup red wine*
Salt and pepper to taste
¼ *cup parsley, chopped*

Prepare eggplants, using Method 1. In a heavy pot, brown eggplant in olive oil, add green and red peppers, onions, and celery. Cook 10 minutes uncovered, stirring occasionally. Do not allow vegetables to brown. Add olives, tomatoes, pine nuts, capers, sugar, and wine, and simmer uncovered for 30 minutes. If too much liquid forms, drain vegetables and put in a separate bowl. Return liquid to stove and boil rapidly about 10 minutes to reduce. Then add the salt, pepper, and parsley, and return the vegetables to the reduced liquid. Spoon into crocks or earthenware jars and chill, or pour into sterilized glass jars while hot and seal top with a layer of melted paraffin. (See To Preserve with Paraffin, page 286.)

EGGPLANT PICKLES WITH CHILI PEPPER
[Mexican]

YIELD: FOUR 1-PINT JARS

2 lbs. very small, slim   10 whole black peppercorns
   eggplants   1 hot chili pepper, seeded and
2 cups water   cut in half*
2 Tbs. sugar   ½ tsp. coriander seeds
2 cups wine vinegar   1 bay leaf
4 tsp. salt

Prepare eggplants, using Method 4. However, since eggplants are very small, do not peel and only parboil for 2 to 3 minutes. Boil together water, sugar, vinegar, salt, peppercorns, chili pepper, coriander, and bay leaf for 5 minutes. Add the eggplants and cook until firm but done. Test after 8 minutes.

Allow eggplants to cool in this cooking liquid. Pour into hot, sterilized jars and seal with paraffin. (See To Preserve with Paraffin, page 286.)

EGGPLANT PICKLES
[Syrian]

YIELD: 7 PINTS

28 to 30 small eggplants   6 Tbs. poppy seeds
2 lbs. sugar   4 tsp. cinnamon
3 pints vinegar   4 Tbs. ground ginger
1 tsp. paprika   6 Tbs. whole mustard seeds
2 Tbs. black peppercorns 6 Tbs. whole anise seeds
4 Tbs. whole cloves

Prepare eggplants, using Method 4, but leave whole and, since the eggplants will be pickled, do not peel. Cook for only 3 minutes. Drain thoroughly.

* Do not touch seeds or they will burn your hands.

Meanwhile, cook sugar, vinegar, and paprika until mixture comes to a boil. Add all other ingredients and cook 1 minute. Then add eggplants and boil 8 minutes.

The shape of the eggplants should be retained. Test after 5 minutes of cooking. Drain and put eggplants into hot, sterilized jars and cover with hot pickling liquid. Seal with hot paraffin wax and store for 2 weeks before using. (See To Preserve with Paraffin, page 286.)

anise

SOUR EGGPLANT PICKLES STUFFED WITH PEPPERS
[*Armenian*]

YIELD: FIVE 1-PINT JARS

3½ lbs. very small eggplants

STUFFING:
½ cup fresh red pepper, seeded and chopped fine
¼ cup green pepper, chopped fine
¼ tsp. dried red pepper flakes
¼ cup parsley, coarsely chopped
1 clove garlic, minced
¼ tsp. salt

BRINE:

¼ cup sugar
3 cups white vinegar
2 cups water
¼ cup salt

Prepare eggplants, using Method 4; however, leave whole but remove stem. Place in a nonmetal colander and weigh down with a
heavy plate. Let drain for 2 hours. Meanwhile mix together the
peppers, pepper flakes, parsley, garlic, and salt. When eggplants are
thoroughly cooled, make a small opening with a knife on one side
of each eggplant and fill with 1 or 2 tsp. of the stuffing, depending
on size of eggplant. Pinch the edges together to hide the stuffing.
Make brine by boiling the sugar, vinegar, water, and salt together.
Place stuffed eggplant in the brine and bring to boil again, lower
heat, and simmer for 2 minutes. Fill hot, sterilized jars and seal
with paraffin. (See To Preserve with Paraffin, page 286.)

PRESERVES AND DESSERTS

EGGPLANT JAM WITH PISTACHIO NUTS   [Moroccan]
CANDIED EGGPLANTS WITH ORANGE FLOWER WATER AND
   VIOLET BLOSSOMS   [Syrian]
EGGPLANT PRESERVES WITH CINNAMON AND CLOVES
   [Armenian]
EGGPLANTS STUFFED WITH ALMONDS IN ORANGE FLOWER
   SYRUP   [Greek]

EGGPLANT JAM WITH PISTACHIO NUTS
[Moroccan]
YIELD: ABOUT THREE I-POUND JARS

2 lbs. very small eggplants
2 lbs. sugar
½ cup pistachio nuts, shelled and broken
4 Tbs. orange flower water*

* Orange flower water can be purchased in Middle Eastern specialty shops.
(See Sources for Ingredients, page 289.)

Prepare eggplants, using Method 4. However, since eggplants are small and will be kept whole, do not peel. Using a heavy pot, put in whole, unpeeled eggplants with the sugar and cook over very low heat for about 1 hour or until mixture is thick. Add the nuts and the orange flower water and simmer for 3 minutes more. Put in sterilized jars and seal with hot paraffin to keep for several months, or keep in a crock or bowl to be used within a month. (See To Preserve with Paraffin, page 286.)

CANDIED EGGPLANTS WITH ORANGE FLOWER WATER AND VIOLET BLOSSOMS
[Syrian]

SERVES 6

12 very small eggplants
2 cups water
4 cups sugar
2 Tbs. orange flower water*
1 whole clove
Juice of 1 lemon

Prepare eggplants, using Method 2. However, leave whole and un-peeled, since they are very small. Drain thoroughly on paper towels, avoiding crushing. Meanwhile, combine water and 3 cups of the sugar; boil until thickened. Add orange flower water, clove, and lemon juice, and stir. When eggplants are thoroughly dry, dip in syrup and then into the rest of the granulated sugar. Place on wax paper to dry further.

These eggplants look beautiful laid out on a round dish like the spokes of a wheel with candied violets scattered over them. The two shades of purple are lovely together. Candied violets can be bought at gourmet specialty shops. (See Sources for Ingredients,

---

* Orange flower water can be purchased in Middle Eastern specialty shops. (See Sources for Ingredients, page 289.)

page 289.) If you would like to candy your own violets, here's how.

CANDIED VIOLETS:

1 large bunch of violets, washed and thoroughly drained
2 egg whites
1 cup fine, granulated sugar

Dip each blossom in egg white and then in sugar. Place on wax paper and, with toothpick, open petals so they do not stick together. Dry in the sun, turning so they dry evenly. Store in air-tight jar.

EGGPLANT PRESERVES WITH CINNAMON AND CLOVES
[Armenian]

YIELD: SEVEN 1-PINT JARS

2 to 3 lbs. very small eggplants   *4 cups water*
2 quarts cold water   *15 whole cloves*
2 Tbs. lime powder*   *2 sticks cinnamon*
6 cups sugar

Prepare eggplants, using Method 2. However, peel but keep whole. Mix lime powder with 2 quarts cold water in a shallow glass bowl. Put eggplants in lime water, cover with a plate weighted down with a stone or other heavy object, and let stand overnight.

Next day, remove eggplants and rinse very well in cold water several times. Drain the liquid from the eggplants by holding each in the palms of the hands and gently pressing out the liquid. Then place eggplants in boiling water (removed from flame) for 5 minutes and let soak. Drain, rinse again with cold water, and repeat the squeezing process in the palms of hands.

* Lime powder can be purchased at your local druggist. Be sure it is lime for cooking.

Make syrup with sugar and 4 cups water. Simmer until fairly thick. Add eggplants and a cheesecloth bag, tied with a string, containing cloves and cinnamon sticks broken into 1-inch pieces, and continue to cook for ½ hour. Remove spice bag. Remove eggplants with slotted spoon and pack into hot, sterilized jars. Pour in hot syrup until jars overflow, wipe, and then seal jars.

EGGPLANTS STUFFED WITH ALMONDS IN ORANGE FLOWER SYRUP
[Greek]

YIELD: 3½ PINTS

12 very small eggplants	*3 cloves*
24 whole almonds, blanched	*One 1-inch stick cinnamon*
3 cups sugar	*1 Tbs. lemon juice*
1 cup water	*2 Tbs. orange flower water**

Prepare eggplants, using Method 4, but leave whole and pierce a slit in the side before preparing. Drain thoroughly on paper towels. When dry, insert 2 almonds into the slit; insert very deeply, or they will fall out while cooking. In a large pot, boil together sugar, water, cloves, cinnamon, and lemon juice. The lemon juice will prevent the syrup from crystallizing. When the syrup has thickened, add the eggplants and bring to a boil again. Remove the pot from the stove and let eggplants cool in the syrup. When cool, remove the eggplants with a slotted spoon and put in a serving dish. Boil the syrup again and let it become very thick. Let cool again and add the orange flower water. Pour over the almond-stuffed eggplants and chill before serving.

* Orange flower water can be purchased in Middle Eastern specialty shops. (See Sources for Ingredients, page 289.)

General
Information

METHOD FOR MAKING
COCONUT MILK OR CREAM

METHOD ONE

Using fresh coconut (for purists)

a. Pierce two of the eyes on the outer hard shell of the coconut with a sharp instrument, like a screw driver, using a hammer to hit the handle of the screw driver to drive it in. Do this in the sink, where it won't be a mess to clean up. Let the liquid from the coconut empty in a bowl, strain, and reserve for another use.

b. Then crack the coconut open with a hammer and remove the white meat, which has a thin brown skin. Peel this brown skin off. Rinse the coconut under cold water and dry with paper towels. Grate the white coconut meat with a grater.

c. For each 2 cups of grated coconut, use 1 cup boiling water. Pour the boiling water over the coconut in a bowl and allow to steep for 30 minutes.

d. Fold a piece of cheesecloth into double thickness and place it over another bowl.

e. Transfer the steeped coconut into this bowl and gather up the ends of the cheesecloth.

f. With the hands, squeeze as much liquid as is possible to extract the milk. Discard the pulp; what is left is coconut milk. To make a richer "cream," steep in boiling *milk* instead of water (step c.).

METHOD TWO

Using canned coconut (for not-so-purists and people in a hurry)

a. Use vacuum-packed, 8-oz. can flaked, unsweetened coconut.
b. Heat 1 cup light cream until hot, but do not boil.
c. Pour hot cream over coconut in a bowl and let steep for 30 minutes.
d. Place double thickness of cheesecloth over another bowl, pull up ends of cheesecloth, and squeeze to extract the coconut cream.
e. For cholesterol watchers, for a lighter coconut cream that is not quite as rich, use milk instead of light cream.

TIPS FOR USING COCONUT MILK IN A RECIPE

1. Make sure the heat is low when adding coconut milk. Add it slowly and stir constantly while adding.
2. Once coconut milk is added to a recipe, never allow it to cook over anything but low heat.
3. Never cover a pot while cooking if there is coconut milk or cream in the recipe, or it will curdle.

TO PRESERVE WITH PARAFFIN

To seal hot, sterilized jars with melted wax or paraffin, the jars should be boiled in water to cover, removed with tongs, and drained on paper towels upside down. Turn right side up with pot holders. Pour food into jars, leaving ½-inch of space on the top. Clean the rim of the jar carefully.

Melt the paraffin wax over hot water. *Do not put over direct heat or it may ignite.* Pour a ⅛-inch-thick layer of melted wax over the surface of the food in the jar. Let it stand to solidify somewhat. Then add a second layer of wax ⅛ inch thick. Clean the rim again. Cover the jar and leave undisturbed overnight before storing in a cool, dry place.

METHOD FOR CLARIFYING BUTTER

Heat 1 lb. butter slowly over very low heat until melted. Let stand, undisturbed, for 10 minutes. Skim off the top and pour slowly into a bowl or crock, leaving the milky residue that has settled on the bottom of the pan. When clarified, butter loses ¼ of its original volume, therefore ½ lb. of butter yields ¾ cup of clarified butter. It has a long refrigerator life, and, when covered and stored in the refrigerator, it will keep indefinitely. Clarified butter does not burn as easily as regular butter and will not spatter the way regular butter does. Therefore, these two advantages make it worthwhile to always have some on hand.

BOILING WATER-BATH METHOD
FOR CANNING

METHOD AND PROCEDURE:
For boiling water-bath method of canning, if you do not have a canning kettle, use a large soup pot or a bucket. It must be wide enough to accommodate a few jars and high enough so that when placed on the rack, water will circulate between the jars, rack space, and at least 2 inches above the jar tops.

Avoid cracked or nicked jar rims, or rusty lids. Select best quality fruit or vegetables. Wash and prepare according to recipe. Wash jars in hot, soapy water and rinse with boiling water. Remove with tongs, drain jars, and fill while hot. Pack jars, leaving ½-inch head space at top of jar. Wipe rims of jars with clean, damp cloth. Cover with lids and screw bands tightly. Place on rack in pot and cover with boiling water. Do not pour the water directly on the jars, but around them. Allow 1 to 2 inches of water above the jars and cover the pot. When the water boils again, start to time the process. When processing time is up, remove jars with tongs and cool on folded towels. When jars are cool, in about 12 hours, test the seal by pressing the center of the lid. If the lid stays depressed, the jar is sealed; if it pops up, refrigerate the contents and use within a few days, or seal with new lids and reprocess.

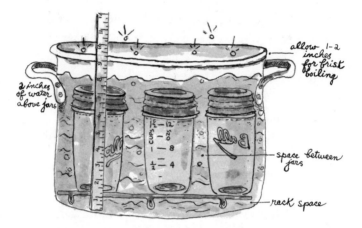

DRY-PACK METHOD FOR FREEZING

METHOD AND PROCEDURE:
Wash vegetables thoroughly, drain and peel, and cut as desired. Place vegetables in a wire basket or steamer and plunge into rapidly boiling water to cover. Cover pot and begin timing immediately. Scald only 1 pound at a time. Then plunge immediately into ice water and let stand same length of time as for scalding. Drain. Spread cut vegetables in a single layer on a cookie sheet and freeze until solidly frozen. Remove and pack in freezer bags. For summer squash, scald 2 to 3 minutes, cool for same amount of time, then freeze and pack. For winter squash and pumpkins, prepare as purée after thoroughly cooking without seasoning; cool and pack for the freezer in containers, freezer boxes, or plastic bags.

For eggplant, it is best to follow the recipe and then use the water-bath method, since eggplant does not freeze as well as winter squash—or summer squash, for that matter. Any recipe or casserole using either eggplant or squash can be frozen after it is cooked.

If you wish to explore canning and freezing methods further and in depth, write to Ball Brothers Company, Muncie, Indiana 47302, and for 35¢ you can get the Blue Book—an easy guide to tasty, thrifty home canning and freezing. Or else write for the Kerr Canning Book, Kerr Glass Company, Sands Springs, Oklahoma 74063.

All of these recipes are adapted for American kitchens. If unusual ingredients are difficult to find, this list of sources for ingredients throughout the country will be helpful. Many of these shops will send mail order on written request.

SOURCES FOR INGREDIENTS

INTERNATIONAL INGREDIENTS:
Barzizza Brothers
351 S. Front Street
Memphis, Tennessee 38103

Antone's Import Foods
2605 S. Sheridan
Tulsa, Oklahoma 74129

Gita's Gourmet
188 Meeting Street
Charleston, South Carolina 29401

International House
712 Washington Avenue, S.E.
Minneapolis, Minnesota 55414

Euphrates Grocery
101 Shawmut Avenue
Boston, Massachusetts 02118

Columbus Food Market
2604 Lawrence Avenue
Chicago, Illinois 60625

CARIBBEAN:
C. Constant
502 Ninth Avenue
New York, New York 10018

GERMAN:
Schaller and Weber, Inc.
1654 Second Avenue
New York, New York 10028

GREEK:
Kassos Brothers
570 Ninth Avenue
New York, New York 10036

MIDDLE EAST:
Malko Importing
185 Atlantic Avenue
Brooklyn, New York 11201

Sahadi Importing Co.
187 Atlantic Avenue
Brooklyn, New York

HUNGARIAN:
Paprikas Weiss
1504 Second Avenue
New York, New York 10021

H. Roth and Son
1577 First Avenue
New York, New York 10028

ITALIAN, INDIAN, INDONESIAN:
Trinacria Importing Co.
415 Third Avenue
New York, New York 10016

ITALIAN:
Manganaro Foods, Inc.
488 Ninth Avenue
New York, New York 10018

Balducci's
424 Avenue of the Americas
New York, New York 10011

SCANDINAVIAN:
Nyborg and Nelson
937 Second Avenue
New York, New York 10022

SOUTHEAST ASIAN:
Sun Sun Co.
340 Oxford Street
Boston, Massachusetts 02111

Min Sun Trading Co.
2222 S. La Salle Street
Chicago, Illinois 60616

Sam Wah Yik Kee Co.
2146 Rockwell Avenue
Cleveland, Ohio 44114

Jung Oriental Foods
2519 No. Fitzhugh
Dallas, Texas 75204

Pacific Mercantile Co.
1946 Larimer Street
Denver, Colorado 80202

Cheng Mee Co.
712 Franklin Street
Houston, Texas 77002

Yee Sing Chong Co.
966 North Hill
Los Angeles, California 90012

Katagiri Co.
224 East 59th Street
New York, New York 10022

Wing Fat Co.
35 Mott Street
New York, New York 10013

Java-India Co.
442 Hudson Street
New York, New York 10014

Wing On Grocery Store
1005 Race Street
Philadelphia, Pennsylvania 19107

Adler's Fine Foods
2012 Broadway
San Antonio, Texas 78215

Mow Lee Sing Kee Co.
730 Grant Avenue
San Francisco, California 94108

Wah Young Co.
717 South King
Seattle, Washington 98104

Mee Wah Lung Co.
608 H. Street, N.W.
Washington, D.C. 20001

SOURCES FOR COOKING UTENSILS

NEW YORK CITY:
These shops will take mail orders. Most have catalogs which will
be sent on request, listing prices and instructions for mailing.

Hoffritz
Mail Order Department
20 Cooper Square
New York, New York 10003

(Specialists in excellent kitchen cutlery, gadgets, and serving
accessories.)

Bazaar de la Cuisine
1003 Second Avenue
New York, New York 10022

Bon Bazaar
149 Waverly Place
New York, New York 10014

(These shops carry fine quality pots, pans, baking utensils,
kitchen gadgets.)

The Bridge Company
212 East 52nd Street
New York, New York 10022

(This shop carries restaurant supplies and the unusual, hard-to-find gadgets, as well as a complete line of kitchen equipment.)

Index

Sheryl London

A native New Yorker and graduate of Cooper Union and other art schools, Sheryl London has worked in graphic arts, sculpture and film. Her artistry also extends to gardening and cooking, and it was an inundation of eggplant and squash in her fertile garden at her Fire Island weekend home that was the inspiration for this book.